STALLED

STALLED

Jump-Starting the Canadian Economy

Michael Hlinka

DUNDURN
TORONTO

Editor: Dominic Farrell
Cover design: Courtney Horner
Interior design: Martin Gould
Cover image: © Don Nichols/istockphoto.com
Printer: Webcom

Library and Archives Canada Cataloguing in Publication
Hlinka, Michael, author
Stalled : jump-starting the Canadian economy / Michael Hlinka.

Includes index.
Issued in print and electronic formats.
ISBN 978-1-4597-2360-3 (pbk.).--ISBN 978-1-4597-2361-0 (pdf).--ISBN 978-1-4597-2362-7 (epub)

1. Canada--Economic conditions--20th century. 2. Canada--Economic conditions--21st century. 3. Stagnation (Economics). I. Title.

HC113.H55 2015   338.971   C2014-908127-8
                                         C2014-908128-6

1 2 3 4 5   19 18 17 16 15

We acknowledge the support of the **Canada Council for the Arts** and the **Ontario Arts Council** for our publishing program. We also acknowledge the financial support of the **Government of Canada** through the **Canada Book Fund** and **Livres Canada Books**, and the **Government of Ontario** through the **Ontario Book Publishing Tax Credit** and the **Ontario Media Development Corporation.**

Printed and bound in Canada.

Visit us at
Dundurn.com | @dundurnpress | Facebook.com/dundurnpress | Pinterest.com/Dundurnpress

Dundurn
3 Church Street, Suite 500
Toronto, Ontario, Canada
M5E 1M2

TABLE OF CONTENTS

INTRODUCTION

Canada has been very good to the Hlinka family.

My grandfather was born in Litminova, Czechoslovakia, a tiny village in the Tatra Mountains, in the year 1900. Litminova was then part of the Austrio-Hungarian Empire. My grandfather came to Canada in 1926 when his first-born son, my father, was three years old. He made a difficult decision and left his family behind to come to the New World. His plan was to take all the risk, establish something, then reunite his family. It took nine years for him to make his dream come true. He brought his wife and two children over and he never looked back.

My father was born in 1923, and came to Canada in 1935 when he was twelve years old. It was in the midst of the Great Depression. Several years ago, I asked him what his first impression of his new home was and he replied: "I couldn't believe that there was so much wealth in the world." That tells you everything about where he came from. My grandfather came to Canada when he was twenty-six years old. He grew to a height of just over five feet tall. My father arrived in Canada at the age of twelve. My father stands about five feet, six inches tall. I was born and raised here and I'm almost six feet, average height for a native-born Canadian. If that isn't a metaphor for what Canada has provided people from all over the world, I don't know what is. This was the Land of Opportunity, and everyone, recent immigrants and the native-born alike, have shared in the country's success and grown, both figuratively and literally, in this great land.

However, I believe that something has happened. Something regrettable. The Land of Opportunity has transformed itself into the Land of

Outcome. Canada has lost the pioneering spirit and appetite for risk that made it so worthwhile, trading the certainty of mediocrity for the possibility of excellence. We're seeing this in many different facets of life but most obviously in the Canadian economy.

There were fifty extraordinary years, from approximately the end of the Second World War to the beginning of the current millennium, where the average citizen — the *average* — enjoyed a quadrupling of his or her standard of living. And I'd argue that the quality of life grew even more exponentially. This was something the world had never seen before, a truly remarkable transformation. Yet, in the past fifteen years or so, the economy has more or less stalled — something that I never thought would happen when I was growing up.

This is a big problem for Canada. But it's one that has a solution. In this book I'll be looking at Canada's stalled economy and suggesting what can be done to fix it.

I will attempt to explain three things:

- What were the factors that drove the Golden Age of growth from 1950 to 2000?

- What caused a once vibrant economy to stagnate over the past decade and a half?

- What will it take to get the Canadian economy growing and moving again so that Canada can provide future generations the same kind of opportunities that were afforded me?

I hope that readers note these words carefully. This is not a doomsday tract, warning that the end is nigh if we don't change our ways. Rather, what I think far more likely is that if we proceed in the current direction (and there's no indication that we're not going to, at least that I can see), most of you reading this book will lead good lives. Older Canadians — and here I include myself — will guarantee that our comforts are provided for, at the expense of younger generations if need be. And to many of my fellow citizens, this might be acceptable.

To me, it's not.

When I undertook this project, there were a couple of questions that I was asked frequently:

- Why are you writing this book?

- To whom is it directed?

The "why" is easy. I've had a lifelong love affair with reading, and several different books have had a profound impact on my life, fundamentally shaping who I am and the roads I've travelled. It may be optimistic to think that this book could have a similar impact on others and I understand that in this desire I may flatter myself … but if I don't, who will?

There's another reason why I'm writing this book. And it's the Number One Reason, hands down. I want *Stalled* to be a bestseller. Or perhaps more accurately: I want it to be a runaway bestseller.

To be considered a bestseller in Canada, five thousand copies must be sold within twelve months of publication. Keep in mind that more than two million people watch Jerry Springer daily. That provides some context about what being a Canadian bestseller signifies. I've been told by industry people I trust explicitly that twenty-five thousand is *huge*.

I've got my own number in mind … and we'll get to it … in a moment.

As for the question of who this book is aimed at, let me answer that in a somewhat roundabout way.

Throughout this book, I'm going to demand more of my readers than most authors. On numerous occasions, I'll be asking you to join me in working through some basic math and exercises in probabilities to illustrate different points.

Here's our first go at it.

Canada's population is approximately thirty-five million. I'm not sure that *Stalled* is suitable for young Canadians (fourteen and younger). That knocks off about 5.5 million people. Let's round things off and say the market is thirty million. My hunch is that if everyone were forced to read *Stalled* through to the end, at least 33 percent of the population would bemoan the fact that capital punishment was abolished years ago. Perhaps 17 percent would go so far as to write their MP and see if Canada couldn't put public stoning to a vote of conscience in the House of Commons. (*Stalled* will ruffle some feathers.) But I've got an even stronger belief that there is a significant number (my hunch is that it's about 33 percent of adult Canadians) who will read *Stalled* and think: *Finally! This is the book I've been waiting years for. Finally, someone has made sense out of what I've been seeing around me, someone has the guts to say what has to be said and state the obvious!*

Warning: There will be a great deal of stating the obvious. In numerous conversations I've had about the book I've found general agreement with my thesis that the economy has gone nowhere lately. There will certainly be less agreement with my recommendations for getting us out of the rut we find ourselves in. But I can live with that, if you can.

As for my target market: anyone who is interested in understanding what turns the economy's wheels. This could include people with "formal" training in economics, either from a college or university. But *Stalled* will have a very different focus than traditional economics courses, because it will stress the importance of microeconomic decision-making and how values impact behaviour and how behaviour in turn fundamentally drives economic performance.

A quick note here: Economics has two branches. Microeconomics, to paraphrase Investopedia, looks at individuals and firms to understand their decision-making processes. Macroeconomics deals with the aggregate economy. But without microeconomics, there is no macroeconomics.… If we understand the former, the latter falls neatly into place.

Stalled might be particularly appealing to those who have a general interest in economic matters but whose life journey hasn't allowed them the leisure to think about these issues as much as I have. People whom I consider experts (here I think of fellow early-morning YMCA-ers like Jay and Bill) will at least appreciate some of the legwork I've done, even if the conclusions are self-evident to them, while others with seemingly superficial knowledge (this includes every Canadian politician I've heard speak over the past thirty years and Bank of Canada governor Stephen Poloz) might at least be enlightened, should they stumble upon a copy.

My belief is that economics is singularly easy to understand. Its basic operations are understood intuitively. I hope to provide a framework to clarify things.

Those who can, teach. Those who can't, teach gym.

Those who can't teach gym become tenured professors (if they're lucky) in Ontario's community college system.

I have been teaching full-time at George Brown College's downtown Toronto campus in the Faculty of Business since the autumn of 2000. To say that I'm happy is an understatement: You couldn't get me out of here with attack dogs and water cannons (more about this later).

I think that for most of the young people I've worked with, it's either "love him or hate him." There is a website, www.ratemyprofessors.com, that posts these assessments from former students:

- "Most stupid teacher I have met, don't waste your time to take this class, waste [of] money and waste [of] time, really really unhelpful."

- "He's the best teacher ever! Some students don't like him or are scared of him, but if you look closely, Mr. Hlinka is the easiest person to deal with. He's [a] very straightforward, no nonsense type of person. Though he's tough, he actually has a heart of gold. Very engaging, intelligent, extremely helpful, & a great motivator...."

- Don't believe what the other "comments" say because he wrote them all. This guy is a waste [of] time....[1]

Let's call it a hung jury and leave it at that. Yet, even though the reviews are mixed, I think that virtually every former student of mine would agree that I test more frequently than most other instructors. There are several reasons for this. Attendance is frequently an issue at George Brown College and I have this crazy idea that attendance and academic success are positively correlated.

A point about this concept. When we say that things are positively correlated, what is implied is that when one increases the other increases or when one decreases the other decreases, and that a causal relationship exists. That is, better attendance leads to higher grades and vice versa. An example of negative correlation might be the relationship between hours spent with Netflix and grades: the more time a student watches movies, the lower his grades. Correlation — both positive and negative — will be a recurring theme in *Stalled* because I'm trying to determine what caused the economy to grow and which factors are responsible for it flatlining over the past fifteen years.

There are other reasons why I test as frequently as I do. It keeps students on top of the material throughout the semester, rather than encouraging them to cram for a single final exam. And because education really should be about the learning (shouldn't it?), testing is a wonderful feedback mechanism. It lets students know whether they understand the subject matter or not.

I am an old dog and testing is one of my tricks. Therefore, I'm going to be testing you, good reader, throughout this book. Interspersed among these two-hundred-and-thirty–odd pages are one hundred questions. I would encourage you to fill them in manually or check them off mentally. Of course, you can ignore them altogether, although I hope you don't.

They will help focus your thinking about whether the arguments I present are persuasive and enable us to agree on a path that will lead to a brighter future for everyone.

But first: seven questions to measure your interest in proceeding. I've already introduced myself as a tenured professor at George Brown College. Some of you might recognize me from my business commentary on CBC Radio. I also teach at the University of Toronto's School of Continuing Studies, running their Chartered Financial Analyst (CFA) and Canadian Securities Course (CSC) programs.

One of the important features of the University of Toronto courses is that they provide students with the opportunity to attend a couple of classes, then decide if the methodology is right for them. If it's not, they get a full refund. I like this policy. It helps students make informed decisions about going forward — or not — because the worst mistake anyone can make in the short time we have on this planet is to waste time.

That's what these questions are about. There aren't right or wrong answers, per se. But they will help you determine at a very early stage whether you should dedicate a good number of hours reading *Stalled*, or do something else from which you'll derive more *value*.

Value and values will be important words in *Stalled*. Robert Pirsig, whom you may know as the author of *Zen and the Art of Motorcycle Maintenance*, followed up with another book, one that I found infinitely more interesting: *Lila: An Inquiry Into Morals*. Pirsig talks a lot about values in *Lila*. According to him, our values express what is most important to us, and what is most important to us determines how we go about acting every day. I agree with him.

So, I've decided it's best to start with a few questions that will help you see if your values and mine are in sync. Now for the questions!

QUESTION 1
Are people rational economic actors?

Allow me to explain why I'm asking this.

My experience has been that people use their reason to help them get what they believe is best for them at a particular point in time. It must be noted that all of us are subject to "bounded rationality." That is, our ability to reason is imperfect and frequently coloured by emotion. The assertion that we're rational doesn't mean that there isn't the possibility of a temporal mismatch, that is, what seems good for us in one instant might not seem so if we adopt a different time horizon. ("Sure, Ben, one more for the road....") That fourth draft at the Crown and Dragon at 10:30 p.m. on Sunday evening sure felt good going down, but it failed to take into account that in six short hours I'd have to rise and shine, bright-eyed and bushy-tailed, for my 6:45 a.m. business commentary on CBC Radio.) It doesn't mean that my decision was irrational — it just wasn't particularly well thought through.

One more thing. The term *rational economic actor* implies the use of reason by a person when making economic choices, not that every decision revolves solely around "profit-maximizing" grounds. Let me return to that "fourth draft" example. I know that if I have that extra brewski, I'm going to have less money in my wallet. But I also believe that my overall utility (a fancy word for well-being) will be enhanced by it, making the decision a rational one.

Bottom line: Being a rational economic actor doesn't guarantee that one makes the "right" decision; it implies only that thought went into the decision before it was made.

QUESTION 1
Are people rational economic actors?

☐   Yes.

☐   No.

QUESTION 2
Would you agree that human nature hasn't changed in the past several thousand years and is unlikely to change in the next few thousand?

☐   Yes.

☐   No.

QUESTION 3
Do incentive systems determine behaviour?

We are at the same time self-interested beings and social animals. Incentive systems are designed to encourage us to act in a manner which is consistent with the general good, which means that frequently they "tilt" against our natural instinct.

Telling the truth, the whole truth, and nothing but the truth may not always be the best thing for witnesses in, say, a courtroom setting. This is why we penalize those who lie under oath. Think of perjury sentences as a stick.

In free and competitive markets, doing hard, dangerous, and high–value added work is rewarded more than doing easy, safe, and low–value added work. Think of the extra compensation as a carrot.

And civil society needs both sticks and carrots.

QUESTION 3

Do incentive systems determine behaviour?

☐　　Yes.

☐　　No.

QUESTION 4

Do you agree that actions speak louder than words and that individuals demonstrate what is truly important to them by the actions they take, not what they say?

☐　　Yes.

☐　　No.

QUESTION 5

Do you agree that self-interest drives principle?

When I was younger and far more naive, I believed that most individuals figured out (by whatever framework made the most sense to them — religious, secular humanist, whatever) what was "right" and what was "wrong," and then this was the North Star that guided behaviour. But as I've become older, I increasingly believe that what most of us (you can pretty much read everyone) do is figure out what serves our self-interest (subject to bounded rationality), and then construct the belief system that best supports it after the fact.

I think — and I'm certain you do as well — that slavery is singularly immoral (we'll return to this topic and the why of it later on). But I'm equally certain that previous generations reasoned that it was perfectly moral, largely because they believed it made their lives better, and came up with the necessary rationalizations to justify it.

QUESTION 5

Do you agree that self-interest drives principle?

☐ Yes.

☐ No.

QUESTION 6

Do you think that Canadian society should be understood as a collection of individuals, rather than a collection of groups?

☐ Yes.

☐ No.

QUESTION 7

Do you think that people should be held accountable for the choices they make?

The city I live in, Toronto, just went through a tumultuous period. Its then-mayor, Rob Ford, caused a great deal of controversy because he allegedly smoked crack cocaine. His defence seemed to be: first, you can't really prove it was crack cocaine, now can you? And even if it was — I was so badly intoxicated that I didn't know what I was doing, so I can't be blamed.

Okay. But he made the choice to drink that much in the first place. An adult should realize that if sufficient quantities of alcohol are consumed, judgment is impaired. Therefore, even if we allow that smoking crack was an unforeseen consequence of alcohol abuse, it doesn't stand as a valid defence.

On the other hand, one may well think that greater forces explain what we do and, if so, it would be unfair to hold individuals responsible for what they cannot control.

Do you believe in free will or not?

QUESTION 7

Do you think that people should be held accountable for the choices they make?

☐ Yes.

☐ No.

Time for full disclosure: I agree with all of those statements. Wait, let me take that back. I *strongly* agree with all of those statements. And everything that follows in *Stalled* will flow out of them as purely and, I hope, forcefully as a mountain stream fed by melting snow in the springtime.

If you don't see the world this way (anything under five out of seven is a red flag), then do yourself a favour: put the book down right now. Let me quote Salt-N-Pepa: "This dance ain't for everybody. Only the sexy people."[2]

On the other hand, if you agreed with at least five out of seven, then fasten your seat belt and enjoy the ride!

Just one last thing: this book is going to be *very* anecdotal. Once you get into it, you'll see that there is no shortage of research. But how we see the world is coloured to a great extent by significant events and single moments. Most of the anecdotes I'm going to relate can't be "proven." In some cases, they come from conversations I had years before. And I suspect that at least a couple of them may seem unbelievable to you because that's how they seem to me, even today.

Skeptics may think I made them up. Critics may accuse me of being a "liar, liar, pants on fire" and I can't defend myself except to say that at least a few of the anecdotes that can be proven are equally unbelievable as the ones that can't.

Here's how *Stalled* is organized.

Part One is a primer in neo-classical growth theory. This school of thought dominates contemporary thinking when it comes to explaining what causes economies to grow over time. Following the primer, I'm going to provide my unique addendum to neo-classical growth theory, because it seems to me that there is a missing link, as it were, in the economic growth evolutionary chain.

With the theoretical framework established, we move on to Part Two. It is divided into five main chapters that deal with the decades of the 1950s, 1960s, 1970s, 1980s, and 1990s. Each of these is followed by a shorter chapter that provides a little more detail about an important topic or idea touched on in the chapter.

My thesis — as I've already alluded to — is that over these fifty years Canadians of my generation enjoyed something unprecedented in human history: a half-century when the average citizen enjoyed a gigantic improvement in his or her standard of living.

I'll be the first to admit that some arbitrary distinctions will be made along the way. Things develop over time. The crisp categorizations I'm making serve the goals of simplicity and clarity. I will be taking a bit of poetic licence (but just a bit) with timelines, et cetera. The purpose is to serve the narrative and to keep our eyes firmly fixed on what this book is about, and that's an *explanation* of the swift economic ascent that followed the Second World War and of the flatlining we're now experiencing.

Part Three covers the period from the year 2000 to the present day.

Part Four offers a set of very specific recommendations to jump-start a Canadian economy that I believe has stalled.

PART ONE

What Is *Supposed* to Make an Economy Grow?

If you were born in Canada in the 1950s — as I was — you pretty much took it for granted that life would always get better.

I was raised in Etobicoke, a western suburb of Toronto. When I was very young, our family bought a window air conditioner. We were one of the first families on the block to have one. Within a few years, who didn't? About a decade after that, we had central air conditioning installed — an astonishing luxury that soon became commonplace.

Progress could be measured in an even more tangible way. In the 1950s, the average North American home measured less than 1,000 square feet. That increased to 1,200 square feet by the 1960s, 1,800 by the 1980s, and 2,400 by the year 2000.[1] And as the houses were getting bigger, the average family was getting smaller — the best of all worlds! Quality of life was improving.

This wasn't always the case in the human experience. The Dark Ages, a period spanning the fifth century A.D. to the fifteenth century A.D., was termed such because there was little improvement (if any) in the lives of average citizens. Since then, economic growth has been uneven, but for most citizens in the developed world life has improved immeasurably. This was particularly true in the half-century following the end of Second World War.

Because our DNA requires a framework within which to understand what we observe empirically, we've come up with theories to explain economic growth, in particular what has lifted the standard of living of those in the developed world. The Cobb-Douglas production function is central to "growth accounting" and the neo-classical framework. The phrase itself implies that there's a way to quantify (or account for) economic growth.

Some of the mathematical functions operate at a high level, but I'm far less interested in the fine details than I am with the broad brush strokes … and they go something like this.

Three factors drive economic growth:

- quantity of labour (think number of hours worked productively);

- amount of capital employed (think machinery used);

- total factor productivity (an encompassing phrase that captures both technological advances and the possibility that we can organize ourselves more perfectly to produce more, given the same hours worked and the same amount of capital employed).

Let's think about the Cobb-Douglas production function with the help of a very simple model. There's a village of two hundred people. Twenty are senior citizens who can't contribute much output at that advanced stage of their lives. Twenty are children who aren't expected to work, either. That leaves 160 people to support the community.

Eighty are men and eighty are women. Eighty toil on farms and the remaining eighty are split equally between doing manufacturing work and performing various services. Everyone is productive: the unemployment rate is zero. The standard work week is thirty-five hours.

One day they come together as a community and agree that everyone will work longer. They extend the work week to forty hours.

QUESTION 8

Everything else being equal, do you think that the decision to increase the work week will increase economic output?

☐   Yes.

☐   No.

I don't know how you answered, but Cobb-Douglas believers would have marked "Yes."

Next question. The work week has increased. Then everyone begins buying machinery to help them do their jobs better. The farmers replace their horses with tractors. The tradesmen trade in their hand tools and buy power tools. The service sector throws out its pens and gets typewriters.

QUESTION 9

Everything else being equal, do you agree that as more machinery is used economic output will also rise?

☐   Yes.

☐   No.

I don't know how you answered, but Cobb-Douglas believers ...

The work week is longer. More capital equipment is being used. And not only is the capital equipment improving as technology advances, the townspeople are figuring out how to organize themselves better. Technicians are specializing rather than being jacks of all trades. Time-motion studies help manufacturers work more efficiently.

QUESTION 10

Everything else being equal, would you agree that the greater the total factor productivity the greater the economic output?

☐   Yes.

☐   No.

I don't know ...

There are just a couple of more things to say before leaving the Cobb-Douglas production function and neo-classical growth theory.

First, increasing hours worked can only get you so far. Yes, this year the village can move from thirty-five to forty hours and maybe next year from forty to forty-five hours. But there is only so much time in a day. You can't grow the economy forever by continuing to increase the work week.

The next important implication is that, in the vernacular of Cobb-Douglas, capital deepening can also only get you so far. Let's keep it simple with this example: There are three carpenters working together, framing houses. Right now, they are all using hand tools. Carpenter One buys power tools and his productivity goes up. Then Carpenter Two follows suit and ditto with his productivity. Carpenter Three is last to the party — but he joins in. It stands to reason that after capital is fully employed, they will be working more efficiently. With hand tools, each framed five houses a month.

That has increased to ten … but as they upgrade their equipment with new and somewhat improved tools, their productivity will exhibit diminishing marginal returns.

Diminishing marginal returns is an important economic concept and one that every recreational runner is familiar with. It's a nice day, so you go out for a thirty-minute run. You cover six kilometres, which means one every five minutes. If you decide to stretch your run out to an hour, it's highly unlikely that you'll cover twelve klicks. Rather, in that time you might run ten. That's an example of diminishing marginal returns. As you add increments (in this case thirty-minute blocks of time), your output (distance) increases, but at a diminishing rate. In that second half-hour, it's taking you seven and a half minutes to cover a kilometre while it took you only five minutes previously.

This teaching from neo-classical growth theory has important implications for a developed country like Canada that is already "deep" in capital. Neo-classical growth theory would predict that we can't rely on capital accumulation alone to drive progress. It will have to be other things: either number of hours worked, total factor productivity, or some combination of both.

One final point: let's say there are two villages that are virtually identical, except Village Two has a better climate. Its growing season is longer, which means that there is more agricultural output per hour worked and per unit of capital. Moreover, Village Two has denser forest around it, providing fuel that is both abundant and cheap. Under those circumstances, wouldn't we expect that Village Two's citizens would enjoy a higher standard of living than Village One's? Absolutely. Yet, at the same time, those natural advantages wouldn't translate into a higher growth rate. Village Two's people would be better off, yes, but the gulf between the standard of living of the two villages would not widen over the years.

Neo-classical growth theory allows for the fact that even if hours worked, capital employed, and total factor productivity are equal, certain jurisdictions — if they're endowed with resources — can and in fact should be better off than another locale not similarly blessed.

To summarize: according to growth accounting and the Cobb-Douglas production function, there may be a different base of wealth between two villages or counties or countries or you-name-it, depending on resource endowment. However, once that is put aside, it's only about hours worked, amount of capital, and total factor productivity. Right?

Not exactly.

It seems to me that neo-classical growth theory misses the single most important factor that has led mankind onward and upward and that is … but before I get to it, let me ask another question, one that I routinely pose to my George Brown College students early each semester.

QUESTION 11

Which country has the higher GDP per capita?

☐   Israel.

☐   Saudi Arabia.

As soon as the words are out of my mouth, I can read the reactions of my students on their faces. "Sir, come on! What do you think we are? Stupid?!" (Some of those comments on ratemyprofessor.com were spot on!) "Saudi Arabia has oil … lots and lots of it."

This is an indisputable point. Saudi Arabia extracts 10 million barrels a day[2] … 417,000 barrels an hour … 7,000 each minute … in excess of 100 barrels of black gold every single second of every single day. Yes, the answer is clear-cut and obvious.

The country with the higher GDP per capita is, by a wide margin, Israel. According to the CIA's *World Factbook*, Saudi Arabia has a GDP per capita of $31,300 while the corresponding figure for Israel is $36,200.[3]

When I let this out of the bag most of the students sit in stunned silence.

How can this possibly be?

They know that Saudi Arabia has oil.

But they don't know what special resource Israel has. Until I tell them.

Israel has … Israelis.

People, properly organized and motivated, are the key drivers of both prosperity and progress.

Uh-oh. My suspicion is that I've already stepped on some politically sensitive toes. But I've got some good news. When I worked for one of Canada's largest publicly traded financial institutions, I attended "sensitivity" training, or as they termed it, a "Respect in the Workplace" seminar.

One of the session's key objectives was to teach me and my colleagues what was and what was not offensive. In *Stalled*, you will *not* encounter phrases like: "Another kick at the cat" (cruelty to animals is an inappropriate subject for metaphor); "Blind as a bat" (the visually impaired and/or crepuscular flying mammals might take umbrage); "It ain't over 'til the fat lady sings" (female endomorphs have feelings, too!); or "Too many chiefs, not enough Indians" (wasn't taking their land enough?!).

Consider yourself warned. Hands up, chin down. We're adults and I plan to speak about all topics honestly, including values and culture. And that's almost un-Canadian.

We're a very polite people. We tend to be uneasy with frank discussions about culture. We're much more comfortable when we trivialize it: "Went to a great Thai restaurant last night. Even used chopsticks instead of a knife and fork! Then to a Brazilian movie (subtitles only, dubbing is just so déclassé!). Capped it off with a cappuccino at an *authentic* Italian café … no Starbucks for me!"

How cosmopolitan can ya get!

I would agree that the foods we eat and our entertainments possess "cultural" elements. But the ultimate truths around culture address deeper questions and more profound issues. They may be discussed aloud around kitchen tables with families, or they may be with us in our thoughts:

- What is most important to us?

- What do we expect from ourselves?

- What do we expect from our friends and neighbours?

- What is the right way to live?

Just off the top of my head, these are some critical cultural questions. I'm sure you've got others. That's the essence of this book. *Stalled* will be a frank discussion of values and the cultural factors that were responsible for the astonishing economic growth from 1950 to 2000. Because how our values have changed goes a very long way toward explaining why the Canadian economy has stalled in recent years.

A quick aside. To the extent that so-called polite society and the chattering classes discuss culture, it's with an *Animal Farm*–like sophistication of "two legs bad, four legs good." Developed cultures are by their very nature flawed. Primitive ones are inherently pristine. I've heard that argument a zillion times and it's hogwash.

This leads us to Question 12, and I think you know how I'd answer it:

QUESTION 12

Do you think that development is a good thing, that economic growth is desirable, and that progress is something we should embrace?

☐   Yes.

☐   No.

PART TWO
The 1950s

When I was sixteen years old, I started a landscaping business. That was what my grandfather did for a living (he ran his own crew), so I had access to the tools and expertise. In mid-March of my second-last year in high school, I went around the neighbourhood, knocking on doors and lining up work for when spring arrived.

One of my first customers was a lovely couple, the Smiths. Mr. Smith was an older gentleman, retired, and didn't have the energy to cut his own lawn anymore. Mrs. Smith was exceptionally kind, treating me almost like a grandson. There was always a glass of cold lemonade on a hot day. One afternoon she invited me into their home to drink it with them. It gave us time to get to know each other better. Up to then it had been mostly business.

It was a modest home — but very much a home — with family pictures everywhere. One of the photographs that drew my attention was of a group of young soldiers; as it turned out, Mr. Smith was one of them. He had been born in 1899 and was fifteen years old when the First World War started. He lied about his age so he could enlist. His unit was among the first of the Canadian contingents to land in France, and Mr. Smith ended up spending four years in the mud and the blood, until the Armistice was signed in November of 1918.

He returned home and married his high-school sweetheart — that was Mrs. Smith — and they started raising a family. Then war reared its ugly head again, and in 1939 Mr. Smith once more volunteered. He spent six years in different combat zones, finally returning home for good in 1945.

At the time, I didn't fully appreciate how truly extraordinary this gentleman was. And he was truly a *gentle* man — you could sense it through and through. Duty compelled him to do what he felt was the right thing, which was to throw himself into the line of fire for his country.

QUESTION 13

In twice volunteering during wartime, Mr. Smith was what?

☐ Noble beyond belief.

☐ A complete sucker.

What Mr. Smith did was extraordinary. But he wasn't alone. A total of 1.1 million Canadians served during the Second World War. More than 40 percent of males aged eighteen to forty-five wore their country's uniform. In addition, one million Canadians worked in essential war industries while two million were engaged in "essential civilian employment," which included agriculture, communications, and food processing. At the time, Canada's population was just over eleven million. This meant that — once you separated out the very young and very old — more than half of all Canadians participated *directly* in the war effort.

And even if you didn't participate "directly," your life would have been affected. Commencing in 1942, basics like meat, sugar, and gasoline were rationed. Everyone was called upon to sacrifice.

However, those sacrifices were trivial compared to the one made by the 45,000 who gave their lives.[1] That represented 0.4 percent of the population. The high school I went to had 1,200 students. Simple probability would suggest that at least five young (most likely) men from Etobicoke Collegiate would have lost their lives. My guess is that most Canadians knew at least one person who never came back. It's a sobering thought. Yet I believe that there were positive consequences. A world view was forged by the fire of war; a common mission unified Canada and laid the foundation for the spectacular success of the 1950s and 1960s.

I try to put myself in the shoes of Mr. Smith and others like him and think what would have driven them when they returned home. I'm guessing it came down to something like this: the Second World War was so horrific that sensible people wanted to do everything in their power to ensure it never happened again. (This desire was made even stronger by the recognition that with the development of nuclear weapons a Third World War might mean the end of civilization as we knew it.) A very clear line could be drawn between the outbreak of the Second World War and the rise of Hitler. An equally clear line could be drawn between the rise of Hitler and Germany's economic ruin after the First World War. Rational, peace-loving people saw the connection between prosperity and peace, and so (as of 1950) 13.7 million[2] Canadians set themselves to building the country.

I wasn't around at the time. But my gut tells me that a general consensus emerged around the following:

- we can't afford another world war;

- we only made it through and won because everyone who was able-bodied did his or her fair share and just flat-out sucked it up when the going got tough;

- after all we've been through, we deserve to enjoy some of the good things in life — but you'll only get those if you work for them. Nothing in this world comes delivered on a silver platter; and

- all Canadians are in this together. Bombs don't differentiate between the rich and the poor.

It was around these principles and the desire for peace and prosperity that the 1950s unfolded.

The desire for peace, the desire not to see another world war led to Canada's enthusiastic support for the United Nations and peacekeeping missions.

And key to the country's economic progress was the view that individuals, not the government, were responsible for themselves and their well-being. Government took care of "peace and order." There was no belief that it was the duty of the government to take care of individuals. That was each person's responsibility.

However, government did play an important role in economic development. It was called upon to provide essential services; then citizens, acting either as individuals or as part of a group — whatever they preferred — would take care of producing the goods and services that made life worth living.

One of the things that government provided was infrastructure. Two important initiatives from that era were the Trans-Canada Highway Act of 1949, which saw the construction of the Trans-Canada Highway begin in 1950, and the building of the Yonge subway line in Toronto. (A quick aside. I've lived in Toronto all my life and it is the biggest city in Canada. I'm using the Yonge line as representative of the kind of projects that were happening all across Canada and, indeed, North America.)

Work on the subway began in September 1949. A technique called "cut and cover" was employed. A large trench was dug into Yonge Street and steel beams were then laid across the trench and covered with dirt and asphalt, which allowed cars and pedestrians to keep using Toronto's main thoroughfare while work proceeded under tires and feet. Fourteen thousand tons of steel, 1.4 million bags of cement, and five years later, there was a line that ran from Eglinton Station to Union Station, allowing more people to get to where they had to go more quickly and efficiently.[3]

The building of the highway system did essentially the same thing: it facilitated activity that produced goods and services of *real* value.

There is a great deal of confusion about *how* infrastructure spending creates wealth. Most people — mistakenly — believe that the value is in the work itself. Nothing could be further from the truth. The value of infrastructure spending is that it creates efficiencies that otherwise wouldn't exist.

Imagine that there are three towns of equal size, located several hundred miles apart. Right now, it's physically impossible to get from any of the three towns to any of the others. This means that each must be self-sufficient in producing what it needs. For example, Town One would have a small factory that makes furniture, a small factory that makes shoes, and a small factory that makes clothing. Let's say that each factory employs twenty people. The same situation is true for Towns Two and Three. They have similar factories of similar size, and altogether 180 people work to make the necessary furniture, shoes, and clothing for the people of the three towns.

Then, a highway is built that joins them. You can now quickly get from Town One to Town Two, Town One to Town Three, and Town Two to Town Three.

Economies of scale are critically important in manufacturing — the opposite of diminishing returns. If it takes twenty people to produce one hundred pairs of shoes a week, it won't take forty to produce two hundred

— it might only take thirty. Instead of needing sixty people to produce the necessary shoes for all three towns, thirty-five might be enough.

Look what just happened. The same output is accomplished with thirty-five people, meaning that twenty-five can turn their energies to something else. This is the kind of efficiency that is fostered by the right kind of infrastructure spending.

Note — and this is important: It wasn't the *building* of the highways that made Canada wealthier.

Again, a simple model helps make the point.

Let's imagine that instead of building a highway that linked Towns One, Two, and Three, the same resources were spent on roads that went nowhere, that were never used by a single person. How can that possibly be understood as adding value? There would have been negative value, because the time and energy wasted could have been used for productive activity — that is, making more furniture, shoes, and clothing!

The subway system or any good public transit system impacts the real economy in a slightly different way. It makes it possible for the human capital of a municipality to be used in the most effective way possible.

Another example: I am a highly skilled carpenter who lives in the west end of a city. But all the factories that need my services are in the east end and I have no way to get there. Meanwhile, there is a highly skilled welder who lives in the east end of that city. But all the factories that need his services are in the west end and he has no way to get there. It might be that I'm okay at welding and the welder is okay at carpentry, so we are able to get jobs close to where we live. However, in this case, human capital is not being maximized.

Public transit systems that get people quickly to and from where they can add the most value are clearly accretive to growth. It's not the spending on infrastructure, per se … it's what the infrastructure facilitates that drives economic progress.

Infrastructure spending was key in propelling the Canadian economy forward in the 1950s. In addition, there was a great deal of attention paid to education, which improved the country's human capital.

My mother graduated with a commercial certificate from an inner-city public high school, the equivalent of a Grade 10 education. She came from a family where neither of her parents were formally educated, and English was not spoken at home. By her own admission, she was an average student. From what I remember about my mother's basic skills in the three Rs, her grammar and spelling were far better than mine ... even with Microsoft's assistance (if you doubt me on this one, please get in touch with my editor), and this after four years of university and a master's degree in business administration.

But as excellent as my mother's communication skills were, they paled compared to her math. I grew up in an era when Canada used the imperial system of measurement. Everything was in ounces, pints, and quarts. My mother grew up in a household where every penny mattered, and this was never lost on her. While she and my father worked as a team to provide wonderfully for me and my sister, my mother was acutely budget-conscious. I have distinct memories of grocery shopping at the local Loblaws, and as we walked the aisles, she would work out to a decimal place — in her head — where the best value would be found, comparing one brand's thirty-two-ounce size with another's forty-eight. If that doesn't speak to the quality of public education at the time, I don't know what does.

In 1955, there were 74,000 Canadians enrolled full-time in post-secondary institutions,[4] which represented a very small fraction of the population. The vast majority of young Canadians (and this included my mother) joined the workforce after graduating from high school, equipped with the basic skills to add value immediately.

This was a *good* thing. Some more simple arithmetic: If you were born in 1930, life expectancy was sixty-one. If you started working straight out of high school at the age of eighteen, 70 percent of the years you had on this planet were spent in productive activity. If you started working after four years of university at the age of twenty-two, that dropped to 64 percent. Aggregate that across a population that numbered into the millions, and it adds up.

Remember Cobb-Douglas: Everything else being equal, more hours worked means higher economic growth.

Something else was going on during that decade. Even while government was ploughing huge amounts of money into infrastructure, the ratio of government debt to gross domestic product was shrinking spectacularly. In 1945, the last year of the Second World War, debt as a percentage of GDP stood at 160 percent. By the beginning of the 1950s, it had come down to a manageable 90 percent; then, ten years later, it was only 40 percent.[5]

How was that possible?

It's easily explained. A growing economy meant that tax revenues were increasing, and given that government limited its role, things took care of themselves.

It's almost impossible to overstate how important it is to minimize debt, whether it be for a household or nation. If you look at the budgets of most governments today, one of the biggest single line items is that for public debt charges. This year in Canada — at the federal level alone — interest payments will cost each Canadian close to $1,000.[6] It was a different story in the 1950s. Even as government revenue was exceeding expenditures and debt was being reduced, even while the standard of living and quality of life of Canadians were improving, the personal savings rate was *increasing*. It ranged between 6 percent and 10 percent throughout the decade,[7] and if there is one thing that history tells us — if we're not blind to the obvious — it's that there's a positive correlation between savings and economic growth. In fact, higher savings rates drive higher growth.

Time for the next question … and this one is a lob ball.

QUESTION 14

Which economy experienced the higher rate of economic growth from 2000 to 2010?

☐　　The United States of America.

☐　　The People's Republic of China.

According to the World Bank, the American economy grew by approximately 2 percent per year while China's clipped along at 10 percent.[8]

QUESTION 15

Which country had the higher savings rate from 2000 to 2010?

☐　　The United States of America.

☐　　The People's Republic of China.

Question 15 might have been even easier than 14. China's gross savings rate for the decade exceeded 50 percent while America's was in the teens.[9] It is unanimously agreed that China's savings rate is the highest in the world.

Wait a second. Isn't it a mantra of conventional economic thinking that spending is "good" and saving is "bad"? When you spend money, aren't you're moving things around and making things happen? Don't you hear this all the time? Aren't we continually told that we'll solve the country's economic ills by getting more money into the hands of consumers?

There's only one problem with this argument — it's simplistic nonsense. Because it confuses the wealth-creation process (working and making goods and services of real value) with the consumption function (using things that have already been made). It puts the consumption cart before the production horse.

There are two logical reasons why higher savings rates contribute to higher economic growth. The first is grounded in the Cobb-Douglas framework. When someone makes money, there are only two things she can do with it: spend it today or save it now to eventually spend down the road. One way or the other, the money will be spent. But a benefit of saving is that it allows pools of capital to accumulate, which facilitates investment and the creation of that much more wealth in the future.

A characteristic of the poorest countries in the world is that their savings rates are very low. This makes sense. If you're living in abject poverty, it takes every single peso or pula to make it through the day. You can't afford the luxury of putting money aside. But what that means, unfortunately, is that tomorrow will be just as bleak as today.

There's another reason why a high savings rate leads directly to higher growth and it's firmly grounded in behavioural economics. Say I currently make $50,000 a year. If I would like to enjoy the lifestyle of someone who makes that much, I will have to spend every cent. At the same time, it's a priority of mine to save 10 percent of my income. I understand that this is what I need to ensure a dignified and comfortable retirement. Seems that I'm stuck between a rock and a hard place. If I save that 10 percent, then I've got only $45,000 to live on.

Except, I've got other options. I can increase my income. I can work harder and longer at my current occupation, putting in overtime. I can get a part-time job. Or I can upgrade my skills, increase my value as a marketable employee, and make that extra $5,555 annually.

Then I can enjoy a $50,000 standard of living *and* accomplish my savings goals.

And drive real economic growth.

Let's get back to the 1950s. One of the most significant events in that decade was the large increase in the number of immigrants that Canada accepted. Of course, Canada is a nation of immigrants, and immigration has always been critical to this country's development. In 1947, Prime Minister Mackenzie King enunciated the principles that guided policy for at least the following decade:

> The policy of the government is to foster the growth of the population of Canada by the encouragement of immigration. The government will seek by legislation, regulation, and vigorous administration, to ensure the careful selection and permanent settlement of such numbers of immigrants as can be advantageously absorbed in our national economy.

It's hard to argue with any of that. A "careful selection" of immigrants and efforts to ensure that immigrants would be quickly integrated into the fabric of Canada would be a win-win situation for both Canadian-born citizens and immigrants.

However, Mackenzie King wasn't finished. He continued, "The people of Canada do not wish as a result of mass immigration to make a fundamental alteration in the character of our population. Large-scale immigration from the Orient would change the fundamental composition of the Canadian population."[10]

This is much easier to argue with, particularly given present sensibilities. But it did reveal something important about the thinking of the day. And that was that most Canadians were more "comfortable" with immigration from Europe than from other continents.

This is something that Canada has struggled with and continues to struggle with — and it speaks directly to one of the questions posed earlier: Should this country be understood as a collection of individuals or groups? Mackenzie King saw it in terms of the latter.

However, one of the positive and unintended consequences of this world view was the policy of allowing many "displaced persons" to enter the country from Europe. With so much of that continent in ruins, many people didn't have a home to go back to. Between 1947 and 1962, 250,000 displaced persons were admitted into Canada, which was more than the rest of the overseas countries (United States, Australia, and New Zealand) combined.[11] This was a case where this country did the right thing and benefitted immensely.

Many of those folks are still alive today, and if you're reading *Stalled* I have one thing to say: "THANK YOU!" Because you helped build what I've enjoyed all my life.

Think about the self-selection process that made someone leave the Ukraine or Germany or Poland and roll the dice in a strange land. It's not right to stereotype, I know, but I'm going to anyway: If there were one single characteristic that bound them all — men and women — it was that they had *cojones* the size of bowling balls. In most cases, these brave people came to Canada with the shirts on their backs and nothing else. The cultural barriers were huge; the social safety net non-existent. All they had were all the disadvantages anyone needs if they want to truly succeed, and succeed they did, making both their lives and those of future generations that much richer because of their hard work and sacrifice.

Before we leave the 1950s, a few anecdotes that tell us so much about the zeitgeist of the age.

The 1950s was the Golden Age of television. Shows like *Gunsmoke* and *Have Gun — Will Travel* were especially popular, and hearkened to a past where individual, strong men did the right thing and ensured that justice was done.[12] Those stories inspired future generations, but none more than the series *Perry Mason*.

It was America's longest running and most successful show about lawyers. Canadian-born Raymond Burr, starring as Perry Mason, week after week took the side of an innocent person accused of murder, and by the end of the hour, not only had he exonerated the innocent, he'd broken down the guilty party and elicited a confession!

Who wouldn't want to be a lawyer? It seemed the noblest profession known to mankind.

Of course, Perry Mason was a fictional character, but there were men doing great things in real life. In his book *The Right Stuff*, Tom Wolfe writes about a group of combat aviators who later became test pilots and ultimately the first American astronauts. A story from the book tells of a dogfight during the Korean War. I'll let Wolfe take it from here:

> Combat had its own infinite series of tests, and one of the greatest sins was "chattering" or "jabbering" on the radio. The combat frequency was to be kept clear of all but strategically essential messages, and all unenlightening comments were regarded as evidence of funk, of the wrong stuff.
>
> A Navy pilot (in legend, at any rate) began shouting, "I've got a MIG at zero! A MIG at zero!" — meaning that it had maneuvered in behind him and was locked in on his tail.
>
> An irritated voice cut in and said, "Shut up and die like an aviator."[13]

"Shut up and die like an aviator."

This era unapologetically saw courage as a virtue and, to some degree, demanded and expected it. It wasn't about being touchy-feely and feeling sorry for yourself; it was about getting it done and showing grace under pressure.

In 1953, Charles Wilson was CEO of General Motors when then-President Dwight David Eisenhower tapped him for Secretary of Defense. In hearings before Congress (there were concerns about his holdings of GM stock and whether he could be objective), he made the following statement: "For years, I have thought that what was good for our country was good for General Motors, and vice versa."[14]

This quote may surprise many of you. There's a widespread misconception that he said "What's good for General Motors is good for the United States, and vice versa." I've heard several people use that statement as an indictment of the 1950s, that is, business came first at the expense of the general good.

Let's revisit Wilson's *actual* words. He was implying that steady, non-inflationary growth, a rising tide that lifted all economic boats, along with peace and prosperity — the phenomenon that people organize into political units to help achieve — would by definition benefit General Motors, which happened to be the biggest consumer discretionary company in North America at that time.

The 1950s taught us that sound public policy dovetails with strong economic growth.

One of GM's rivals was AMC, the American Motor Company. Its CEO from 1954 to 1962 was George Romney. When he took the helm, AMC was floundering and there's a compelling argument that he saved it from bankruptcy, before making it extremely profitable.

The company's board of directors believed that he should be rewarded. Romney was making a salary of $225,000 (this was at a time when the median family income was $5,600) and they thought he deserved $100,000 on top of that (equivalent to $1.5 million in today's dollars) — Romney refused.[15] His argument was that no one needed any more money than he was already getting.

What do you think that did for morale at AMC? I'm sure there were some workers who thought, *Look, the guy is already making so much money that he can't know what to do with it!* But I'm equally certain that there were more than a few who argued: "He didn't have to turn it down. Pretty righteous thing to do, if you ask me."

Romney was making about forty times the median family income. According to the Canadian Centre for Policy Alternatives, Canada's one hundred top-paid CEOs make 171 times more than the average Canadian worker. By 1:11 p.m. on January 2 — the first working day of the year — members of this select group have earned more than the typical working stiff makes in twelve months.[16]

There has always been income disparity in North America. It is likely that there always will be. But a symbolic gesture like the one Romney made *matters* and was a sign of the times.

The 1950s in fifty words: Immigrants join the native-born in building the country. Massive wealth-generating infrastructure projects are initiated, even while government reduces debt. Individuals take responsibility for their own futures, saving mightily. And while Canada's population went up by 30 percent, real GDP per capita increased at an annual rate of 2.5 percent for each year.[17]

And the next ten years would be even better.

Wealth Generation – and What Makes Wages Go Up

GDP per capita went up sharply during the 1950s, which was a good thing. We want the lot of the average person to improve as time goes by.

However, as much as we crave wealth generation, there is very little systematic thought into what *really* drives it.

Let's establish a few basic principles.

There is a small community that consists of three families. They have organized themselves such that one family provides basic food for everyone, another basic clothing, and the third basic shelter. They trade basic food, basic clothing, and basic shelter, and everyone's needs are satisfied.

However, in addition to the basic clothing provided by the second family, it makes especially good clothing for itself. This means that the overall wealth of the community is higher than it was before. The other two families decide that they would also like especially good clothing for themselves.

There are several alternatives. They could illegally take the clothing. But this would mean that the community's total wealth is unchanged — they're better off at the expense of the first family.

Another alternative would be to organize themselves politically and "legally" expropriate it. The argument could be that this family doesn't deserve all the good clothing itself. It should be forced to share. But this would also mean that the total wealth of the community is unchanged.

Or the families could strike a bargain: *If we offer especially good food and especially good shelter, would you be willing to exchange some especially good clothing?* If the answer is "yes," wealth is being created. Everyone wins. And it illustrates the single key point about wealth generation: It is achieved through *voluntary* exchange.

In this example, I've used goods rather than services. But the framework is the same. What if the first family, in addition to providing basic food, were particularly good entertainers? And what if they were willing to put on shows to enrich the lives of the other families in exchange for especially good clothing and especially good shelter? Moreover, what if the other two families would prefer to see an entertaining show than to have especially good food? Once again, everyone wins if everyone voluntarily agrees. There is no meaningful distinction between the provision of services rather than goods: The model holds.

On the other hand, what if the first family were terrible entertainers? And what if they spent an equal amount of time rehearsing, but the other families refused to exchange clothing and shelter to see them? Just because the first family spent a great deal of time in their artistic pursuits doesn't mean that wealth is created.

Wealth creation isn't a function of hours worked; it's a function of hours worked *productively*.

This leads us to several key understandings:

- by definition, wealth-generation it is *not* a zero-sum game. Growing the pie benefits multiple parties;

- wealth generation works only if production is directly responsive to the needs and wants of other parties. This means it is the most selfless exercise known to mankind: to the extent you provide exactly what other people crave most, you benefit the most;

- wealth generation works best when executed through voluntary arrangements, allowing each party to customize the benefit it will receive.

The majority of Canadians are employed rather than self-employed. This means they rely on somebody making the voluntary decision to pay them more if they want to get ahead. Therefore, what drives real wage growth should be of acute concern.

I'm going to go back in history to demonstrate this process in action. In 1914 the average industrial wage in the United States was $1.75 a day. That year, Henry Ford shocked the business world by paying his workers $5.00 a day — almost tripling the average wage paid at the time.[1]

The question is *why*. Why did he do that?

I'm going to present two different interpretations. Just so you know in advance, one of them is mine. But I'm not going to tell you which one yet. I'll let you read them first.

QUESTION 16

Which of the following statements provides the more reasonable interpretation of why Henry Ford paid his workers almost three times the prevailing industrial wage?

☐ Ford was neither a madman, nor a socialist, but a smart capitalist whose profits more than doubled from $25 million in 1914 to $57 million two years later.... Ford understood the basic economic bargain that lies at the heart of a modern, productive economy: workers are also consumers.[2]

☐ Ford was neither a madman, nor a socialist, but a smart capitalist whose profits more than doubled from $25 million in 1914 to $57 million two years later.... Ford understood that if you paid workers above-average wages, you would attract the best and they would be motivated to work hard.[3]

The choice couldn't be clearer: Did Henry Ford pay his workers well because in doing so he would create a market for his products, or did he pay his workers well because he would get more work out of them?

☐ I agree with the first interpretation.

☐ I agree with the second interpretation.

I've tried to be as fair as I can. I've let you make your selection before I reveal which one of the two is mine, because there is a fundamental problem with the first interpretation: It makes sense only if one is incapable of performing simple arithmetic.

In 1914, Ford was a privately held company. That meant that every dollar of profit went into Henry Ford's pocket. He could pay his workers $2 a day (a slight premium to the average wage), which meant $500 annually, or $5 a day, which meant $1,250 — a premium of $750. At the time, a Model T — the company's flagship brand — retailed for between $450 and $550.[4] Let's split the difference and call it $500.

Ford chose to pay his workers $1,250 because this gave them the extra money they needed to buy one of his autos, thereby putting $500 back in his pocket, right? Well, not exactly. Because anyone who knows the first thing about business understands that owners keep the profit, not the revenue. Let's be generous and imagine that the profit margin on a Model T was 25 percent. Ford gets back 25 percent of $500, or $125, while he paid out an extra $750 in wages that year! And that's the first year. Because unless these workers buy a new car every year, from that point forward it's pure expenditure on Hank's part, with no benefit flowing back to him.

Then there's the second interpretation, which is not only my argument, by the way, it's the one you'll find put forward as the "primary" motivation on the Ford Motor Company website![5] Because it's the one that makes sense. There's a term for it: the "efficiency wage."

The premise of the efficiency wage is that it is enlightened business practice to pay workers more than the bare minimum because more generous pay packages result in greater output and higher profits. If you pay someone the absolute minimum needed to get a warm body, you'll get an untalented person who will give you minimum effort. In a market economy, wages are determined by many factors, but the value-added component is decisive. The more value added that is directly attributable to your efforts, the more money you'll make. It's why athletes like Sidney Crosby and LeBron James earn more than the average player; they more directly boost their team's revenue. And if I may paraphrase the words in the first interpretation, *that* is the basic economic bargain that lies at the heart of a modern, productive economy.

The first interpretation should be at least a bit troubling. In place of hard analysis, we have wishful thinking. It might be nice if everyone were paid more money (because we're all consumers, aren't we?), irrespective of whether anyone works harder and/or smarter and adds more value. But it's not how any economy works. Wages move in lockstep with productivity and anything that enhances productivity leads to higher wages. And the reason why wages grew so robustly in the 1950s was a combination of capital deepening and a workforce that flat-out busted its @ss.

It just occurred to me. I haven't told you who wrote the words for the first interpretation. It was Robert Reich, who is currently Chancellor's Professor of Public Policy at the Goldman School of Public Policy at the University of California, Berkeley. He was formerly a professor at Harvard University's John F. Kennedy School of Government and Mr. Reich served as Labor Secretary during the Clinton administration.[6]

You can't make this stuff up.

The 1960s

John Fitzgerald Kennedy was an inspirational figure. My parents loved Canada, grateful for the opportunity it had provided them, yet they still had a small bust of JFK that sat on a living room table. If there was one person who symbolized the 1960s, it would be Kennedy, and there is one single quote that defined him above all else: "My fellow Americans, ask not what your country can do for you, ask what you can do for your country."[1]

The words inspired a continent, at least temporarily. The irony is that before the decade was out, this quote had been turned on its head: North Americans were increasingly asking what their country could do for them, and expecting more and more.

JFK had a wonderful ability to turn a phrase. If the "ask not" quote is his most famous, perhaps number two was "Those who make peaceful revolution impossible will make violent revolution inevitable."[2] The years after JFK's death were turbulent, but there was a peaceful revolution that had been going on since the middle of the Second World War, and the ripple effects were felt in both the developed and developing worlds.

It was the so-called "Green Revolution," referring to improved agricultural practices that started in Mexico in the 1940s, and spread across the globe over the next two decades. This revolution's George Washington was an American scientist, Norman Borlaug. He developed new, disease-resistance strains of wheat. These products, combined with mechanized farming, made the United States, a country that had previously had to import half of its wheat, a net exporter by the decade's end.

The Green Revolution involved more than developing new and more robust strains of plants. It also crossed into fields as diverse as agronomy, soil science, and genetic engineering.[3]

Almost unbelievably — because of the latter in particular — there is some "controversy" around the Green Revolution. There have been criticisms levelled against it, including that increasing food production has led to overpopulation (suggesting it would be better if more people starved to death?) and that some places — specifically Africa — have not benefitted to the same extent as others because of a lack of infrastructure and corrupt governments (clearly Borlaug's fault!).

QUESTION 17

Which do you think a critic of the Green Revolution is more likely to have?

☐   A full stomach.

☐   An empty stomach.

The Green Revolution was — and is — an unmitigated good and if there ever was someone who deserved a Nobel Peace Prize, it was Norman Borlaug, who received the award in 1970.[4]

Canada benefitted from the Green Revolution. One of the consequences was that fewer people actually produced more food. In 1951, 2.9 million Canadians lived and worked on farms. That number was cut in half by 1971.[5] This change freed them to do other things; that is, to provide other goods and services, enabling the economy to grow even faster.

A transition was continuing. Canada, which had had an economy based on agriculture in the nineteenth century, was becoming increasingly more reliant on manufacturing, and its single most important sector was automobiles.

General Motors, Ford, and Chrysler were a tight oligopoly that controlled the North American automotive market. They manufactured on both sides of the border and all faced the same problem: there were stiff duties on both imports and exports. This meant that in order to sell Thunderbirds in Canada, Ford had to produce Thunderbirds in Canada.

Otherwise, the tariffs made the cars prohibitively expensive. This hindered the economies of scale that are required to manufacture efficiently.

A compromise solution was eventually reached — the Auto Pact of 1965.

Its key points were:

- for tariff-free entry of Canadian automobiles or original equipment parts into the U.S., automobiles must contain at least 50 percent North American (U.S. or Canadian) content;

- for tariff-free entry of U.S. finished vehicles or original equipment parts into Canada, manufacturers in Canada must satisfy the following criteria:

  - manufacturers must maintain a certain ratio between the net sales value of vehicles made in Canada and the net sales value of vehicles sold in Canada;

  - the amount of Canadian value added for all classes of vehicles made in Canada must be at least as great as the amount achieved in the base year.[6]

The Auto Pact created a unified North American market that discriminated against manufacturers located off this continent. It meant, practically speaking, that if Canada accounted for 10 percent of the North American auto market revenues, 10 percent of the total value of all cars sold in a calendar year had to be built here. This allowed a company like Ford to do all of its production of one model in Detroit, and sell them across North America, as long as it did all of its production of another car in Windsor, Ontario.

This was good for both countries, but the impact was more pronounced in Canada: the productivity gap between Canadian auto plants and U.S. plants narrowed markedly in the wake of the Auto Pact.[7]

Geography — as well as culture — made it inevitable that the United States would be our most important trading partner (and vice versa, though many Americans are unaware of this fact).

A trade relationship can be impacted significantly by exchange rates.

A quick step back in history. Coming out of the Second World War, there was a desire for the developed countries of the world to maintain the value of their currencies. I still remember a picture from my high-school history textbook of a German man in the 1930s pushing a wheelbarrow full of bills in order to purchase a single loaf of bread. The painful lesson was that runaway inflation could lead to economic and social chaos that in turn could lead to horrendous political solutions. Therefore, exchange-rate stability was a paramount goal of international policy in the 1940s and 1950s. This led to the Bretton Woods agreement.

The U.S. dollar (USD) was established as the global reserve currency, the benchmark against which other currencies were valued. Exchange rates were fixed for the world's currencies, with one important exception — the Canadian dollar.[8] From 1950 to 1959, the Canadian dollar (CAD) was allowed to float, and for much of that time it traded at a slight premium to the USD. However, in 1960 it started to fall sharply. Canada returned to a fixed exchange-rate system from 1962 to 1970, with a new rate of 0.925USD to buy 1CAD.[9]

The combination of a fixed dollar and managed trade wasn't optimal. If Canadian productivity was lower (it was), a depreciating CAD would have levelled the playing field.

Here's how. There's an American who makes twenty-four car parts in a week. There is a Canadian who makes twenty car parts in a week. The American is 20 percent more productive than the Canadian.

To keep the arithmetic simple, let's start off with the two currencies trading at par: 1CAD = 1USD. If each worker made $200 per week, the cost contribution from labour on the U.S. side is $8.33 per widget ($200/24). On the Canadian side, it's $10 per widget. However, if the U.S. dollar appreciated by 20 percent, the labour cost per widget would be equal.

This is the benefit of freely floating exchange rates and why (sensibly) most developed countries embrace this as public policy. It helps correct imbalances.

Yet here's the overriding point: In spite of the fact that our currency was fixed against the U.S. dollar for most of the decade, manufacturing still took off. That shouldn't surprise anyone who's stuck with the thesis of *Stalled* so far.

There are four factors that drive economic growth: labour, capital, total factor productivity, and motivation. It's difficult to draw too direct a line between exchange rates and any one of them.

You can make the argument that the 1960s really started with the election of JFK on November 8, 1960. Richard Nixon was Eisenhower's vice-president and even then seemed much more a product of the 1950s and the Cold War. JKF represented the future ... hope. Then he was assassinated on November 22, 1963.

I have no recollection of that day. But one of my most distinct early memories is of watching JFK's funeral with my mother. I was in kindergarten at the time, which meant I spent mornings in school and afternoons at home with her. My sister was in Grade 2, so my mother and I were alone in the basement of our house. I was playing with my toys on the hardwood floor and she was ironing my father's shirts. Tears were streaming down her face. I asked her why she was crying. She said that what was on TV was upsetting her. I asked her why she didn't change the channel. She just shook her head and cried even harder.

It was the first time I had seen my mother cry.

JFK's assassination traumatized our southern friends and neighbours. There were two major consequences of his assassination: a significant change in the manner in which the Vietnam War was conducted and the launch of the Great Society program. At the same time, the United States wrestled with a terrible historical injustice — slavery.

> We hold these truths self-evident, that all men are created equal; that they are endowed by their Creator with certain unalienable rights; that among these are Life, Liberty, and the Pursuit of Happiness.[10]

These stirring words were written by Thomas Jefferson, who throughout his lifetime owned six hundred slaves.[11] Not for the first time — or last — would a politician talk the talk, yet fail to walk the walk. Perhaps we shouldn't judge Jefferson too sharply. It was the world he was born into.

QUESTION 18

In a world of slaves and masters, which would you choose to be?

☐   A slave.

☐   A master.

A bloody civil war was fought, in part at least, to end the abomination of slavery, although a more sober reading of history might suggest that the real motive was to preserve the Union. After the Civil War ended, the United States struggled with race relations, and it came up with the doctrine of "separate but equal."

The politicians passed the laws. Then the Supreme Court put its stamp of approval on the policy with the 1896 decision *Plessy v. Ferguson*. Not only was it legal to provide separate facilities for blacks and whites, if you defied the law you were considered a criminal. That was the law of the land until the 1954 decision *Brown v. the Board of Education*. Following that decision, the policy of "separate but equal" was against the law.

Prior to Lyndon Johnson's assumption of the presidency following Kennedy's assassination, both Eisenhower and Kennedy had used the federal government's power to trump the states when the rights of blacks weren't being adequately protected. Little Rock, Arkansas, 1957. James Meredith, University of Mississippi, 1962. These actions were necessary to reverse obvious wrongs. Wrongs, by the way, that would never have occurred had America defined itself as a collection of individuals rather than groups. But I digress. The result was that fair-minded people, seeing what good the federal government had done with respect to this issue, started reflexively siding with the federal government. Power was increasingly being concentrated in Washington D.C., at the expense of the states and, ultimately, individuals.

On May 22, 1964, Lyndon Johnson delivered his famous Great Society speech at the University of Michigan's commencement ceremony. It's a wonderful piece of oratory and established the foundation for public policy for decades to come — I would argue — on both sides of the forty-ninth parallel. I'll summarize it, using LBJ's words as much as possible.

> For half a century, we called upon unbounded invention and untiring industry to create an order of plenty for all of our people. The challenge of the next half century is whether we have the wisdom to use that wealth to enrich and elevate our national life.

LBJ was right that in the early half of the twentieth century plenty had been created for most of the American people. Yet even as late as the early

1950s, hunger had been widespread in parts of the United States. That was no longer true by 1964.

LBJ then proceeded to explain how he planned to "elevate" national life:

> The Great Society rests on abundance and liberty for
> all. It demands an end to poverty and racial injustice,
> to which we are totally committed in our time. But that
> is just the beginning.

The three pillars of the Great Society, according to LBJ, were taking care of the cities, nurturing the countryside, and improving the classrooms of America. He ended the speech with a series of rhetorical questions:

> So, will you join in the battle to give every citizen the full
> equality which God enjoins and the law requires, what-
> ever his belief, or race, or the colour of his skin?
> Will you join in the battle to give every citizen an escape
> from the crushing weight of poverty?
> Will you join in the battle to make it possible for all
> nations go live in enduring peace — as neighbours and
> not as mortal enemies?
> Will you join in the battle to build the Great Society,
> to prove that our material progress is only the foundation
> on which we will build a richer life of mind and spirit?[12]
> I don't know what you were doing as you were reading
> those words, but I was standing on top of my desk and
> shouting: "YES! ... YES! ... YES! ... YES!!!"

Only one problem: the legislation that came out of the Great Society program accomplished exactly the opposite.

LBJ wanted the Great Society to be his legacy; I would argue that what actually came to define his presidency was the Vietnam War. The United States got sucked into a quagmire, and just as in previous wars, there was a shortage of volunteers, so it had to rely on the draft to fill the military's ranks. The country was torn apart, divided along class lines. Working class/blue-collar America generally supported it. The intelligentsia and the privileged were against it.

I'll be the first to admit that this is a crude characterization. But I'm guessing that Oliver Stone's *Platoon* was accurate: those who were sent to die in Southeast Asia, were, for the most part, those who benefitted *least* from the system.

The decision to go to war is the most profound one that any country faces, but it's a particularly significant one for States that consider themselves democracies. The ultimate sacrifice that anyone can make for his or her country is to die for it. There are some people who willingly put themselves in harm's way. I would characterize them as extraordinarily brave, but I suppose there are other ways to describe them. However, there aren't enough people like that. So there has to be some kind of system to fill the ranks. The consensus in America at the time of the Vietnam War was that the fairest method was a lottery system, which was what the draft represented. But during Vietnam, the elite turned their backs on fairness, and gamed the system with deferments or draft-dodging or desertion … and, most importantly, they got away with it.

QUESTION 19

How would you describe the soldiers who served in Vietnam?

☐   Noble.

☐   Complete suckers.

It was clear how the American elite of the late 1960s and early 1970s would have answered that question. In fact, a the poster-child of that group, Vassar-educated Jane Fonda, travelled to Hanoi in 1972, sat on anti-aircraft guns, and posed for pictures. She called POWs who spoke of torture "hypocrites and liars" and was cheered by many Americans.[13]

An important line had been crossed.

Every society has its elites. The important questions are:

• Who are they?

• Where does their self-interest lie?

• In pursuing that self-interest, at whose expense will it be?

The New Elite that was emerging in North America was university-educated, concentrated in urban centres, disproportionately made up of those trained as lawyers, and tended to work in the public rather than the private sector. And it understood that its economic interests were tied far more closely to the political process and the redistribution of income than to wealth generation.

I've spent a great deal of time speaking about the United States when this book is *supposed* to be about Canada. There's a reason: we tend to mimic the United States.

Canada has a complicated love-hate relationship with its southern neighbour. I think of it like this: the United States is the cool, older teen-aged brother (let's call him Lance): captain of the football team; dates the head cheerleader; drives a souped-up Camaro; C-student, true, but with a larger-than-life persona — you get the idea. Meanwhile, Canada is the nerdy younger brother (given name, Les): not very athletic; wears braces; straight A student, but who cares about that except Mom and Dad? We envy and resent the success of Lance, and even while we'd like to be him, we know we can't, because after all, we are Les. There's more than a little bit of an inferiority complex at work here.

Meanwhile, Lance doesn't think too deeply about the relationship. But then again, Lance doesn't think deeply about very much! He just goes on his merry way, gets away with what he wants because he is captain of the football team ... and often leaves a mess in his wake that other people have to clean up.

So, what was happening in Canada during this decade? Along with the increases in efficiency in agriculture and the further development of the industrial sector, cemented by the Auto Pact, there were two State-sponsored initiatives in the 1960s that contributed to Canada's strong economic performance. "Socialized" medicine was brought to Saskatchewan in 1962[14] (by 1966 it had spread across the land) and the Canada Pension Plan (CPP) was established in 1965.[15]

There is a solid economic rationale for why the State should operate the health care system. There are certain industries where "natural" monopolies exist. It wouldn't make sense to have several different private companies provide water to a city, for example — it would mean multiple sets of pipes. That's wasteful. A similar argument can be made for health care. The single-payer system has administrative efficiencies. The single-payer system results in greater buying power and the ability to negotiate lower prices with suppliers. And the proof is that in 2012 total per-capita spending on health care was half as much in Canada as it was in the United States.[16]

The logic underlying the CPP is impeccable. Everyone needs to save for retirement, yet most people don't have the expertise or the sophistication to do it for themselves — not to mention that many don't have the discipline either. The CPP is designed so that citizens benefit to the extent that they contribute to it. Its size (particularly as it stands today, with assets well in excess of $125 billion) means that there are economies of scale. It costs about 0.3 percent of assets under management to operate,[17] which means that if it returns 7 percent before fees, 6.7 percent of that goes to the Canadian people. Most actively managed mutual funds charge around 2 percent, which means that if the assets return 7 percent, the investor sees only 5 percent. And from the beginning the CPP was a defined-benefit plan, eliminating longevity risk — the possibility that your money will run out before you die.

When they were introduced, both State-run medicine and the Canada Pension Plan were almost perfect. However, each has failed to adequately change over the years. In 1962, no one could have foreseen how expensive medicine would become. The Canada Pension Plan was established when life expectancy was much lower. In 1965, the fact was that many people who paid into the CPP over the years would never live to receive anything from it.

While the State-run medical insurance and pension plans set up in Canada in the 1960s created great benefits for all Canadians, the same cannot be said for many of the changes made to the education system.

In 1967, the Province of Ontario eliminated Grade 13 departmental examinations. Up to then, every student who graduated from an Ontario high school wrote the exact same examination, and the result was critical in determining who would proceed to post-secondary education.

Those tests hold special significance for the Hlinka family. My grandfather was a man who never set foot in a school, except to ensure that his children received the education he never had. But he was damn sure that his son would go to university. He didn't believe that there was the same need for his daughters. Fortunately, his children were as stubborn as he was and one of my aunts did an end-run around her old man: she wrote the departmentals, achieved the best mark in the province, and received a full scholarship to the University of Toronto. If there was one thing my grandfather hated more than anything else, it was turning down something free. His youngest daughter received the university education she so desperately wanted.

This scholarship wasn't means-based. The daughter of a landscape gardener and the son of the moneyed classes were equally eligible. It was decided on sheer merit. This spoke to the *values* of the time.

In 1968 I was watching the U.S. Track and Field Championships. The winners would compete in that year's Olympic Games. I remember a discussion that the commentators had after a favourite was upset, which meant he would not be going to Mexico City. One questioned the wisdom of the U.S. system. The Soviet Union did it very differently, he said. A committee got together behind closed doors and *decided* which athletes would wear their country's colours. He argued that this method made a lot of sense. It probably meant more medals, and that was the point of the Games, wasn't it?

His colleague was mortified. No, the Olympics was about providing everyone a *fair* opportunity to compete. And if that meant fewer medals, so be it.

QUESTION 20

How should Canada's Olympic team be decided?

☐   Via open and transparent competition.

☐   Via committees meeting behind closed doors.

What the Canadian education system did in 1967, if I may extend this metaphor, was move from an open and transparent, objective-merit, American-style Olympic-selection process to a closed, subjective-merit, Soviet-style one. If your name was Betty Hlinka ("What's *wrong* with these people — can't they even afford enough vowels for their names?") and you weren't raised in the right neighbourhood, it would become that much harder to compete.

Then, in 1968, education in this province took a huge step back with the acceptance of the Hall-Dennis Report. Its key conclusion was that education was about things like "self-actualization" and "fulfillment" rather than meeting the needs of the marketplace.[18] I personally felt the impact two short years later.

I was in Grade 8. Every Friday afternoon our teacher had us move our desks, which were in traditional rows, and create a rectangle around the perimeter of the classroom — like a large conference table. Then we would — and I kid you not — have to say something "nice" about someone else in the room.

There were a couple of different ways we went about this. Sometimes you could pick whom you wanted to compliment ("Johnny, you have a *very* nice personality"). Sometimes, we went around the room clockwise ("Susie, I think you're *very* nice") or counterclockwise ("Jimmy, you're *very* good at sports"). And sometimes, he would direct us to heap praise on someone specific ("Mary, everyone thinks you're *very* smart").

The exercise was about building "self-esteem," and to this day I think my teacher was well-meaning. But kids aren't stupid. Everyone saw how ridiculous it was, and it led to one of the funniest things I've ever seen in my life.

There were three short boys in the class. I was one of them. But I was accepted because I was a good athlete and that earned me sufficient cred. The other two short boys were Roger and David. They hated each other with a passion. Roger was a very smart kid, while David was … the polite word back then was "slow." One day, after we arranged our desks, it happened that the two ended up beside each other, and David was called upon to say something nice about Roger.

There were four stock phrases. I've already given them to you. David had to say something nice about Roger. But he couldn't come up with anything. He started, "Roger is …" He stopped himself. He ran his hands through his hair, then clenched his fists, as if he was trying to force an idea out of his cranium. You could almost see the smoke coming out of his ears as he tried to come up with something — anything — good to say.

Meanwhile, the other kids (we were all between twelve and fourteen) were laughing until tears streamed down our faces. Finally, the teacher said: "David, say something nice about Bobby instead."

David immediately responded, "Bobby has a *very* nice personality."

I left public school aware that:

- I had a *very* nice personality;

- I was *very* nice;

- I was *very* good at sports;

- everyone thought I was *very* smart.

That's what I knew. What I didn't know was the difference between a noun and a verb, or an adverb and an adjective.

The assault on educational excellence had begun.

If real economic growth was strong in the 1950s, it was explosive in the 1960s. The following are U.S. numbers, but they are indicative of the situation in Canada as well. In 1960, there was one passenger car for every three Americans. By 1970, it was one for two.[19] Houses were getting bigger and better. The "official" numbers indicate that real per capita income jumped by just over 3 percent compounded annually over those ten years,[20] and poverty had been virtually eradicated from both the United States and Canada — Lyndon Johnson noted as much in his 1964 speech at the University of Michigan.

I am very lucky. I don't know what it is to be hungry. But I'll never forget a story my grandfather told me, a story from when he went back to Czechoslovakia for the last time to bring his family to their new home in Canada. He had spent the day working in the fields with his brothers and sisters. It was harvest time and everyone had to pitch in. He returned to the shack they called home, and there was a glass of milk on the table. Except it wasn't really a glass; it was more like three ounces. He was exhausted and hungry and he went to drink it. My grandmother, seeing what he was doing, said, "No. If you have that, there's nothing for the children tomorrow." So he put it down and went to bed.

Three lousy ounces of milk. That's poverty.

There were very few situations that extreme in Canada, even back in the 1930s. There was nothing like that in 1968. The war on poverty had been won, but some people were arming themselves for a new battle.

Welcome to the low income cut-off (LICO) metric.

It was determined that in 1959 the average Canadian family spent 50 percent of its income on basic food, clothing, and shelter. The 1968 low income cut-off said that if a family spent 70 percent of its income on basic food, clothing, and shelter, that it was "low-income." What happened is that the LICO, for all intents and purposes, became Canada's "poverty" line. And this framework guarantees that we will always have people living in "poverty" — no matter how wealthy all of us are.[21]

A bit of basic math.

It is 1968. The average Canadian family brings in $8,000 per year. It spends $4,000 on necessities, which means that $4,000 is left for luxuries.

A low-income family brings in $5,333 (67 percent of the average) and must spend $4,000 (75 percent of its income) on necessities. This means that it is below the low income cut-off, even though its needs are covered and there is $1,333 (25 percent) left over for luxuries.

The decades pass. If real economic growth averaged 3 percent (and it did during the 1950s and 1960s), then in thirty years the average Canadian family brings in $20,000 in inflation-adjusted dollars. We'll assume that it spends $10,000 on necessities and $10,000 on luxuries. The low-income family continues to earn 70 percent of what the average family earned, which means that it earned $14,000. It's required to spend $10,000 on necessities (71 percent) and $4,000 on luxuries. *So even though the low-income family is spending on luxuries what the average family did a generation ago, it is still considered low-income, with the logic being that it is deserving of social assistance.*

The LICO framework is a fraud.

QUESTION 21

Before reading these preceding paragraphs, I understood how "poverty" is defined in Canada.

☐ Yes.

☐ No.

And for the sake of novelty if no other reason, can we be honest and agree that very few "activists" ever mention LICO. They use the much more emotionally charged word, "poverty."

QUESTION 22

Which term are "activists" more likely to use?

☐ LICO.

☐ Poverty.

QUESTION 23

Do you agree that a poverty "activist" will do anything in his/her power to eradicate poverty, short of putting in an honest day's work?

☐   Yes.

☐   No.

The LICO was designed to redistribute income and perpetuate government bureaucracies that generate nothing of value. And there would be many, many more of those departments created in the decade that was to follow.

The 1960s in sixty words: Immigration continues, but not at the same rate as experienced in the previous decade. Fewer people are needed to work in agriculture, and in the wake of the Auto Pact, manufacturing becomes much more efficient. State-run medicine will benefit the country for years to come. But there are storm clouds gathering as Canadians begin to expect more and more from government.

A Primer on
Fiscal and Monetary Policy

John Maynard Keynes is the most important economist of the twentieth century, and his imprint remains to this day. He came to prominence during the Great Depression, a prolonged slump that — at least according to Keynes — couldn't be explained by "traditional" economic thinking.

In his day, the consensus was that if the economy went into a slump for any of a variety of reasons, it would self-correct — at worst this would occur in the long term; more likely, it would do so in the short term. The 1930s seemed to disprove the "short term" theory, and Keynes famously quipped, "In the long run, we are all dead."[1] He advanced the theory that government should intervene actively.

When an economy is agriculture-based, Nature determines whether times are good or bad. However, by the 1930s the transition from an agriculture-based economy to a manufacturing-based one had already occurred. Manufacturing, by its nature, is different. There are periods where capacity expands at a strong rate (booms) and times when inventory levels build up and have to be reduced (busts). The latter are accompanied by rising unemployment.

Keynes advanced the proposition that government, with its power to tax and spend, should act in a counter-cyclical manner. If the economy was slow and unemployment was rising, taxes should be cut and spending increased to eliminate the recessionary gap. Then, as things picked up, taxes would naturally increase and spending could be curtailed to balance budgets over the business cycle. The power to change taxes and spending is understood as fiscal policy and is one important tool that public authorities have at their disposal to manage the economy.

Monetary policy is the other tool. The root of the word *monetary* is money, and monetary policy is all about the cost of money. This is influenced by central banks through their control of interest rates. If I would like a $25,000 loan to renovate my house, I might go to my bank and ask for a line of credit. The bank will tell me what interest rate I'd have to pay. If the interest rate is low, the money I am borrowing is "cheap"; if the interest rate is high, the money is "expensive."

Monetary policy is very intuitive. If a central bank (in Canada, it's the Bank of Canada; in the United States, it's the Federal Reserve) believes that the economy is sluggish, it will react by putting more money into the system. Increasing the supply, everything else being equal, leads to a lower price. Conversely, if the economy is operating past capacity and seems to be inflating, central banks drain liquidity, reducing supply, leading to higher interest rates.

The most important tool at a central bank's disposal is the bank rate (Canada) or Fed Funds Rate (U.S.). In the course of the day, there is a lot of money sloshing around the system, and banks charge each other based on what the bank rate or Fed Funds Rate is at any given time. They are reference rates on which other interest rates tend to be based.

All central banks give themselves wide discretion with respect to changing the level of interest rates in order to achieve their particular goals. In a perfect world, those goals would always be steady, non-inflationary, real growth, but the world is anything but perfect.

It's apparent why the political classes embrace Keynesianism, treating it as if it were written on tablets brought down from the Mount. This ideology gives them carte blanche to tinker with the economy in any way, shape, or form. The intellectual fig leaf was provided by Keynes: the economy will *not* self-correct. Assertion metastasizes into proof. All parties, New Democrat, Liberal, Conservative, Republican, Democrat, sing from the same hymn book. Only their choice of psalm is different.

It's equally obvious why central bankers embrace activist monetary policy. It justifies their existence. It gives them at least the veneer of importance, and important people can ask to be (and likely will be) well compensated for the "work" they do, even if it adds no real value.

The promise was that activist fiscal and monetary policy would be the solution to the economy's woes. However, an objective reading of economic history since 1970 tells us that activist fiscal and monetary policy has, in fact, more often been the problem.

The 1970s

On January 2, 1970, the Dow Jones Industrial Average, the most closely watched indicator of stock market activity, opened at 809.20. Almost exactly ten years later, December 31, 1979, it closed at 838.74.[1] The stock market went nowhere over that decade because the economy went nowhere, and the belief was that it would continue to go nowhere.

The stock market is closely watched. But I suspect that it's broadly misunderstood. What it indicates, at any point of time, isn't so much where we are, but where we think we'll be in the future.

When you buy shares of a company, you're laying out a known amount of money today for an uncertain payback in the future, which could be in the form of dividends or capital gains on the sale, or a combination. It stands to reason that if you're optimistic about what that future income will be, you'll pay more right now. If you're pessimistic, you'll pay less.

The stock market served as a wonderful metaphor for the 1970s. After two decades of spectacular growth, North America experienced a time of retrenchment. I grew up in that era, and the pessimism was palpable.

The Vietnam War had a lot to do with this air of pessimism. Popular mythology sprang up around why the United States had sent its poorest and least privileged to die in the paddies of Southeast Asia. There were profiteers — *war profiteers* — who were manipulating the system to their benefit. I remember a James Michener novel, *The Drifters*, that captured the disaffection of a generation. One phrase in particular caught my attention: "War is good business. Invest your sons."[2] I was a teenager at the time, and I fully bought into this narrative.

I wasn't the only one. As a result of the belief that America was fighting an unjust war — one that resulted in the deaths of both Vietnamese villagers and American soldiers who came, overwhelmingly, from poor backgrounds — all for the benefit of big business, there seemed to be a turning away from the free enterprise system that had led to the explosive growth in wealth over the past twenty years.

The feeling wasn't totally unwarranted. In 1965, Ralph Nader wrote *Unsafe At Any Speed*. His thesis was that the North American car companies made conscious decisions to cut back on safety features in order to maximize profits.[3] In the 1950s, a lot of people — not everyone, but a lot of people — accepted Charles Wilson's slogan: "What's good for America is good for General Motors." Many were far less sure after Nader's book.

What brought the issue to a literally explosive head, however, was the Ford Pinto case.

The story started in 1968, with the introduction of a new subcompact car, the Pinto. In an effort to get it to market quickly, Ford Motor Company rushed its design and development. The Pinto was launched in September of 1970, and eventually assembled in three different North American plants, including one in St. Thomas, Ontario.

It was a very small car, a subcompact. At the time of production, it was customary to place the gas tank between the rear axle and bumper to provide more trunk space. Pinto's designers put the gas tank *beside* the rear axle. On the rear axle's transfer case (the device that converts the rotation of the driveshaft into power for the rear wheels) were bolts that stuck out, facing the vehicle's rear bumper. When the Pinto was rear-ended — a frequent enough accident — the gas tank was forced up into the rear axle and those bolts punctured the gas tank. A rear-end collision caused the Pinto to crumble, meaning the other car would plough through to the rear axle, often causing an explosive fire.

In May of 1972, an elderly woman, Lily Gray, was driving her 1972 Pinto in Orange County, Florida, with her thirteen-year-old neighbour Richard Grimshaw. Her car was rear-ended at approximately thirty miles an hour. Lily died upon impact and Grimshaw was seriously burned. In the aftermath, the disclosures were shocking.

It was revealed that Ford knew about the Pinto's defects and after a cost-benefit analysis, determined that a recall wasn't warranted. The company calculated that it would cost $11 per vehicle to make the necessary changes, and after applying that $11 to 11 million cars and 1.5 million trucks, it determined that the cost of the recall would be $137 million.

Now for the other side of the equation. Ford believed that recalling the cars would result in 180 fewer burn deaths; 180 fewer serious burn injuries; and 2,100 fewer burned vehicles. Then it applied a cost of $200,000 per death; $67,000 per injury; and $700 per vehicle to determine that the benefit of the recall was only $49.5 million. It was cheaper to leave those Pintos on the road.[4]

It's very easy to argue with that kind of arithmetic, and it made people question — profoundly — the legitimacy of big business and many of the structures around which North America was organized.

If the actions of companies like Ford caused many consumers to lose faith in big business, the performance of the economy made many lose faith in capitalism itself. There was a huge shock to the economy in the 1970s, one that hit all consumers exactly where it hurts most — in their wallets.

At the end of September 1973, oil was about $3 a barrel. In the wake of the Yom Kippur War and American support for Israel, however, several Arab states curtailed oil production by five million barrels a day. Other countries were able to increase production by a million barrels a day, but that still left a shortfall of four million barrels. Market forces took over. Within months, oil was $12 per barrel and this (according to popular wisdom) led to economic misery and *stagflation*.[5]

Now, based on the law of supply and demand, one would expect that as the price of oil rose, demand would diminish. However, oil is an essential item for the world's economy, and the price of oil is highly inelastic in the short run, which means that it takes very large price increases to reduce the quantity consumed. No such thing happened; the price of oil remained high, causing economic chaos.

The Misery Index was a term coined by economist Arthur Okun.[6] There are two economic ills: unemployment and inflation. Adding them together gives a measure of economic distress, which is measured by the Misery Index. After never being higher than 9 percent in the 1960s, the index hit double digits in nine of the ten years of the seventies, peaking at 17.7 percent in 1975.[7]

No one had even heard of stagflation in the 1950s and 1960s. It was a made-up term to describe stagnant growth that is combined with inflation. At the time, there was a popular theory, credited to New Zealand economist John Phillips, that for any developed country, the price of strong economic growth is inflation, and the price of economic weakness is unemployment. You would have one but not the other.[8] The oil shock seemed to disprove that theory. Or did it?

Something else *does* explains stagflation — remember, we're talking about unemployment *and* inflation — and that's rigidities in labour markets. During the 1970s, unionization exploded in Canada, rising from 2.173 million in 1970 to 2.876 million by 1975. That year, almost 11 million person-days were lost due to strikes and lockouts, compared to 739,000 in 1960.[9]

I have belonged to three unions in my life. For close to a year in the early 1980s, I worked in a Planters peanut factory before returning to school. Currently, I'm a member of two unions — one through George Brown College and the other with CBC Radio. I've seen first-hand how they are uniquely capable of accomplishing what Phillips deemed impossible. If there is one institution that by its very nature leads to stagnant growth and inflation, it is closed-shop labour unions.

Reckless government spending causes demand-pull inflation (i.e., inflation caused by demand outstripping supply) and there was ample evidence of that behaviour on both sides of the forty-ninth parallel during the 1970s. When LBJ left office in 1970, the national debt of the United States was $348 billion. By the end of the Nixon/Ford presidency in 1974, it had grown to $620 billion. When Jimmy Carter got booted out in 1980, he'd run it up to $908 billion.[10]

Something similar happened in Canada. When Lester Pearson left office in 1968, the national debt was $18.75 billion. By the time that Joe Clark was ousted in 1980, our national debt was $77.4 billion, an annualized increase of 12.5 percent.[11]

What government did — on both sides of the border — was turn Keynesian economics on its head by running large deficits during good economic times and humongous ones during leaner years.

Excessive government spending contributed mightily to the stagnation of the 1970s. If it was going to spend like that, it should have been finding ways to generate revenues, but, instead, the minority Liberal government in Canada repealed one particular tax, and it spoke volumes about the new values that were emerging in North America.

I'm talking about the inheritance tax.

If someone stands to inherit a great deal of money, it likely means that throughout their entire lives they've had more advantages than most others. If someone stands to inherit a great deal of money, it likely means that through connections alone they should have had an insurmountable head start on the rest of the field. If someone stands to inherit a great deal of money, haven't they already benefitted enough?

One of the most important justifications for inheritance taxes is that they help level the playing field. The revenue from these taxes helps the government to provide support and services to less-privileged citizens.

These taxes don't really penalize those who inherit large amounts of money, however. Let's keep in mind that inheritance taxes take only a small fraction of money that the heirs didn't actually earn. It's not like they are left with nothing — just not quite as much.

Pierre Trudeau — born into a very wealthy family, and so had lots of skin in this game — and his Liberal Party abolished inheritance and gift taxes at the end of 1971.[12] You have to hand it to the guy: He knew how to look after himself first.

With the end of inheritance taxes an important signal was sent: there would be — if the New Elite had anything to do with it — less economic and social mobility in Canada in the future than there had been in the past.

QUESTION 24

Is economic and social mobility, both upward and downward, desirable?

☐   Yes.

☐   No.

Inheritance taxes were eliminated. Yet Canada's government was spending money like it never had before during peacetime and therefore had to come up with ways to find extra revenue.

Why not State-sponsored lotteries?

In February 1975, the Ontario provincial government created the Ontario Lottery Corporation (OLC). The money, the government declared, would go to good causes. The first lottery in the province, WINTARIO, directed the money toward sport, culture, and recreation. In its first year, it returned $43 million in profits to the citizens of Ontario.[13]

The argument can be made that lotteries are one of the "fairest" taxes that exist. No one holds a gun to anyone's head and forces them to play. Going in, everyone buying a ticket knows that the expected return is negative; still, many people have no problem with that. As a result, the revenues for the government lottery corporation are very large. So, too, are the profits. In fact, if you look at the latest annual report for the Ontario Lottery and Gaming Corporation, the successor to the OLC, you'll learn that the *profit* margin on lotteries is 28 percent.[14]

The revenue from lotteries is important for the Government of Ontario. However, the argument can be made that lotteries are not only not one of "fairest" taxes that exist, they are, in reality, one of the "unfairest." They tend to be highly regressive. If you are a low-income Canadian, taking home $20,000 per year, and spend $10 per week on lottery tickets, that is about 2.5 percent of your total income. On the other hand, if you're a middle-class Canadian making $50,000, spending the same amount on lottery tickets only amounts to 1 percent of your total income. That's one strike against lotteries.

I look at the issue differently. I look at the message that is sent and the values that are communicated when the State runs the lottery.

The consumption of both tobacco and alcohol is taxed heavily because there is the belief that these behaviours are bad for you and they should be discouraged. Prohibition, of alcohol at least, was attempted in the United States during the last century and failed because too many people like to drink. Most people can control their own drinking, too.

There are good reasons why for a very long time the State didn't want to get involved in the gambling business. The regressive nature of taxes was surely one. However, there was a more profound reason: lotteries, by holding out the possibility of getting rich quick, act as a disincentive to getting rich slow, through hard work.

Despite all this, lotteries proliferated across North America in the 1970s, with governments encouraging their spread at the same time that economic growth was slowing. This looks like a case where it is difficult to distinguish between cause and effect.

Another government-sponsored work avoidance program is Unemployment Insurance. Anyone who has taken even a cursory look at it understands that it serves as a disincentive to work. Unfortunately, this program mushroomed in the 1970s.

The history of Unemployment Insurance and its development speaks volumes about how attitudes have changed in Canada, and what those changes have wrought for economic growth. In 1940, the federal government passed the Unemployment Insurance Act. It covered about 42 percent of the workforce but excluded a number of different occupations — and anyone who earned more than $2,000 a year. To be eligible for benefits, someone had to prove they were unemployed, available for suitable work, and had contributed to the program for the last 180 days. The length of time a claimant could receive benefits was based on the number of days he/she had contributed to the program: One day of payments was offered for every five days of contributions, up to a maximum of one year. In other words, if you worked for five years, you could enjoy one full year of benefits.

Fast-forward thirty-one years to the Unemployment Insurance Act of 1971.

Under the new regime, if you worked EIGHT weeks in the previous fifty-two, you were eligible for fifty-one weeks of benefits.[15] In 1940, it took 260 weeks. In the wake of this new legislation, an unemployment rate that had averaged under 5 percent from the end of the Second World War to 1971 spiked, so that from 1976 to 1990, it never fell below 7 percent.[16]

QUESTION 25

Did the changes to Unemployment Insurance made in 1971 contribute importantly to higher unemployment rates in the period from 1976 to 1990?

☐ Yes, it was the the changes to Unemployment Insurance.

☐ No, it was something other than the changes to Unemployment Insurance.

Let me repeat a question I posed earlier:

QUESTION 26

Are people rational economic actors?

☐   Yes.

☐   No.

Some people don't like to work. Not everyone. But some. And that cohort is more than happy to work the minimum to qualify for unemployment benefits. Since the changes to the UI Act in 1971 made that easier, what we started to see in Canada during the 1970s was a huge amount of voluntary unemployment, which served as a much more serious drag on growth than higher oil prices ever were.

Government intervention in the marketplace through programs such as Unemployment Insurance almost invariably leads to higher unemployment. Likewise, government intervention in the market through economic stimulus programs almost invariably leads to inflation. Markets — as long as they are unencumbered — know how to deal with both high unemployment and higher prices.

When resources or products are scarce and demand exceeds supply, the invisible hand of the marketplace works its magic. The price will increase, and fewer will be used. Consumers will adjust. If gasoline becomes more expensive, people will drive less and look for more fuel-efficient vehicles. Resources are allocated to those who value them most.

But in the 1970s, meddlers on both sides of the forty-ninth parallel couldn't leave well enough alone.

On August 15, 1971, Richard Nixon announced a "freeze on all wages and prices throughout the United States."[17] I suppose you could call the result a success, if you define success as lower production. The only discernible consequence was that output fell, and of course, everything else being equal, with less supply, the logical adjustment is always higher prices.

Smart people learn from other people's mistakes. But I would never accuse Canadian politicians of being particularly smart. We had our own episode with wage and price controls, and how they came about should make any thinking person despair about the democratic process as it is currently conducted in the developed countries of the world.

In the 1974 election, the Conservatives under Robert Stanfield proposed wage and price freezes for the Canadian economy. The Liberals, led by Pierre Trudeau, opposed those measures. However, once elected, Trudeau did an about-face. But where, in his finite wisdom, Richard Nixon limited the controls to several months, our fearless leader and the same gaggle of deep thinkers who thought that eight weeks of work deserved fifty-one weeks of unemployment benefits, imposed a three-year limit on wages, starting at 10 percent in the first year, then tapering to 8 and then 6 percent.[18]

A period of disinflation occurred after these controls were introduced, which might lead some to conclude that wage and prices controls were a success. But that idea is wrong-headed, because inflation is always a monetary phenomenon. This means that there is too much money chasing too few goods and services, leading to prices being bid up to clear the market.

The best way to combat inflation is to control the money supply and embrace pro-growth policies. But every policy initiative the Liberals introduced in the 1970s was anti-growth. The most glaring example was the explosion in the size of the public service. In 1970, there were fewer than 200,000 Canadians working in that sector, but by 1975 it had mushroomed to 273,000.[19]

It was nice that all those folks had jobs. It would have been nicer if they had been doing something to make the pie bigger.

The 1950s demonstrated that large-scale government spending isn't necessarily a problem. It depends, however, on where the money is going. Similarly, government regulation isn't necessarily a problem. It just depends on what's being regulated.

The year is 1970. If you were listening to AM radio at that time — as I did — you enjoyed a wide range of music. But the government decided that not enough of the music being played on the radio was ours, and so it devised the MAPL rules to promote Canadian content.

According to the rules, which came into effect in January 1971, 30 percent of the content played by a radio station had to be "Canadian." Under the MAPL system, this meant:

• Music (M) — it must be composed by a Canadian;

• Artist (A) — the music or lyrics must be principally performed by a Canadian;

- Production (P) — the musical selection must consist of a live performance that is either recorded wholly in Canada or performed wholly in Canada and broadcast live in Canada;

- Lyrics (L) — the lyrics must be written by a Canadian.[20]

It wasn't enough for the cultural busybodies to control what we listened to, though. They wanted to control what we watched as well.

In 1974, the Canadian Audio-Visual Certification Office (CAVCO) was created to administer the Capital Cost Allowance Program (CCA) as a means to increase private sector investment in the film industry. Special capital cost allowances were provided to encourage investment. If someone put money into a "certified production," it allowed investors a 100 percent tax deduction.[21] Think of it as a free lottery ticket that might provide some ancillary benefits.

It's 1975. There's a middle-aged man who's making a very good wage — let's say $50,000 — and he's paying $15,000 in taxes, leaving him with $35,000 to live on. He puts $5,000 into a "certified production" and now he pays $10,000 in taxes and he still has $35,000 for himself. If the movie is a smashing success, *Yabba-dabba-do!* And if it's not, no skin off his nose.

He can tell his friends at the club that he's financing a feature film. Perhaps he can go to a day of shooting, hang around the set, strike up a conversation with the nubile starlet. Sounds good to me.

The purpose of MAPL and CAVCO film credits was to generate make-work projects for the New Elite and its sons and daughters, masquerading under "culture."

This is a problem. Any behaviour that doesn't benefit others through wealth creation ultimately results in the pie shrinking; and as it does, the fight gets fiercer over the size of the piece that each of us gets.

Something else was at work here, too, something that characterizes this New Elite. It *thinks* it knows better than anyone else what everyone else should listen to and watch. It thinks that its sensibilities are more refined than everyone else's. There is a smugness, an unwarranted sense of moral and intellectual superiority, that permeates institutions like arts councils and other grant-giving bodies. Such bodies believe that they — not the market — should decide what is produced and what is seen.

I have no difficulty if citizens — of their own free will — choose to give money to support the arts. I have a great deal of difficulty having the government expropriate money from the unwilling to fund projects that are frequently impossible to justify.

There never will be a shortage of "arts" in Canada — or any country for that matter. People like to sing. People like to dance. People like to play music. People like to paint pictures. People like to write books (you should see the smile on my face right now!). People will do all of these things whether or not the State subsidizes them. Subsidies attract people with negligible talent, giving them the opportunity to self-actualize off the public teat. Meanwhile, the talented artists (that is, the ones who sell) are penalized because they have to compete with a bunch of people who stink at what they do but are great at filling out forms and sucking up to those who hold the purse strings.

Public funding for the arts creates more positions for bureaucrats. Someone has to monitor what is being played on the airwaves. Someone has to sift through the CCA forms. More and more people draw paycheques, while doing nothing that adds any value.

The lessons we should have learned from the 1950s and 1960s went out the window in the 1970s:

- Focused, cost-justified infrastructure spending contributes importantly to economic growth. Otherwise, government should intrude minimally in markets.

- It is possible to enjoy strong growth and for governments to run surpluses at the same time. And, in fact, surpluses *lead to* growth because they contribute to the most efficient allocation of resources.

There was not a single year in the 1970s where the federal government of Canada balanced its budget. A deficit of $1 billion, 1 percent of GDP in 1970, ballooned to $13 billion and 3 percent by 1978, and there were worse years to come.[22]

The 1970s in seventy words: The oil shocks of the 1970s were used as a convenient excuse for economic underperformance, while the real culprits in Canada were a government that distorted the labour market by changing the rules around Unemployment Insurance, and a union movement that contributed directly to stagflation. Deficit spending fuelled inflationary fires, and an economy that had grown robustly over the past twenty years passed through a decade where it went nowhere.

An Economic Understanding of Unions

A couple of years ago, I was asked to be part of a panel that talked about the problems young people were having finding good jobs. I made the self-evident comment that one of the headwinds they faced was the presence of unions. By their very nature and structure (given the laws of the land today), they lead to artificially high prices in labour markets, contributing to unemployment at the same time.

I could sense that I was about as popular as the proverbial porcupine in the nudist colony. One audience member, during question period, asserted — and I paraphrase — "unions have been responsible for the wage growth that workers have enjoyed in the past." The statement was greeted with hearty applause.

I recognized the speaker. He will remain unidentified. However, I will ask you to speculate on his profession.

QUESTION 27
Who do you think the man who claimed that "unions have been responsible for the wage growth that workers have enjoyed in the past" was?

☐   An ex-politician.

☐   An ex-entrepreneur.

QUESTION 28
How would you describe the claim that "unions were responsible for the wage growth that workers have enjoyed in past generations"?

Before you answer, let's discuss unions within a strictly economic, rather than ideological, framework.

There are several different ways to characterize markets: perfectly competitive, dominated by oligopolies, and controlled by a monopoly, among others.

Perfectly competitive markets have many different players, each of which provides an identical good or service.

Oligopolies have a few large and powerful players.

And in a monopoly, there is only one.

In the early days of industrialization, both suppliers of labour (workers) and buyers of labour (business) operated under conditions something akin to perfect competition. Many small businesses were bidding for labour. The automotive industry serves as a perfect example. Between 1896 and 1930, it was estimated that over 1,800 car manufacturers existed in the United States.[1] There were far more workers, but it's reasonable to assume that there was robust competition for the best, which explains Henry Ford's decision to pay his employees so much more than the average wage.

However, the nature of mass manufacturing and the returns to scale that exist for market-share leaders meant that most industries evolved to form an oligopoly-like structure. This put the power in the buyers' hands, leaving the suppliers at a distinct disadvantage.

Hence the move by workers to form unions. Unionization turns the power relationship on its head. Instead of an oligopoly getting its most important input, labour, from a perfectly competitive market, the oligopoly is forced to deal with a labour monopoly, with the playing field tilted heavily in the monopolist's favour because of "closed-shop" provisions. Once a union is certified, the employer *must* make the union its sole supplier of labour.[2]

This is absurd. Imagine that ABC Company buys 1,400 tons of steel a year from Steel Incorporated, paying $1 million, and it pays its employees $1 million. What if, instead of closed-shop provisions, there were "closed-vendor" provisions? That is, ABC Company was forced to buy the steel it needed from Steel Incorporated ... no matter what Steel Incorporated charged! It's a ridiculous proposition, but that's exactly what ABC Company faces when its labour force is unionized.

Now I'm going to do something I promised myself I wouldn't do in this book — and that's draw some graphs. Economists love them the way a rooting hog loves its corn — forgive me on this one, but it helps demonstrate the impact of unionization.

But before we get to those graphs, I need to mention something. There are two fundamental laws in economics, the Law of Demand and the Law of Supply. The Law of Demand says that the more expensive something becomes, the less demand there is for it. The Law of Supply says that the more expensive something becomes, the more people will be willing to supply it.

QUESTION 29

Do the Laws of Demand and Supply pertain to labour markets?

☐   Yes.

☐   No.

Now for those graphs!

Demand

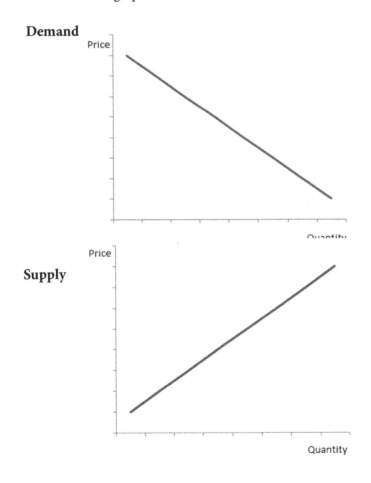

Supply

The demand curve is downward sloping (higher prices, less demand) and the supply curve is upward sloping (higher prices, more demand). When they are overlaid on top of each other, there is an intersection point which represents market equilibrium, where people only work for wages that they are satisfied with.

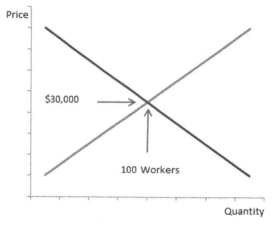

Let's set this up with a very simple model. The only input costs in the production process are labour, fixed overheads, and the return required by investors. Under competitive market conditions, one hundred workers make $30,000 per year (labour expense is $3 million) and each worker makes 1,000 widgets a year, meaning 100,000 are produced. The variable cost per widget is $30. Fixed production costs are $1 million, $3 million of capital is employed with a required return (after-tax) of 10 percent, and the tax rate on corporate profits is 50 percent.

Here's what the income statement would have to look like to realize that $300,000 profit:

Revenue	$4,600,000	(each widget costs $46)
Fixed Costs	$1,000,000	
Labour	$3,000,000	
Earnings Before Tax (EBT)	$600,000	
Taxes @ 50 percent	$300,000	
Profit	$300,000	(achieving the minimum required return)

Everybody is happy. The one hundred workers are. The providers of capital are. They're getting the return they need. There's so much happiness, people are spontaneously breaking into group hugs!

Then the factory unionizes and wages increase from $30,000 to $36,000. Now the supply and demand curves look like this:

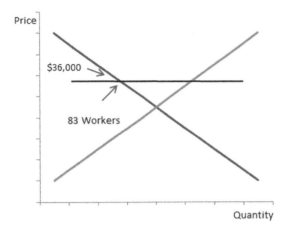

There are far more people who would like to work for that $36,000 wage, but the business can afford only eighty-three workers.

Are those eighty-three workers happier now than they were before? Of course. But it's at the expense of the seventeen who are now unemployed. And it changes the production function dramatically.

The best-case scenario is that now eighty-three workers will produce eighty-three thousand widgets. Now the income statement would have to look like this in order for the same profit to be realized ... but this time we'll work *backward*:

Profit	$300,000	
Taxes @ 50 percent	$300,000	
EBT	$600,000	
Labour Expense	$3,000,000	
Fixed Costs	$1,000,000	
Revenue	$4,600,000	(83,333 x $55.42)

Hmm. Seventeen workers were let go (higher unemployment) and instead of widgets costing $46.00, they're $55.42 (higher inflation) ... doesn't this look like stagflation?

QUESTION 30

What does this model demonstrate?

☐ Stagflation results when labour markets become uncompetitive through unionization.

☐ Nothing except that Hlinka hates working-people!!!

I'm the first to admit that there are serious flaws in this model. The biggest one is that it presents an unrealistic best-case scenario, because as the price increased by 20 percent, the quantity demanded decreased by exactly 17 percent, meaning that it is revenue-neutral. It's far more likely that the demand for widgets is elastic, which means that a price increase of 20 percent will result in a decrease in widgets demanded in excess of 20 percent. What if, instead of eighty-three thousand widgets demanded, there are only seventy-five thousand consumers who are price-insensitive and will pay-up for more expensive widgets? Now seventy-five workers are needed to make widgets, making our income statement looks like this:

Revenue	$4,300,000	(75,000 x $57.33 per widget)
Fixed Costs	$1,000,000	
Labour	$2,700,000	
EBT	$ 600,000	
Taxes	$ 300,000	
Profit	$ 300,000	

This scenario is far more likely. That is, there is even *higher* unemployment and *higher* inflation.

There's another scenario that is also entirely plausible: the price that the market will bear for widgets is $46 and that is that.

The variable cost per widget is $36. That means that in order to make the required $600,000 pre-tax profit:

$$(\$46 - \$36) \times Q - \$1,000,000 = \$600,000$$
Therefore: Q = 160,000.

But here's the problem: market demand is only 100,000.

$$(\$46 - \$36) \times 100,000 - \$1,000,000 = 0$$

There is no return for investors and it's time to close the factory.

Yet practice is even *worse* than theory.

Unions are productivity killers because they systematically slay the motivation of their members.

Allow me to reflect on my experience with Planters Peanuts. I was young and strong and knew I wouldn't be there for long, so perhaps I approached my job with more enthusiasm than many of the lifers. Plus I've always had a very high motor — I can't go half-speed at anything even if I want to.

There was a slowdown in business. The shop foreman approached me one Friday afternoon, tears in his eyes, and told me that as of Monday, I'd be laid off. It wasn't because I wasn't a good worker; it was simply because I was a recent hire. To this day I remember him mumbling to himself as he walked away, "It just isn't fair…. It just isn't fair…. It just isn't."

Yes, he was a member of the union. But his values weren't being represented by it. The foreman *valued* hard work and thought it should be rewarded; the union *valued* seniority.

Hard work propels an economy. Seniority does not.

For a wide variety of union jobs, there is not only no incentive to work hard, there are *disincentives*. You're not going to be paid more (that's the no-incentive part) and the loafers will resent you and make your life miserable (that's the disincentive part).

I've heard the sophistic argument made that unions enhance productivity because if labour is more expensive, less of it is used and capital is substituted. The problem with that argument is that when a workplace unionizes it stands to reason that capital will become more expensive also, because there is more risk associated with the operation. The only certain outcome of unionization is that both capital and labour become more expensive.

We know that unions are resistant to technologies that enhance productivity because the adoption of such technologies results in workers being let go, and the prime directive of a union is to serve the interests of its members, not the public interest. The very nature of the institution is to fight a rearguard action against progress if that progress means greater efficiencies.

Let's go back to Cobb-Douglas one more time, to evaluate the impact of unions within an *economic* framework. These are organizations that resist improvements in total factor productivity, these are organizations that increase the cost of capital for businesses, these are organizations that negotiate on behalf of their members to reduce the number of hours worked, and these are organizations that do everything in their power to demotivate their members.

QUESTION 28

How would you describe the claim that "unions were responsible for the wage growth that workers have enjoyed in past generations"?

☐ It is an accurate interpretation of North American economic history.

☐ It is a statement so asinine that only an ex-politician could possibly think it is true.

It would be intellectually dishonest not to acknowledge that in the *short run*, immediately after a workplace unionizes, the remaining workers are better off than they were before. It would be equally intellectually dishonest not to acknowledge that in the *long run* (for all the reasons previously cited) unions cost workers … and we can find the proof with the Ford Motor Company.

In 1914, Henry Ford paid his workers $5 a day. If over the past century, wages for auto workers had increased at the same rate as nominal economic growth, assembly-line workers at Ford Motor Company would today be making approximately $3,300 a week.

The 1980s

On January 2, 1980, the Dow Jones Industrial Average, the most closely watched indicator of stock market activity, opened at 824.57. Almost exactly ten years later, December 31, 1989, it closed at 2,753.20. The stock market went through the roof that decade because the North American economy went through the roof that decade.[1]

With the benefit of 20/20 hindsight, we can understand the reasons why times were so good: one had everything to do with public policy and the other had nothing to do with public policy.

The 1970s was a time of deep pessimism and self-doubt in the United States, and that spirit of malaise had an impact on all the developed countries of the world.

We appreciate this on a micro level. There are points in our lives when we don't feel very good about ourselves. This leads to a downward cycle, one that's very hard to break. Sometimes that cycle is broken by a change in circumstances; sometimes the help of another person is needed. The same is true for nations. When we're talking about the macro level, the condition of a country, change for the better will sometimes occur as a result of things beyond the control of any one person. Sometimes, however, it takes special leadership to lift the spirit of a people. With the election of Ronald Reagan in 1981, the United States had a leader able to do just that. Reagan is, I believe, the most extraordinary politician to serve in my lifetime, in several ways. Yes, there was his natural optimism and superb communication skills, but he also possessed something even more important.

Ronald Reagan is the only North American politician I can think of who embraced free markets, understood what drives an economy, and believed in everyday people — qualities that resulted in him being hated with passion by the New Elite.

When Reagan took office in 1981, the highest marginal tax rate was 70 percent. One of his first legislative acts, the Economic Recovery Tax Act of 1981, lowered it to 50 percent; over the next two years, it was lowered to 38.5 percent, and finally to 28 percent.

Let me explain what a marginal tax rate is. This is what is imposed on your last dollar of income. Let's step back in time to 1981. Someone taking home $100,000 is given the opportunity to work extra-hard and make an additional $20,000 on top of that. With a marginal tax rate of 70 percent, that would translate into an additional $6,000 in her pocket. Not much after taxes! Reagan understood this; he knew that high tax rates serve as a disincentive for workers to exert themselves. As an actor during the Second World War, he had seen first-hand what impact high marginal tax rates (at that time 92 percent)[2] had on him and his colleagues. They would work until hitting the upper limit, then take the rest of the year off.

It's not so bad for an economy if actors stop working. There will always be an army of waiters and waitresses who can step into the breach. It becomes more problematic when skilled workers like doctors and engineers make the same rational economic choice: Why work hard if there is little benefit to be gained from it?

QUESTION 31

What is the most likely result of high marginal tax rates?

☐   Fewer hours will be worked.

☐   The same number of hours will be worked.

☐   More hours will be worked.

Common sense tells us that at some point, high marginal tax rates put a damper on wealth-creating activity.

Common sense should tell us something else. At some point, lowering marginal tax rates doesn't impact the work-leisure decision. This is completely unscientific, but my instinct (and behaviour), tells me that as long as I'm keeping more than half, it's worth my while to burn the midnight oil. Cutting the marginal tax rate from 70 percent to 50 percent generated real economic growth. I feel certain saying that. I'm less positive that the two other cuts did much else but increase the U.S. national debt.

However, tax policy shouldn't be only about finding the necessary revenue to fund vital government programs. A kind of rough-and-ready justice should factor in as well. If two citizens are provided with the same benefits by the State, is it right that they are treated very differently when it comes to footing the bill? We don't extend this argument to anything else in civil society. We understand that when we go into a restaurant, we should be responsible for paying for what we order. When we ride the subway, the cost of a ticket is the same for all adults because the approximate benefit is the same for everyone. Steeply progressive income taxes are politically popular, but to call them "fair" is to rely on an argument whose roots are in ideology, not logic.

There was another important provision in the Economic Recovery Tax Act. It involved new rules around the expensing of depreciable property. Businesses are taxed on the profits they earn. Expenses incurred, whether they involve an outlay of cash or not, reduce the profit that a company reports and the taxes it has to pay. Imagine that a business buys a machine for $10 million that will be used for the next ten years. Before the Tax Act of 1981, it was required to expense $1 million a year for the next ten years. After the Tax Act, it could expense (in some cases) approximately $6.77 million in the first year. The impact was predictable: companies started investing heavily in capital equipment.[3]

Ah! More machines (everything else being equal) lead to higher real growth. There's a good argument to be made that if wasn't for the Tax Act of 1981, Silicon Valley wouldn't have become what it did.

I know that all of this occurred in the United States, not within Canada's borders. But let me quote Canada's prime minister at the time, as he described the relationship between the two countries: "Living next to you is in some ways like sleeping with an elephant. No matter how friendly and even-tempered is the beast, if I can call it that, one is affected by every twitch and grunt."[4]

That was Pierre Trudeau, of course. And while his counterpart in Washington was focusing his attention on laying the foundations for a stronger economy, Trudeau and his cronies were redefining the relationship between individual citizens and the State with the Charter of Rights and Freedoms.

Rather than enhancing rights and freedoms, it has had exactly the opposite effect.

Read through it and you've got lots of your basic Motherhood and Apple Pie. But what is not included is as significant as what is.

The Charter guarantees several "fundamental" freedoms:

a) freedom of conscience and religion;

b) freedom of thought, belief, opinion, and expression, including freedom of the press and other media of communication;

c) freedom of peaceful assembly; and

d) freedom of association.[5]

There is no mention of property rights. And there is a very good reason for that.

The dictator Frederick the Great summed it up wonderfully: "My people and I have an agreement which satisfies us both. They are to say what they please, and I am to do what I please."[6] That's the reason they called this guy "the Great" and not "the Above-Average." As an authoritarian ruler, he totally got it.

What he "got" was that giving people one type of important protection — the protection from State prosecution if they said something deemed unpopular — allowed him to take away another equally important protection — the protection of property rights.

In the discourse about politics, the distinction is generally made between left-wing and right-wing. The NDP is Canada's "left-wing" party. The Liberals are in the "centre" and Conservatives are on the "right." In the United States, the Democrats are the southpaws and Republicans inhabit the right. This classification misses the point: The only meaningful distinction between political parties is that of authoritarian versus libertarian.

The premise of libertarianism is that individuals should be empowered to the fullest extent possible to make their own decisions and then deal with the consequences.

The premise of authoritarianism is that some body or group should be empowered to make decisions on behalf of individuals and that they should then have the right to shove those decisions down everyone's throat.

I've already introduced the notion — and this is central to *Stalled* — that a New Elite started to emerge in North American during the late 1960s. It believes strongly in authoritarianism and seeks to crush libertarianism.

In addition to the fact that the New Elite tend to be well educated, overrepresented in the liberal arts and law, secular humanist (rather than religious), and liberal in personal matters while being highly interventionist in economic affairs, there is another important characteristic its members share: they're useless at producing things of real value.

Tool-and-die makers aren't part of this New Elite. Lawyers are. The New Elite doesn't drive trucks. They shuffle paper in government offices. The New Elite aren't harvesting crops. They sit in interminably long committee meetings and come up with new and creative ways to expropriate the wealth generated by the tool-and-die makers, truck drivers, and farmers. The New Elite understand that its economic interests are *best* served by an ideology that favours the redistribution of income, not its creation, because it isn't capable generating wealth. That is not its skill set.

And in order to expropriate wealth, the political ideology must be one that champions authoritarianism … and at the same time crushes a libertarian framework that protects both freedom of speech *and* property rights.

QUESTION 32

Do you agree that slavery is one of the most evil institutions in the history of mankind?

☐   Yes.

☐   No.

My guess is that everyone agrees. But what exactly is the essence of that evil? Isn't it that a majority uses force to make a minority work for the majority's benefit?

QUESTION 33

Do you agree that the essence of the evil of slavery is that it involves a majority using force to make a minority work for the majority's benefit?

☐   Yes.

☐   No.

Any discussion of slavery — at least in North America — quickly gets tinged by the issue of race. It was a white majority (in the United States) that enslaved a black minority. But what if, instead of white people enslaving black people, 90 percent of white and black people joined forces to enslave 10 percent of the other white and black people?

QUESTION 34

How would you compare slavery not based on race to slavery based on race?

☐　　Less odious.

☐　　Equally odious.

☐　　More odious.

If you believe that society should be understood as a collection of individuals, rather than groups, you have to believe that whether slavery is based on race or "something else," it is equally wrong. If you believe that it is fundamentally wrong for a majority to expropriate wealth (read: steal) from any minority, then you have to believe that any document like the Charter of Rights and Freedoms, supposedly meant to protect minorities — any minority — from the whims of the majority — any majority — should address property rights. However, the Charter fails miserably in extending one of the most important protections that any citizen needs, and that's with respect to seizure of property by the State.

That's a very serious omission. Then there's a glaring change to the same Charter, and it's in a "marginal note" to Section 15:

- **15.** (1) Every individual is equal before and under the law and has the right to equal protection and equal benefit of the law without discrimination and, in particular, without discrimination based on race, national or ethnic origin, colour, religion, sex, age or mental or physical disability.

- Marginal note: Affirmative action programs

- **15.** (2) Subsection (1) does not preclude any law, program or activity that has as its object the amelioration of disadvantaged individuals or groups including those that are disadvantaged because of race, national or ethnic origin, colour, religion, sex, age or mental or physical disability.[7]

This clause forever made Canada a nation of groups, not individuals. And it provides groups the incentive to play the "victim" card to "ameliorate" their condition, rather than embrace the remedy that had worked so well in the past: If you want to make your lot in life better, try setting your alarm clock fifteen minutes earlier. To this day, the Charter encourages political solutions if members of certain groups aren't "getting ahead," solutions that have everything to do with the transfer of wealth, not its creation. In the wake of the Charter, what would matter less and less was the content of your character and what would matter more and more would be an accident of birth, that is, where your ancestors came from.

QUESTION 35

Do you agree that Canadian society should be understood as a collection of individuals, rather than a collection of groups?

☐   Yes.

☐   No.

The Charter's world view led — in a direct line — to a conversation I had several years ago with an admissions officer from my alma mater, the University of Toronto.

A particular joy in teaching is the relationships I get to forge with young, bright, energetic people. One of the best students — no, let me take that back — one of the best *people* I've ever encountered is Adam, who was my student ten years ago. It's a long and convoluted story about how we met; suffice it to say that I was his instructor and he was one of a group of thirty that had no shortage of truly spectacular minds.

Adam's background was in computer science/mathematics. Born overseas, he landed in Canada with an undergraduate degree. He was passionate about mathematics and applied to a master's program at the University of Toronto. He was on a waiting list, his student visa was about to run out, and he asked me if there was anything I could do to help. I told him that I was more than happy to contact anyone involved with the admissions process. He provided me a number and after the introductions were made, the conversation went something like this:

> *Me:* I'm calling on behalf of an ex-student of mine, Adam.
>
> *U of T:* Ah, yes, I know him well.
>
> *Me:* That's wonderful. My understanding is that he is on a waiting list for your math program. The purpose of this call is to vouch for his work ethic and attitude.
>
> *U of T:* Thank you. We are giving Adam serious consideration, but …
>
> *Me:* But?
>
> *U of T:* But it is a highly competitive program — I'm sure you can appreciate that.
>
> *Me:* Of course I do. However, as a fellow academic, I would think that you'd agree that the most important considerations are that the candidate is capable of doing the work, and then after graduation, he'll reflect well on the institution that admitted him.
>
> *U of T:* I agree that those are important but there are other things to consider.
>
> *Me:* Other things?
>
> *U of T:* Other things.
>
> Silence. Until it became uncomfortable.
>
> *U of T:* It's important that the program is "balanced."
>
> *Me:* Balanced?
>
> *U of T:* Balanced.
>
> An even longer, more uncomfortable silence.
>
> *U of T:* What I mean is that when we're putting together a class, we want it to be representative.
>
> *Me:* Representative?
>
> *U of T:* Representative.
>
> By then, I had a pretty good idea where this was heading.

Me: I'm sorry. I don't quite understand what you mean by "representative."

U of T: I'm not quite sure how to put this …

Me: May I ask a question?

U of T: Please.

Me: If Adam had been born in Africa instead of China, would you admit him immediately?

U of T: Yes. [Pause.] But we wouldn't want that to get out.

Let's return to the Charter of Rights and Freedoms, this time with emphasis added:

- **15.** (1) *Every* individual is *equal* before and under the law and has the right to equal protection and *equal benefit* of the law without discrimination and, in particular, *without discrimination based on race*, national or ethnic origin, colour, religion, sex, age or mental or physical disability.

- Marginal note: Affirmative action programs

- **15.** (2) Subsection (1) does not preclude any law, program or activity that has as its object the *amelioration of disadvantaged individuals or groups including those that are disadvantaged because of race*, national or ethnic origin, colour, religion, sex, age or mental or physical disability.[8]

Recall the words of Mackenzie King: "Large-scale immigration from the Orient would change the fundamental composition of the Canadian population."[9]

Our Charter makes everybody equal before the law; it's just that some are more equal than others.

QUESTION 36

How does this anecdote make you feel?

☐   It makes me ashamed of this country.

☐   It reconfirms my belief that both Mackenzie King and Pierre Trudeau were great prime ministers.

Several years later, I recounted this story to a Harvard-educated, self-described "civil rights activist," somewhat older than me, who very patiently explained that *we* (by that he meant people who had similar complexions to one of the two of us) *had* to support that sort of admissions policy because *they* (meaning people of Asian descent) were built differently than we were.

I needed clarification because I was totally lost.

Their body types, he went on, were designed to form fit into desks and chairs so that *they* could spend more hours studying. It was an insurmountable genetic advantage that required State intervention to level a playing field that was patently unfair.

And he was serious.

Gibberish? Yes and no. Once a multi-ethnic society understands itself as a collection of groups, then it needs to rationalize its behaviour when it discriminates against those who happen to be in one of the "wrong" groups.

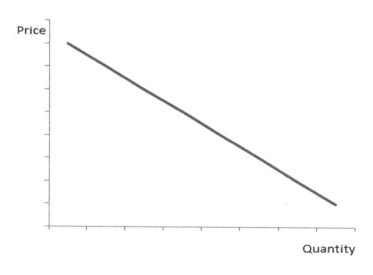

It's pretty clear by now that I oppose any sort of arbitrary discrimination based on things like race, gender, and sexual orientation. Individuals should be recognized for their specific talents and capabilities, not prejudged based on the group they belong to. One of the positive developments in the 1980s was that gender equality took huge strides forward. There was a broadly based recognition that women should enjoy equal opportunity in the workplace. When I was in primary school, which pretty much spanned the decade of the 1960s, the majority of mothers in my neighbourhood stayed at home during the day. This changed gradually over the years — as this chart that tracks the employment rate of women since 1976 indicates:[10]

A confluence of factors led to this development. In many "blue-collar" manufacturing occupations, women (if I may generalize) were at a distinct competitive disadvantage compared to men: it was frequently much more about brawn than brains. On the other hand, in many "white-collar" service occupations, women (if I may generalize) are at a distinct competitive advantage compared to men; as long as it's more about brains than brawn. Attitudes about what was "proper" had changed, and as more talented women joined the labour force, the economy moved to a higher plane.

The increasing participation of women in the workforce occurred at the same time a revolutionary change occurred in the workplaces of the Western world. On August 12, 1981, IBM unveiled the world's first personal computer, the 5150, and things were never the same.[11]

Manufacturing had become more and more efficient over the decades, which meant that more people were toiling in the service sector. The PC had a dramatic effect on how a myriad of jobs in the service sector were done.

My first office job was in 1982. It was after my first year of MBA studies. I was hired for a summer internship with National Grocers, a division of the Loblaws Group of Companies, and subsequently stayed on full-time, delaying the completion of my graduate degree. When I started working there, there were no personal computers.

Instead, there were secretaries and typewriters.

If a manager wanted to send something out — let's say the agenda for an upcoming meeting — here's what the workflow looked like.

He (and in those days, it was almost always a he) would either write something out longhand or bring his secretary into his office and dictate what he wanted written, then she (and in those days, it was always a she) would type it out.

The secretary would bring the agenda back to the manager to proofread.

He would edit and make corrections on the paper.

She would retype it.

He would read it again, and provided it met his satisfaction, would send it out. Of course, if there was something he didn't like …

The PC simplified and streamlined work processes, meaning that more was done by fewer people in less time.

Before I leave my National Grocers experience, let me explain what I and nineteen other MBA students were hired to do. A new president had been hired. National Grocers was a food wholesaler that operated out of eleven distribution centres scattered across the province of Ontario. It sold a wide variety of products: dairy, meat, fruits and vegetables, and canned goods to thousands of different stores. Accounting was done at the distribution-centre level only. So, the president knew what gross profit was on sales of dairy products out of Ottawa and what gross profit was on dairy sales out of Chatham, but he had no idea what the overall gross profit for dairy was across the entire company.

Imagine that! It's 1982 and you're president of one of the biggest businesses in Canada — and you don't know what margins are firm-wide. What did we do that summer? We added up the information manually. Twenty students sat from dawn to dusk, logging literally tens of thousands of hours, compiling data that an Excel spreadsheet would soon do in seconds, with accuracy to innumerable decimal places.

The computer revolution jump-started a North American economy that had gone nowhere during the decade of the 1970s.

Along with technological advances, there were also significant changes in how businesses operated, which helped to improve economic conditions during the decade.

Early in the 1980s, there was a great deal of trade tension between the United States and Japan. Japanese car makers were increasingly taking market share from their American rivals, and early in 1981, the Japanese Ministry of International Trade and Industry announced that Japanese producers would limit their annual shipments to the United States to about 1.7 million vehicles.[12]

The Japanese producers had already seen the writing on the wall. Even before the Japanese government committed to limiting exports, Honda had already decided to build the first "transplant" in Ohio, a state that bordered Michigan, the epicentre of the U.S. auto industry. Soon thereafter, Nissan Motors indicated that it would open its first assembly plant in the United States. And the location was more than a bit surprising: Smyrna, Tennessee.[13] Nissan chose Tennessee for a very sound strategic reason: Tennessee's labour laws were very business-friendly.

The United Auto Workers had crippled the Big Three, pushing Chrysler to the brink of bankruptcy in 1980. The Japanese auto makers were not going to let the same thing happen to them. They were determined to establish profitable plants in North America, and in doing so, they provided North American consumers with more choice, and workers with much-needed employment.

Yet, even as good things were happening in the real economy, it seemed like the political classes were doing everything in their power to screw things up. In Canada, the federal Liberals went on a spending spree that saw deficits increase from $14.6 billion to $32.4 billion in 1983. Then, after the Conservatives under Brian Mulroney took over, they made an even bigger mess of it — the deficit averaged $31 billion over the next six years.[14]

And where did the money go?

I think by now you realize that I'm non-partisan. I think that virtually every politician is equally useful, which means that I think that virtually every politician is essentially useless. There is an unfortunate self-selection process that attracts people to this occupation, just as there is a self-selection process that determines who will be interior designers and who will be mixed martial artists.

There was a consensus in the 1980s among politicians that their electoral interests were served by spending lavishly today, then letting someone else deal with the fallout down the road. Irresponsible? I think so. But it wasn't irrational behaviour. If your time horizon is the next election, and the consequence of acting this way is being returned to office, then it's mission accomplished.

There was one good piece of legislation that came out of the 1980s, and its passage explains much of the country's success in the years thereafter: the Free Trade Agreement between Canada and the United States, which eventually developed into a more comprehensive North American deal that included Mexico (NAFTA).

The purpose of the Canada-United States Free Trade Agreement was to:

- eliminate barriers to trade in goods and services between Canada and the United States;

- facilitate conditions of fair competition within the free-trade area established by the agreement;

- significantly liberalize conditions for investment within that free-trade area;

- establish effective procedures for the joint administration of the agreement and the resolution of disputes; and

- lay the foundation for further bilateral and multilateral co-operation to expand and enhance the benefits of the agreement.[15]

This was a very different approach than the 1960s Auto Pact. That was managed trade. This would be as close to free trade as possible.

I still remember how vitriolic the opposition was at the time. A collection of essays was released: *If You Love This Country*.[16] The New Elite, who benefitted most when the power of the State was greatest, went ballistic, wrapped themselves up in the Canadian flag, and started throwing mud balls ... prompting many Canadians to recall Samuel Johnson's quote: "Patriotism is the last refuge of a scoundrel."[17]

Free trade agreements reduce government's arbitrary decision-making ability. Free trade puts power directly in the hands of individuals. It takes the power away from institutions and politicians.

The New Elite, with their authoritarian bent, hate anything that promotes freedom, because it makes them as irrelevant as they should be.

While the New Elite were opposing greater freedom in Canada, a much greater force, one clamouring for greater freedom, was helping to liberate Eastern Europe from the tyranny of Communist rule. On November 9, 1989, the following announcement came from the East German government: "Permanent relocations can be done through all border checkpoints between the GDR (East Germany) into the FRG (West Germany) or West Berlin."[18]

The Berlin Wall was coming down.

The greatest accomplishment of Ronald Reagan's presidency was winning the Cold War — without firing a single shot. The arms race had prevented the U.S. economy from achieving its full potential; however, it collapsed the State-run Soviet economy.

This outcome should have convinced every citizen in the Western world that when it comes to government involvement in the economy, *less is more*. It was precisely to the extent that the West was freer and its resources were allocated more efficiently that our productive capacity was able to overwhelm that of the Soviets. In North America, we had both lots of guns and lots of butter — while there was a dearth of both on the eastern side of the Berlin Wall.

The impact of the Wall coming down would be felt in the decade that followed, and it was all for the good.

The 1980s in eighty words: Ronald Reagan's tax reforms provided the incentive for Americans to work more and invest in wealth-generating capital equipment. Canada was fortunate to be caught in the updraft of the strong growth that started in the United States. NAFTA led to greater trade opportunities and better allocation of resources continent-wide. But the single most important development was the PC and, more generally, computer technology. This allowed the increasingly important service sector to boost its efficiency in ways previously not possible.

And there was an even more important technological breakthrough on the horizon.

Understanding How
Free Trade Benefits EVERYONE

There are many well-intentioned Canadians who believe that free trade between Canada and the United States benefits only the United States because it is the bigger of the trading partners. There are many well-intentioned Americans who believe that free trade between the United States and China will benefit only China because it is the poorer of the trading partners. Both of those beliefs are mistaken.

Imagine that there are two neighbouring countries that do not trade with each other. One is bigger and wealthier and the other is smaller and poorer. For the sake of simplicity, let's assume that Bigger and Wealthier (B&W) has twice the number of citizens as Smaller and Poorer (S&P).

B&W can use all of its resources and in a day produce either forty-eight tons of peanut butter or forty-eight tons of jam, or a linear combination of the two. As everyone knows, the perfect peanut-butter sandwich requires an equal amount of peanut butter and jam, so B&W produces twenty-four tons of each.

S&P isn't as blessed as B&W. If it allocates all of its resources to peanut butter, it can produce twelve tons of peanut butter, and if it allocates all its resources to jam, it can produce six tons. The citizens of S&P similarly agree that the perfect peanut-butter sandwich has equal parts of peanut butter and jam, which means that it will produce four tons of peanut butter (which takes eight hours) and four tons of jam (which takes sixteen hours).

This is where we stand right now. B&W produces twenty-four and twenty-four and S&P produces four and four, and the combined output is twenty-eight and twenty-eight. On a per capita basis B&W is better off, enjoying twelve and twelve versus four and four, after adjusting for the population differential.

Okay. We've established that B&W is better at making peanut butter (one ton per hour, population adjusted, versus one ton per two hours) and it's also better at making jam (one ton per hour, versus one ton per four hours). But *comparatively* speaking, B&W is better at producing jam because it's four times as efficient. And that means that S&P has *comparative* advantage in the production of peanut butter.

Huh? Didn't we just say that B&W makes twice as much peanut butter in an hour as S&P? Yes. But because it makes four times as much jam in an hour, it should allow S&P to direct its resources to make peanut butter, because comparatively speaking, being half as efficient is better than being one-quarter as efficient.

The two countries agree on the following: S&P will use ALL of its resources to produce peanut butter. That means twelve tons. B&W will divide its resources: It will spend fifteen hours a day to make thirty tons of jam and nine hours to produce eighteen tons of peanut butter.

Now the combined output is thirty and thirty and the two countries decide to split the extra production down the middle: Now, instead of enjoying twenty-four pounds of peanut butter and twenty-four pounds of jam, B&W's citizens have twenty-five and twenty-five and S&P's have five and five.

This is comparative advantage in action. As long as one of the trading partners has a comparative advantage in one good or service, both benefit from free exchange. In the real world, things are slightly more complicated, with the operative word being "slightly." What we find is that certain countries are really good at lower end manufacturing (think China), some countries are really good at precision manufacturing (think Germany), and other countries are wonderful at design (think Italy). Allowing them to trade freely means everyone benefits.

Canada is good at lots of things. The United States is good at lots of things. Mexico is good at lots of things. And all benefit from NAFTA, and all would benefit from more trade relationships with even more countries.

The 1990s

The 1990s didn't start off auspiciously. A recession in 1990 dragged on for a couple of quarters.[1] It shouldn't have been totally unexpected. There was a pattern in North America, with a slowdown occurring about every ten years. The previous recession was in 1982, so the time seemed to be just about right for another one.

There are different theories about what causes recessions. However, there is more-or-less universal agreement that they are exacerbated by the inventory cycle. Let me explain.

Things are chugging along with the economy producing exactly 100,000 gizmos a month and also selling that many. Stores, because they never want to run out of gizmos, start each month with 100,000 gizmos in their inventories.

The economy starts to grow for all the reasons we've talked about before: capital deepening, more hours worked, and/or improvements in total factor productivity. Businesses anticipate that next month they'll need 105,000 gizmos, so they start producing more now. Production is 105,000 in a month when only 100,000 are sold. The ramping up of inventory means that more supplies are bought and people work more hours, giving them the ability to buy even more gizmos. As long as the economy continues to expand, production in the current month will always be greater than consumption in that month, because business wants to stay ahead of the curve.

Several months pass. Now 125,000 gizmos are being produced in a month where it is anticipated that 120,000 will be sold. But something happens. A shock of some sort or other occurs, and only 100,000 are sold. So, there is excess inventory of 25,000. This means that to correct the inventory imbalance only 75,000 will be made next month, if business anticipates that demand will stay at 100,000. Jobs are slashed, and the same multiplier effect that expanded the economy on the way up is felt even more intensely on the way down.

Understanding the inventory cycle is critical to understanding why recessions were once as prolonged as they were. But the 1990s saw a technology emerge that would help businesses manage their inventories in a way never before thought possible.

The 1980s was the PC decade.

The 1990s was the Internet decade.

QUESTION 37

Which of the following men should be credited with creating the Internet?

☐ Albert Gore, U.S. vice-president, 1993–2001.

☐ J.C.R. Licklider, director, U.S. Department of Defense, Director of the Information Techniques Processing Office.

Opinion is split on this one. In an interview with CNN's Wolf Blitzer, Gore said (and I quote fully so as not to take his words out of context): "During *my* service in the United States Congress, *I* took the initiative in creating the Internet."[2] That's Al Gore making the case for Al Gore.

Allow me to make the case for Licklider.

As early as 1962, Licklider formulated ideas for global networking in a series of memos that talked about an "Intergalactic Computer Network." A year later, while serving in the Pentagon, he spearheaded an Internet predecessor, the ARPANET. A paper he wrote in 1968 illustrated his vision of network applications and predicted the use of computer networks for communications. This was revolutionary thought. Conventional wisdom was that computers would primarily be mathematical devices that would speed up computations. In addition to Licklider, scores of other brilliant scientists kept pushing the ball forward. The Internet eventually eclipsed the ARPANET, which was shut down in 1990, the same year that Dr. Licklider passed away.[3]

Internet adoption was slow at first. I distinctly remember a conversation I had early in the 1990s with a research analyst at one of Canada's leading investment dealers. We were kicking around the idea of whether the Internet was for real or just a passing fad. We both agreed that it was here to stay, but it wasn't a slam dunk. In 1995, only about 14 percent of Americans had access to the Internet,[4] but by 2000, it had grown to 55 percent.[5]

This technology enhances productivity in any number of ways. Snail-mail is slow and expensive. Hard resources have to be used, where email transmission costs virtually nothing (just some bandwidth). There were tremendous efficiencies in supply chain management as a result of the Internet: inventory levels came down dramatically, boosting real economic growth in the process.

This is how it works. You're running a retail store and sales are $5 million per year. You're pulling out $250,000 in cash based on those sales. The inventory you need, pre-Internet, to generate that revenue is $1 million.

Then you get this amazing tool that helps you manage your inventory better. And you realize that you can get away with $900,000 of inventory. Even if your sales remain flat, it means that you can pull $350,000 in cash out of your business. You've just upped your cash flow by 40 percent! This is exactly what North America saw through the entire supply chain starting in the early 1990s. Computers, and more specifically Internet technology, led to efficiencies, which meant that you could do more with less, and whenever that happens, the economy is sure to grow.

Not only did the economy benefit as a result of the growth of the Internet during the 1990s, there was also the peace dividend.

Since the 1950s, Western democracies, led by the United States, were engaged in a Cold War with the Soviet Union. The expenditure was necessary, but it consumed valuable resources. Let's go back to our village example. If 10 percent of the able-bodied men are taken away from farming, manufacturing, and the production of services to serve in the military, the community will be poorer. By similar logic, if 10 percent of the men who had been in the service return to farming, et cetera, then output will increase.

Military spending fell sharply in the United States in the early 1990s and by the end of the decade, in inflation-adjusted dollars, it was just two-thirds what it had been at the start of that ten-year period.[6]

While the economy was benefitting from the growth of the Internet and peace dividend that accompanied the ending of the Cold War, other, less beneficial, changes were occurring — ones that would have real, long-lasting negative effects on the economy and on society as a whole. Some of the worst of these were the result of judicial decisions.

There are some things I don't understand and never will. One is the knee-jerk respect that is paid to judges and courts, particularly the highest court in the land, the Supreme Court.

QUESTION 38

On balance, do you trust lawyers?

☐ Yes.

☐ No.

QUESTION 39

On balance, do you trust politicians?

☐ Yes.

☐ No.

My hunch is that if a poll of Canadians were taken, the majority would say "no" to both of these questions.

How about this one?

QUESTION 40

On balance, do you trust judges?

☐ Yes.

☐ No.

My hunch is that if this question were asked of Canadians, the majority would say "yes."

People, judges are ex-lawyers who have been appointed by politicians!

The year is 1990. Francis Lavigne is a teacher in Ontario's community college system. Every time he gets paid, union dues are deducted from his paycheque. Neither he nor anyone else in the system has a choice, by the way. Workers in a unionized environment are forced to pay dues, even if they choose *not* to belong to the union.

Whoa, Nellie! Isn't one of the fundamental freedoms that is supposed to be guaranteed according to the Charter "freedom of association"? At times it is, at times it isn't. In this case, if you choose not to associate, you're still dinged.

Let's imagine if this principle were extended to everything in life. Last night, I went out to dinner. I chose not to eat dessert. But the restaurant charged me for it, and when I squawked, the courts ruled in its favour.

The root of this problem goes back to 1946, and one of the true mental midgets this country has ever produced, Justice Ivan Rand. In an arbitration decision, he ruled that everyone in a workplace should be forced to pay dues, whether or not they wanted to be part of the union. He justified this by invoking the "free-rider" argument: non-paying workers would receive the same benefits as dues-paying members.[7]

The reasoning is specious. Even the dullest pencil in the pack should have been able to see how both union members and non-union members can coexist peacefully in the same workplace. Pay dues and receive the benefits conferred by union membership, such as being represented if you have a grievance, being entitled to strike pay, or protection in the case of layoffs through seniority. Choose not to pay dues, you're on your own. The remedy is obvious.

That wasn't even what Lavigne was challenging. Very narrowly, his complaint centred around the union's right to use his dues to support political causes. He objected to seeing his money go to the New Democratic Party, disarmament campaigns, and striking coal miners in the United Kingdom. A trial judge agreed with him. The Ontario Court of Appeal reversed that decision. Then it fell into the Supreme Court's lap.

The decision came down on June 27, 1991. The appeal was dismissed. Lavigne's dues would go wherever the union wanted them to go.

There's no point spending much time on the reasons the court gave. Three of the seven justices agreed that the Rand Formula violated Section 2(d) — Freedom of Association — but that it was acceptable to limit freedom of association because any right or freedom is subject to "reasonable limit prescribed by law." The other four said that there was no violation of the Charter, but even if there had been, it was perfectly acceptable to in this case limit freedom of association because ... you see where this is going.[8]

The Supreme Court of Canada "liked" unions and would bend the Charter and law like Silly Putty to protect them.

After reading the arguments the court presented, I would be tempted to credit it with bovine intelligence, were it not insulting to all the Holsteins and Angus cattle that are grazing around the globe right now.

On February 27, 1992, seventy-nine-year-old Stella Liebach, who was a passenger in her grandson's car, bought a cup of coffee from a drive-through McDonald's in Albuquerque, New Mexico. Her grandson pulled the car forward and came to a full stop so that she could flavour it with cream and sugar. Ms. Liebach put the coffee cup between her knees and while attempting to take the lid off, spilled the hot liquid into her lap.

Her clothing absorbed the coffee and held it against her skin. As a result, she suffered third-degree burns to 6 percent of her body, had to spend eight days in the hospital, and underwent skin grafting. When she and McDonald's were unable to settle, the case went to trial. A jury awarded Liebach $160,000 in compensatory damages and an additional $2.7 million in punitive damages. (This was subsequently reduced to $480,000 by a judge.)[9]

There was a new way to strike it big in America; and not only for the Stella Liebachs, but also for the lawyers who represented them.

In 1960, the United States had one lawyer for every 627 people. That ratio had shrunk to one for every 339 by 1988.[10] And if there were one person to blame, I'm putting the finger on Raymond Burr ... that Perry Mason character!

There's an axiom in economics known as Say's Law, popularly understood as "supply creates its own demand." There were lots of lawyers and they needed work. Lawyers are disproportionately represented in legislatures. People tend to take care of their own. The promise of the legal system became: "Find an excuse to sue and you might become rich." North America was becoming increasingly litigious, with the United States leading the way.

The origin of class-action lawsuits predates the formation of the United States; they started in England during the seventeenth century. But no one has mastered the art quite like Americans. Class-action lawsuits reached a whole new level in 1994 with a $3.4 billion settlement over breast implants.[11]

Reasonable people should agree that breast implants are not medically necessary. Thousands of women exercised their free will and had the operation because they thought it would make them more attractive. Thousands of doctors were more than happy to perform the surgery because it helped pay for the house in the country. And government regulators gave implants, if not a green light, then at least a flashing amber one that seemed to say *Proceed ... at your own risk.*

In 1976, the Food and Drug Administration (FDA) permitted breast implants because they had already been on the market for fifteen years, reserving the right to make manufacturers "prove" they were safe.

It was a curious regulatory response. If the FDA believed that there was a reasonable likelihood of danger, you would hope it would have erred on the side of caution. Instead, the FDA waffled. In January 1982, it proposed to reclassify breast implants, but that went nowhere. In June of 1988, the FDA required pre-market approval, and then in 1991, it convened a panel of experts and decided that the devices should stay on the market temporarily and with limited access.

Meanwhile, the manufacturers started being hit with lawsuits.

In December 1992, a Houston jury awarded Pamela Jean Johnson $25 million — $5 million in actual damages and $20 million in punitive damages for symptoms that experts and lawyers alike conceded were similar to a "bad flu." But that was chump change compared to what the lawyers who represented the plaintiffs in the breast-implant class-action lawsuit received.

The presiding judge decreed that "at least" 75 percent of the $3.4 billion had to go to the women who claimed damage, leaving a staggering $850 million for their commission-based agents.[12]

From the plaintiff's perspective, the litigation game is a "Heads, I win, tails, I don't lose" proposition. The worst possible outcome is that a judge dismisses the case before it comes to trial. But let's consider where the court's interest lies. Is it really in turning away business?

There is an overwhelming systemic bias that encourages all lawsuits, including frivolous ones, because you never know how the litigation cookie will crumble.

Postscript to the breast implant case: Virtually every subsequent study determined that breast implants caused neither disease, nor increased risk of connective-tissue disease, nor was any link found between silicone breast implants and neurological disorders. In June of 1999 the U.S.-based Institute of Medicine released a four-hundred-page report prepared by an independent committee of thirteen scientists. They concluded that although silicone breast implants may be responsible for localized problems such as hardening or scarring of breast tissue, implants do not cause any major diseases such as lupus or rheumatoid arthritis. The Institute of Medicine is part of the National Academy of Sciences, the United States' most prestigious scientific organization. Congress had asked the institute to set up the committee. The committee did not conduct any original research; they simply examined past research and other materials, and conducted public hearings in order to consider all sides of the issue.

Yet even after the truth came out, no one was compelled to return one red cent to the real victims, the shareholders and employees of those companies that made the devices women chose to put into their bodies.

QUESTION 41
Should people be held accountable for the choices they make?

☐ Yes.

☐ No.

I don't think that in the 1950s we would have seen a jury award Stella Liebach $2.7 million. I don't think that the manufacturers of breast implants would have agreed to a $3.4 billion shakedown in the 1950s. What changed?

The answer is how we think about personal responsibility.

During the decade in which I was born, people understood that coffee was served hot and if you spilled it on yourself, it could burn you. The accident that befell Stella Liebach was a result of her mistake, not McDonald's. If you believe that people should be accountable for their actions — in Liebach's case, this involved buying a product she knew was hot (there was never a suggestion that this was the first time she had bought McDonald's coffee), then choosing to hold it between her knees while she took the lid off — then the case should have been dismissed.

The same is true for the breast implant case. If you believe that people should be held accountable for their choices — in this case, having a gel-like product inserted into their bodies for no sound medical reason — then it would be impossible to find the manufacturer guilty.

Attitudes have changed.

Lawsuits were one way to get rich quick in the 1990s. Investing in the stock market was another, and there was a boom in the equity markets during the latter half of the decade.

NASDAQ (the National Association of Securities Dealers Automated Quotation Systems) was established in 1971 as an alternative to the New York Stock Exchange. While the NYSE had a physical presence — the "floor" — NASDAQ was a telecommunications network that linked thousands of market participants who were scattered across the globe.[13]

Its listing fees were much lower than those charged by the NYSE, and soon it became home to most of the start-up tech companies of the 1980s and 1990s, including Microsoft, Apple, and Cisco Systems, to name just a few. In its early years, NASDAQ's growth was typical of equity markets — 10 percent compounded annually over the period from February 1971 to July 1995, when it broke through 1,000 for the first time.

By 1998, NASDAQ had doubled in value to stand at 2,000. It jumped another 50 percent and was 3,000 as of November 3, 1999. Before the year was out, it had surpassed 4,000, and by March 3, 2000, NASDAQ hit its all-time high of 5,046.86.[14]

This spectacular growth made men like Bill Gates of Microsoft and Larry Ellison of Oracle fabulously wealthy. There were many more ordinary working people — at large publicly traded companies ranging from Enron to Northern Telecom — who were also enjoying the buoyant markets … and the fact that they were becoming rich beyond their wildest dreams.

The attractiveness of markets such as NASDAQ and the growth in the number of people possessing personal computers and using the Internet led to the day-trader phenomenon. From their homes, people logged onto the Internet and watched their computer screens, moving in and out of the market quickly, sometimes holding positions for minutes or even seconds.

These day traders reasoned that they could make more money and enjoy better working conditions buying and selling shares than by toiling in mines or factories. That kind of labour grows the pie, while day trading results only in the re-slicing of what has already been made. Still, day trading attracted a lot of people, and soon more and more were making their living shuffling paper, rather than producing it.

Growth was real in the 1990s, however, and it helped Canada get its fiscal house in order. In the 1980s there were large federal deficits each year. In order to stem the tide, the Goods and Services Tax (GST) was introduced in 1991.[15]

The GST was sold to the Canadian people as a replacement for the manufacturers' sales tax that, according to Brian Mulroney, prevented Canadian companies from competing successfully with U.S. rivals. There was an element of truth to that. But more importantly — if there is such a thing — the GST was a "good" tax.

There is consensus in the economic community that good taxes are ones that do not discourage people from producing goods and services of real value. When you tax income, you discourage production. When you impose a sales tax, you discourage consumption. And it should be clear to everyone that both individuals and nations become wealthy because of production, not consumption.

Concentrated taxes on manufacturing could well have moved businesses out of Canada, particularly in the wake of NAFTA. But a 7 percent tax on goods and services? Nobody would work less because of it.

Sales taxes raise revenue without discouraging productive work. And they can be progressive as well, provided there are intelligent exceptions made for necessary goods and services.

A simple model.

Citizen One makes $25,000 a year and spends the entire $25,000 on necessities. Citizen One would pay zero GST.

Citizen Two makes $50,000 a year and spends $25,000 on necessities and the rest on luxuries. Citizen Two would pay $1,635 in GST (based on 7 percent).

Citizen Three makes $100,000 a year and spends $25,000 on necessities and the rest on luxuries. Citizen Three would pay $4,906 in GST.

Citizen Three, who makes 57 percent of the income, pays 75 percent of the GST, while Citizen One, who makes 14 percent of the income, pays 0 percent of the GST.

Consumption taxes are the smartest and fairest types of taxes.

The workings of the GST are proof that tax policy matters. Here's an even better example: the emergence of Ireland as "the Celtic Tiger."

The first documented use of that phrase was in a Morgan Stanley report released in 1994. In the 1990s, Ireland's per capita gross domestic product doubled and its unemployment rate fell from 16 percent to less than 5 percent, largely due to a tax code that supported foreign direct investment. The tax rate on corporate profits, which was 40 percent in 1990, was slashed and it stood at only 10 percent for manufacturing companies by the end of the decade. It was no wonder that multinationals poured money into the Emerald Isle, leading to an economic boom and the moniker Celtic Tiger.[16]

An important lesson was provided: A State can establish a decisive competitive advantage with an enlightened tax policy.

The 1980s and early 1990s saw government debt balloon at the national level. This turned around in the middle of the decade. The introduction of the GST helped, since it poured some extra money into the federal government's coffers. International investors were partially responsible as well. They started demanding higher interest rates for buying Canadian bonds. But there was another factor at work, and it was Quebec nationalists. Even though it wasn't part of their agenda, their actions had "unintended consequences."

In 1995, the country was shaken to its core when the people of Quebec voted on the following proposition:

> Do you agree that Quebec should become sovereign after having made a formal offer to Canada for a new economic and political partnership within the scope of the bill respecting the future of Quebec and of the agreement signed on June 12, 1995?

The margin was razor-thin: 50.8 percent voted "no."[17] For the time being, at least, Quebec would remain within the nation. In the wake of the decision, some serious questions were raised. What would have happened if Quebec had decided to go its own way? Who would be responsible for the national debt? The rest of Canada was looking for a pro-rata split while *la belle province*'s position seemed to be: "It's Canada's debt. And we're not part of Canada anymore. It's your problem."

It was a sobering wake-up call. For the first time since Pierre Trudeau served as prime minister, it hit home that running large federal deficits could have negative consequences. For the first time in a generation, there was the political will to behave in a fiscally responsible manner.

As it turned out, the stars aligned very nicely. The deficit the year of the referendum (1995) was $30 billion; it shrank to $8.7 billion the next. The year 1997 saw the first of a string of eleven straight surpluses.[18] During the late years of the nineties, a robust U.S. economy meant that demand for Canadian products increased, and our dollar weakened against the greenback. The average exchange rate was about $0.73 from 1994 to 1996. From 1997 to 1999 it dipped to $0.67 and finally bottomed out in the $0.64 between 2002 and 2003.[19] When one currency weakens against the other, it is a sign of weaker relative performance. But that doesn't necessarily signal that things are going badly; for example, if one trading partner is growing very robustly and the other is growing strongly, but not as robustly, the former's currency will appreciate against the latter's. That's what we saw during the 1990s.

The United States was going gangbusters; we were doing very well, and our weakening currency was a boon to manufacturing, specifically the auto industry.

We haven't addressed exactly what "currency" represents. Well before my time — 1914 — it was possible for a Canadian to enter a bank, hand over a dollar, and receive the equivalent amount of gold. The First World War ended that.[20] The United States ceased backing its currency during the Great Depression; private ownership of gold was prohibited on January 30, 1934.[21] And from that point forward, both Canadian and U.S. dollars were fiat currencies. Nothing tangible backstopped them.

Most introductory economics textbooks explain that money is a medium of exchange, a store of value, and a unit of account. I'm not disputing that. But most fundamentally, money is a belief system. It's the belief that you'll be able to give someone these flimsy and colourful (in Canada's case) pieces of paper, and you'll get things of real value in return.

But here's the truth about any fiat currency. At the end of the day, you can only be sure that it will be accepted in the country of issue. Many Canadians have had the experience of travelling to the United States and trying to pay for purchases with our dollars. Good luck! Americans usually have their currency accepted here, but that's only because of the relative size of the markets, and the knowledge that we'll be able to take those U.S. dollars and convert them into Canadian dollars at any bank on any street corner.

Here's where any discussion about currency gets highly theoretical, but it's the only sensible way to understand money. What a Canadian dollar represents, at any instant, is a fractional ownership of all the productive capacity of this country, both in the present and stretching into the future.

Let me try that again. This time in English. There is no inherent value in money. Rather, it represents value. Imagine if everything in Canada vanished — Poof! — and there was nothing to buy, and there was the universal belief that nothing would ever be produced within these borders for the rest of humankind. In that case, a Canadian dollar would be worthless.

Second hypothetical scenario: Everything in Canada has vanished, but there is the belief that the country will rebuild in short order. The currency would then hold at least some value.

So when you're holding a loonie in your hand, what you have is a small claim on what Canada has produced in the past and is expected to produce in the future. Same thing holds for one U.S. greenback.

Therefore, when currencies freely trade against each other, as our currency does with the U.S. dollar, the appreciation of one and the matching depreciation of the other represents the consensus view of the two countries' relative fortunes.

This was what the appreciation of the USD and depreciation of the CAD was about: The opinion that America's future was brighter than ours.

From 1991 onward, the U.S. economy grew at a compounded real rate of 3.0 percent, something that North America hadn't seen since the 1960s, and our performance — 2.7 percent growth — wasn't much shabbier.[22]

The 1990s in ninety words: Coming out of the recession of 1990, North America experienced the longest continuous expansion in its history. The key driver was technology, the Internet in particular; the allocation of resources away from the military to the goods and services producing sector spurred growth as well. The depreciation of the Canadian dollar helped a variety of export industries, and the strong performance of the private sector, coupled with the introduction of the GST, enabled the federal government to reduce debt, which meant that interest payments started coming down in lockstep.

And as we headed into the new millennium, there was every reason to believe that the decade to come — the 00s — would be equally as good, or even better than, the one before, as long as we could survive Y2K.

Efficiency – and the Race to the Top

Several years ago, I needed some repairs done to my condominium. I called two different contractors and got quotes.

After meeting with them, I judged that they were equally professional and would deliver work of similar quality. One was going to charge $1,000, the other $1,250. Clearly, it made sense for me to select the contractor who charged less, because he was the most *economically* efficient.

I didn't ask either of the contractors how long it would take them to do the work. But let's say for the sake of argument I had. One estimated it would be forty hours and the other guessed fifty.

Would this influence my decision? Of course not. If the contractor who quoted me $1,000 was going to take fifty hours, I would go with him, even though I understood he was less *technologically* efficient.

When the rubber hits the road, economic efficiency trumps technological efficiency in short-run, microeconomic decision-making. In the long run, countries get wealthier because of technological efficiency. That process is driven by economic efficiency.

People generally don't get better at things unless there is some reason for them to do so. There's an axiom I recall hearing years ago: "Necessity is the mother of invention but invention is the mother of them all." That gets it right. It's not easy to invent and we tend to do so only when our backs are against the wall.

Back to the two contractors. I select the cheapest one and, for the sake of argument, let's say he's the one who requires only forty hours of labour. He's working for $25 per hour. Contractor Two, who was also charging based on $25 per hour, would, presumably, lose out on contract after contract and would either have to reduce his hourly wage (which he'd be loath to do), figure out how to work more productively, or realize that he's competing in the wrong market and find something else he can do better. In all cases, it's a win-win for the macro-economy.

On the other hand, let's say that Contractor Two quoted me the price of $1,000. Contractor One would, presumably, lose out on contract after contract and would either have to reduce his price and earn a competitive wage (which he'd be loath to do), figure out how to work more productively, or find an occupation that commanded an hourly wage of $31.25 an hour.

No matter what, economic efficiency leads to technological efficiency.

Let's try another scenario: Both contractors quote a price of $1,000 and I tell them that I can't afford that much, and that if they want the work, they'll have to drop the price.

Contractor One digs in his heels and says his price is $1,000 and I have to take it or leave it. Meanwhile, Contractor Two reasons that he'll still make a reasonable profit at $950.

I've heard this type of competitive activity described as a "race to the bottom," and that is sheer nonsense. Contractor Two must be making money at $950 or he wouldn't have dropped his bid. But, as we just discussed a moment ago, my request for him to lower his price puts all the positive pressure in the world on him to figure out ways to become more technologically efficient to get his profit back to what he would have made had the market borne the $1,000 price.

Look at it from my point of view. I'm paying $50 less. I can afford to go to AAA and have a couple of Boneshakers and the best ribs in the history of the world, stimulating that much more economic activity.

This scenario illustrates a race to the top, not the bottom, that race being one in which more goods and services of real value are generated by the same amount of resources.

My hunch is that I haven't convinced everyone. If you really believe that the competitive process that forces out excess profits leads to a "race to the bottom," then the next time you're in a grocery store and see something you were already going to buy on special, find the manager and insist on paying the full price.

I think *now* I've convinced everyone.

PART THREE

The 2000s and Beyond

I awoke on January 1, 2000, rolled over in bed, and looked at my alarm clock.

Seemed to be working okay.

I got out of bed and opened the refrigerator door.

Everything under control.

Then I flipped on the TV, found CNN … according to the scroll at the bottom of the screen, there hadn't been any nuclear launches in the past eight hours.

It appeared that the world had survived Y2K, after all.

Does anyone else remember how many people were terrified that computers would malfunction after the year turned from 1999 to 2000? The theory was that to save memory space, computers generally represented a year by its last two digits only. For example, 1999 was saved as 99. So when we got to 2000, some computers would not be able to tell whether "00" meant 1900 or 2000.[1]

And, at least according to some, the results were going to be apocalyptic. But as it turned out, it was just another case of the boy crying wolf.

There had been a number of those false alarms in the past twenty-five years. When I was in high school in the mid-seventies, a physics teacher convinced me that a new Ice Age was imminent because mankind was screwing up the ecosystem with CO_2 emissions. Then the ozone was dissipating and there would be a global epidemic of skin cancer.

In retrospect, these can be viewed as harmless entertainment for us in

North America: There's something in the human spirit that responds to a good old ghost story. But in at least some of these instances it seemed like people wanted to manufacture a crisis to serve their personal agendas.

It was a harbinger of what we'd see later in the decade when it was determined — at least by some — that my high-school teacher had it backward: What we should have been worrying about was global warming, not cooling.

In January 2000, however, there was nothing but rational exuberance on both sides of the forty-ninth parallel.

Arthur Okun's Misery Index, U.S. style, stood at a miniscule 6.3 percent at the end of 1999. Unemployment was at a thirty-year low of 4.1 percent.[2] Inflation was a benign 2.2 percent, almost smack dab on the 2 percent target that every developed country's central bank establishes as the "optimal" rate.

Closer to home, things weren't quite that good, but the trend lines were moving in the right direction. We ended 1999 with unemployment standing at 7.6 percent[3] (it had been well over 10 percent just five years earlier) and given that inflation was 2.6 percent, our Misery Index wasn't very far north of 10 percent.[4]

The stock market was going strong, particularly in the States, hitting new highs day after day.

And yet.

And yet the times they were a-changing and there were new factors and forces that would contribute to the stagnation we've lived through over the past fifteen years. Some were out of our control — headwinds that we would have had to navigate our way through, even if we'd minded our Ps and Qs:

- The Demographic Challenge: An aging population meant that there were fewer people of working age to support retired workers;

- Infrastructure as Albatross: All of the civic infrastructure that had been built in the past fifty years (and earlier) needed upgrading, and this would take a huge economic toll;

- The World Flattens: China (in particular) and India emerge as world economic powers, requiring North America to rethink the sectors where it enjoys comparative advantage.

But the other, more important factors were (and are) well within our control and have everything to do with why we're stalled:

- Debt: The ballooning of public and private debt both contributed to slowing growth;

- The Welfare State: A culture of dependency had taken root;

- Upper-Middle-Class Entitlements: The elite had increasingly figured out how to game the system;

- The Inheritance Retirement Plan: Working hard and saving for your own retirement no longer became important for those who were going to be handed everything on a silver platter;

- Behavioural/values-based roblems: A dramatic decline in taking personal responsibility resulted in problems as diverse as obesity, disintegration of the family, and substance abuse.

We will discuss all of these issues later in the chapter, but first I'd like to mention how the decade began for me. Early in 2000, I made the best decision of my life and left the private sector, accepting a full-time, tenure-track position with George Brown College in its financial planning department.

I had been involved with the securities industry since 1993. I got very lucky and blundered into an opportunity selling mutual funds through a 1-800 number, then spent several years working in discount brokerage, learning everything I could about how stock markets functioned. It was the perfect world for me, one of probabilities, rather than certainties. In 1998 I felt confident enough to start managing other people's money and joined HSBC as a rookie investment advisor (IA).

But how to differentiate myself? I knew that the competition was fierce, and I also realized that in the midst of a bull market — that's smack dab where I found myself in October 1998 — people are hesitant to change advisers. I thought that having the imprimatur of an academic institution ("He teaches securities courses at George Brown College — he must know what he's doing!") would help me market myself.

One teaching assignment led to another, and by September 1999 I had a full-time course load. At the same time, I was managing a growing book of business. This was my dilemma: I liked being an investment adviser, but teaching was so much more fun! It also had many other benefits. When given the chance to instruct full-time, I jumped at it.

That decision — and some of my reasons for it — were representative of serious structural problems in the Canadian economy. More about that later.

When the decade began, inflation was benign. We've discussed how monetary policy can and should be used to deal with inflation. If the economy is overheating, it is prudent to raise interest rates to cool things off before an inflationary spiral sets in. Although inflation was not a problem, the United States central bank, the Federal Reserve, started raising rates in 2000. An increase of one-quarter of 1 percent in February was followed by an increase of similar proportion in March. Finally, in May, the Fed said: "The hell with it — let's bump 'em up a full half of a percent," and as of May 16, 2000, the Fed Funds Rate stood at 6.5 percent.[5]

The reason the central bank of the United States raised interest rates was to deflate the stock market bubble that it believed had formed. With the benefit of 20/20 hindsight, it's hard to argue with its assessment. But there were other, more effective ways to address this problem. Loan values for securities could have been decreased; this would have led individuals and institutions to de-leverage their investment portfolios. There could have been a special tax levied on speculative day trading. Any of these would have been better solutions. Because an asset bubble should never be that important. There will be winners and losers, but nothing of real value is either destroyed or created. Here's an illustration of that fact:

Four people live in a city and they are the only ones who trade stocks. Each one has $100,000 cash in his or her portfolio — and the total investable wealth looks like this:

Investor One	$100,000
Investor Two	$100,000
Investor Three	$100,000
Investor Four	$100,000
Investable Wealth	$400,000

Investor One puts $25,000 into the market, when it's at a level of 2,500. When it goes up to 5,000, he sells his holdings to Investor Two for $50,000. Now Investor One has $125,000 and Investor Two has $50,000 in cash and $50,000 worth of stock. When the market goes up to 7,500, Investor

Two sells to Investor Three. Which means that Investor Two has $125,000 and Investor Three has $75,000 worth of stock and $25,000 in cash. Then when the market goes to 10,000, Investor Four buys out Investor Three for $100,000 which leaves Investor Three with $125,000 cash and Investor Four with $100,000 worth of securities ... and then the market crashes, falling back down to 2,500.

Now investable wealth would look like this:

Investor One	$125,000
Investor Two	$125,000
Investor Three	$125,000
Investor Four	$25,000
Investable Wealth	$400,000

The increases and decreases in the stock market only lead to a redistribution of wealth.

Using the Fed Funds Rate to address an overheated stock market made as much sense as using a meat cleaver to remove a sliver from your finger. It may have done the job, but it caused much greater suffering than necessary.

The negative effects began to be felt immediately, and by 2001 the damage to the economy was becoming pronounced. This should have provided an important lesson to the bank. Milton Friedman had warned for years that erratic monetary policy was the cause of both inflation and boom-and-bust cycles. A central bank should grow the money supply at a rate that matches long-term economic growth. The Fed didn't do this. Its actions provoked the opposite effect: its interest rate hikes of 2000 led to a mild recession, commencing in 2001.

The year 2001 was also the year that George Bush Jr. was inaugurated as the forty-third president of the United States of America. There was no shortage of optimism after George Bush triumphed over Al Gore in the 2000 election. For one thing, Bush Jr. was the first president in history with a master's degree in business administration, a degree that he'd received from no less an institution than Harvard University![6] If anyone would understand the workings of the economy, it would be George Walker Bush.

Here's something you may not know about George Bush. When he ran for president, he was asked to release different bits of confidential information, one of which was his GMAT score for admittance to Harvard Business School.[7]

Some of you may not be familiar with the GMAT. The letters stand for Graduate Management Aptitude Test. It's a standardized test that everyone writes under the same conditions — I went through the experience myself before attending business school at the University of Toronto.

What's the purpose of the GMAT? It provides the only opportunity in the admissions process to level the playing field. Typically, when you apply for business school, you provide your undergraduate transcripts. But different programs and different teachers rate things differently — how can anyone actually compare them intelligently? You can submit a letter or essay introducing yourself — but who knows who actually wrote it? But that's not possible with a GMAT score. Finally, there's nowhere to run, nowhere to hide.

George Bush Jr., was asked to reveal his GMAT score … and he refused.

Why do you think that was? I suppose that there are a couple of possible explanations. Because I'm generally one who sees the glass as half full, not half empty, and I like to give people the benefit of the doubt, it could be that he had an incredibly high score. I mean he might have knocked his GMAT out of the ballpark and he was just being modest. He didn't want to put it out there because people might have thought he was being boastful.

Or maybe it's because it was embarrassingly low and he didn't want people to know that he had no business being admitted into Harvard Business School in the first place and he could thank his lucky stars that his father was born before he was.

QUESTION 42

What do you think of the last sentence?

☐ It's a clever lampooning with oh-so much truth to it.

☐ It's a scurrilous attack on a great American president.

Why should a GMAT score even matter? Because it speaks directly to how a society's most treasured prizes are allocated. A pure merit-based system — which is what the GMAT represents — had been replaced by something else. In Bush Jr.'s case, it was family connections.

This would cause problems because the new millennium required someone with the vision to see that, for a variety of reasons, things were very different and that the conventional responses to economic difficulties were no longer effective. Particularly after the attack on the World Trade Center.

Do you remember where you were on the morning of September 11, 2001?

My memories of that day are so distinct. It was astonishingly beautiful in Toronto, with a sky so blue it made you wonder if it wasn't heaven shining through.[8] I walked to class, as I generally do, to arrive for the 8:00 a.m. start time. About an hour after it began, a habitually late student strolled in with a smirk on his face and glibly announced: "World War III just started!" No one had any idea what he was talking about until we took our break and I checked the news on the Internet. After class, I headed to a local bar that I knew had televisions, watched the footage that looked like special effects from a Hollywood movie, and tried to learn as much as I could about what happened and why. I remember thinking at the time, *What's next?*

The fallout in the world's financial markets was immediate. The New York Stock Exchange couldn't open that day and remained closed until the following Monday. The price of both gold and oil spiked. When the European bourses opened the next day, losses were sharp, ranging from 3 percent to 8 percent.[9]

Very soon after the attacks in New York and Washington we learned that Osama bin Laden and al Qaeda were responsible. By October 7, U.S. and U.K. troops were on the ground in Afghanistan, trying to bring him to justice. The belief is that in December of that year, he slipped through their fingers at Tora Bora, and made his way into Pakistan. Had he been captured, political history might have been very different, but I suspect it would have only pushed back the day of economic reckoning.

While this was going on, the Federal Reserve acted decisively, accelerating the interest rate cuts that it had been executing over the previous nine months. The Fed had pushed the Fed Funds Rate to 6.5 percent on May 16, 2000, in order to deal with a perceived stock market bubble. As mentioned earlier, there were immediate negative effects as a result of the rise in the bank rate. The next January, rates came down a full 1 percent to stand at 5.5 percent. There were five more cuts through August of 2001, and when the planes hit the World Trade Center, it was 3.5 percent.

The fear was that business activity would contract even more in the wake of the destruction, and in order to prevent that, the Federal Reserve became even more aggressive: An emergency meeting on September 17 brought the Fed Funds Rate down to 3 percent, and by June 2003, it was an unprecedented 1 percent.[10]

At the same time, there were sharp tax cuts. Keeping a campaign promise, George Bush inaugurated the first round in 2001, reducing the top marginal rate of 39.6 percent to 35 percent, with the other five brackets reduced by 3 percent. Further changes to the tax code, made in 2003, focused largely on reducing the inclusion rate for both capital gains and dividend income, and scaling back inheritance taxes.[11]

The 2003 cuts sent exactly the wrong message. From now on, Mr. and Ms. American Taxpayer would receive special treatment precisely to the extent that their income was unearned.

Not only did the changes to the tax code send the wrong message about the value of work, they also threatened the government's financial stability. I've made it very clear that one of the most important priorities of a national government is to balance budgets over the business cycle. If taxes are going to be cut, the government had better reduce spending. But during these years, taxes were cut and spending was increased.

And even while interest rates were lower than a snake's belly and deficits soared like eagles, the United States exhibited only moderate growth. It should have been apparent to anyone — *even* one of Harvard's finest — that there were bigger issues with the American economy.

The early years of the decade were better for Canada, for a couple of reasons. The fiscal discipline that started under the Liberals continued under the Conservatives. Surging resource prices (we'll get to this later) benefitted the Canadian hinterland. And more and more Canadian companies — commencing around 2003 — took advantage of a quasi-loophole in the tax code and started converting from a corporate structure to a trust structure.[12]

Most people are familiar with the corporate structure because this is how most for-profit businesses are organized. A corporation is a legal entity, separate and apart from its owners, the shareholders. The corporation raises capital and then tries to generate profit. If it does make a profit, it will pay tax and can then return the excess value to shareholders, either in the form of dividends or (theoretically) an increase in the share price.

Here's a simple model to demonstrate: I have this great idea for a business but need $20 million to launch it. Let's imagine I raise $10 million from investors (100 people pitched in $100,000 each) who are willing to take the risk and I borrow the other $10 million, paying 10 percent interest. After one year, the income statement looks like this:

Revenue	$10.0 million
Operating Expenses	$7.0 million
Interest Expense	$1.0 million
Profit before Tax	$2.0 million
Tax @ 30 %	$0.6 million
Net Profit	$1.4 million

That $1.4 million belongs to the investors (my compensation would be part of the operating expenses) and there are three things that can be done with it. It could be reinvested in the company, it could be returned to shareholders in the form of dividends, or it could be used to buy back shares from existing investors so next year when the profit is made, it is divided (perhaps) ninety-five ways, rather than one hundred.

Doesn't it stand to reason that the manager's preference would be to retain the entire $1.4 million? If the company is bigger, I can argue that I need more compensation because there's more on the line. And if I'm being compensated with share option plans, the value of the entity will grow, simply by holding that amount of cash in the company coffers. It is well documented that the corporate structure frequently creates tension between the owners (shareholders) and managers, to the detriment of the former.

Let's pretend that I'm Mr. Integrity of CEOs and I agree that the entire $1.4 million should be given to the shareholders as dividends. If you're a high-income Canadian (even with the dividend tax credit considered), it means that for your $100,000 investment, you'll get $14,000 after the business tax has been deducted, and then you're clipped at a rate of about 40 percent (combined federal and provincial taxes) leaving you $8,4000.

This is double taxation. The profits are taxed at both the corporate level and the individual investor level.

Hence the ascension of the trust structure. As long as the majority of earnings were paid out in the form of distributions (think dividends) to unit holders, the structure itself was not subject to tax. This meant that even if an investor's marginal tax rate was 50 percent, now she was able to keep $10,000 from her investment, rather than $8,400.

There were any number of benefits that flowed from income trusts. First, it had the effect of reducing a company's cost of capital. People were more likely to invest in trusts, since what they care about is what they make after tax.

QUESTION 43

If you have two investment options, which would you choose?

☐ Investment 1, which provides a pre-tax return of 10 percent and an after-tax return of 6 percent.

☐ Investment 2, which provides a pre-tax return of 8 percent and an after-tax return of 7 percent.

The answer is obvious. And it demonstrates something important: If the market's required rate of return is 7 percent after tax, a business could go ahead with Investment Two while it could not go ahead with Investment One. The trust structure created employment opportunities that would otherwise not have been there.

There are other benefits. The trust structure imposed discipline on managers. Now they couldn't retain earnings in order to create their own little empires. To avoid taxes, the trust was required to pay out between 50 percent to 80 percent of earnings. This is a much higher ratio than you'll see from most corporations. If a business had expansion projects, it could go to the market and raise money. There was nothing stopping the trust from issuing additional units.

Think of what this means in practice. An oil refinery has been operating profitably for years with its existing plant. Now it wants to expand. If it's a corporation, it could have been retaining earnings for years, earnings that it can now use to finance the expansion. But if it's organized as a trust, it will have been paying out virtually everything as it went along. In order to attract additional investors, the trust would have to make a specific case that this particular expansion plan is cost-justified. It's a much more rigorous vetting process, which means that capital is employed more efficiently, and efficiency is always a good thing.

Finally, the trust structure had the entirely unintended consequence of moderating CEO compensation. The pay packages that at times seem obscene to everyone (including me) are almost invariably a result of stock options. Paying out earnings in the form of distributions and rewarding shareholders with cash payments had the direct consequence of moderating the capital appreciation of those trusts.

I can't quantify how beneficial the income trust structure was to Canadians in the early years of the 2000s, but I am sure that its impact was significant. This is why I was thrilled that in the 2006 election the Conservative Party pledged to "preserve income trusts by not imposing any new taxes on them."[13] Finally, there seemed to be a political party in Canada that seemed to understand that efficiency drives prosperity.

But as it turned out, all the Conservatives understood was that you say what you think will help get you elected, then do whatever you want once you're in office. There is no meaningful accountability. Fewer than nine months after the election, the finance minister did a 180-degree turn on Halloween and killed the tax advantage that had resided within the trust structure.[14]

Trick or treat, Canada. Trick or treat.

If the benefits allowed corporate trusts in Canada proved to be fleeting, there were other changes to the economy taking place that were profound and long-lasting. In the year 2000, a barrel of oil averaged $27.39. By 2010, it was $71.21.[15] In the year 2000, an ounce of gold averaged $279.11. By 2010, it was $1,224.53.[16] There were several factors that drove this surge in commodity prices and a major one was the emergence of China and India as global economic powers.

I first sensed China's immense potential when I began instructing full-time at George Brown College. It was September 2000. My hunch is that if I had gone into my local Canadian Tire store at the time and tried to find something made in China, it would have been possible — but it would have taken me a long time to do so. China didn't seem to register much then.

Back to George Brown. It was an 8:00 class, and when I arrived at 7:45 for it, there were twelve students in the room. Five of them were Chinese. Four were sitting together in the front row. At the back of the class, there was another Chinese man. He was hanging out with a mixed group of Canadian students, so I assumed he'd been born here, his parents of Chinese descent.

Class started promptly at 8:00. And very soon into it, the Chinese man at the back of the class raised his hand and asked a question. I was surprised. His English — while very good — was heavily accented. Clearly, Mandarin was his first language.

I try to get to know my students and soon got to know the Chinese student who had sat at the back of the class. Our relationship developed, becoming something much more like that of friends or even older brother/younger brother than teacher-student.

Sen's life story was remarkable. He was born into abject poverty in northern China. At a young age, he was tested by the State for athletic aptitude. It was discovered that he had remarkable flexibility in his shoulders, a natural gift that would immensely benefit him if were to become a competitive swimmer — especially if he specialized in the backstroke. His parents were approached: would they allow their son to join one of the country's elite swimming programs in two years?

A family meeting was convened. The parents explained to Sen's older brother the opportunity that had come Sen's way. They wanted to support their younger child as fully as possible — but only with the older one's consent. They had determined that if they scrimped and saved, they could afford to buy eight ounces of milk each day and they wanted to know if it was acceptable to the elder if they gave all of it to Sen to help develop his body as fully as possible.

The older brother agreed.

If you've been paying attention, you understand why this story resonated so powerfully with me.

Sen joined that program and eventually medaled in a major international competition. But months before the Olympic Games he had spent his life preparing for, he blew out his shoulder. That ended his competitive swimming career. He started coaching and ended up in California, before coming to Toronto to open his own swim school. Smart, entrepreneurial, with a work ethic that was astonishing, he symbolized the potential of that great country. And to think that China's population numbered 1,271,900,000.[17]

The Chinese economy's transformation started in the late 1970s. Agriculture was de-collectivized. Farmers owned the land and got to keep what they grew after paying a share to the State. That policy was largely responsible for avoiding the famines that had killed millions during Mao's Great Leap Forward. Soon private businesses were allowed. There was gradual reform, with the next major change occurring in 1997 and 1998 when large-scale privatization occurred.

The developed countries of the world should have been watching. The developed countries of the world should have noted that China was advancing precisely to the extent that its government was reducing its role in the economy.

What is so hard to understand about that?

A watershed event for China occurred on December 11, 2001, when it became the 143rd member of the World Trade Organization (WTO).[18] The WTO's founding and guiding principles remain the pursuit of open borders, the guarantee of the most-favoured-nation principle and non-discriminatory treatment by and among members, and a commitment to transparency in the conduct of its activities.[19]

The idea of open borders and global free trade is one of the key themes of Thomas Friedman's *The World is Flat*, published in 2005. It's a brilliantly entertaining discussion of a "flat" world, where there is both greater competition and greater opportunity for those who are unafraid to embrace the challenge.

For me, the most memorable part of the book is a quote that Friedman finds hanging on the wall of a small manufacturing facility in rural China:

> Every morning in Africa, a gazelle wakes up. It knows it must outrun the fastest lion or it will be killed. Every morning in Africa, a lion wakes up. It knows it must run faster than the slowest gazelle, or it will starve. It doesn't matter whether you're the lion or a gazelle — when the sun comes up, you'd better be running.[20]

The Chinese were waking up earlier and running further and faster than their counterparts in the developed world, and it showed in any number of industries. In 2000, China produced 128,500 tons of the world's 848,934 tons of steel, or 15 percent. Ten years later, its production and percentage had soared to 567,842 and 46 percent.[21] In 2013, China produced more cars and commercial vehicles than the United States, Mexico, and Canada combined.[22]

All of this production, all of this productivity, was a boon to Canada's resource sector, and it led to a significant change in the locus of economic power. If at the beginning of the decade it was difficult to go into a Canadian Tire store and find something that was made in China, by 2014 it was even more difficult to go into a Canadian Tire store and find something that wasn't. Manufacturing-centric central Canada was becoming less important than resource-rich Alberta, Saskatchewan, and Manitoba. Ontario slipped from being a "have" province to a "have-not" province, with per capita income below the national average. The same was true for Quebec. Ontario and Quebec do have one thing going for them, though. Together these two have-not provinces represent 62 percent of the population and currently have 59 percent of the seats in Parliament, meaning what they can't produce, they can always take.

Another important result of China's emergence as a manufacturing juggernaut was the anti-inflationary effect it had on the global economy. Commodities like oil and gold were surging in price, and others had similar price increases. Had this occurred in previous decades, there is no question that we would have seen the Consumer Price Index (more about this later) move up sharply. The oil shock of the 1970s resulted in double-digit inflation. Imagine what would have happened if all other commodities had similarly increased!

Yet inflation remained benign from 2000 to 2014. It makes sense if you give the matter a bit of thought. It's true that materials like oil and steel are important inputs into the manufacturing process. However, there is a far more important one — labour. Chinese workers made less, and even while China's manufacturing sector grew explosively, fewer people were being employed in it. [23]

It was sort of like déjà vu all over again ... we'd seen the same thing happen on this continent, first with agriculture and then with manufacturing. Fewer people doing more work equals productivity gains, which leads to lower prices. And lower-income Canadians, who disproportionately spend more of their budgets on the basic necessities that China was increasingly providing, benefitted the most.

By the early years of the decade, both Canada and the United States were running large trade deficits with China. And there were claims made, particularly in the United States, that China was doing something wrong. It was nonsense, but at least for some populist politicians, it distracted from the real issue at hand.

That issue was the huge amount of debt, both public and private, that the United States was amassing. We've discussed the Bush tax cuts of 2001 and 2003. At the same time that tax revenues were falling, the government was spending more, in no small part because of an ill-advised war in the Middle East.

On the morning of September 12, 2001, something happened that I hadn't seen in my lifetime: the United States, the world's foremost super-power, was seen more as victim than victimizer. Public opinion, from Tokyo to Toronto to Timbuktu, was four-square behind it. Everyone I knew believed that the U.S. was well within its rights to violate the territorial integrity of Afghanistan in order to bring bin Laden to justice.

Okay. The Allies failed in that effort. Afghanistan is a difficult country and he had the advantage of knowing the terrain. Once again, everyone I knew believed that the United States should continue to do everything in its power to prevent anything like the attack on the World Trade Center from happening again. And it seemed clear where the problem lay, at least if you checked the passports of the attackers.

Bin Laden was a citizen of Saudi Arabia. Of the nineteen hijackers, fifteen carried Saudi passports, two were from the United Arab Emirates, one was Egyptian, and one was Lebanese. We've done a lot of math together so far, so your skills must be razor-sharp by now. Numbers alone identified where the problem lay.

But the United States didn't attack Saudi Arabia. It attacked Iraq.

I don't know what motivated George Bush and the Republican Party to declare a War on Terror and decide that the key battleground was Iraq. And it doesn't matter. Because the motivation is far less important than its impact.

The American people — like most who have it reasonably good — are a peace-loving lot. They had to be led into war. In fact, the war was sold to them as something that was going to be painless for them.

About two weeks after the attack on the World Trade Center, this is what Bush urged Americans to do, in order to combat al Qaeda: "Get down to Disney World in Florida. Take your families and enjoy life, the way we want it to be enjoyed."[24]

Let's flash back in history to another time, another continent. It's June of 1940. Dunkirk has just been evacuated. Winston Churchill is about to address the House of Commons. A nation is on pins and needles, wondering what should be done to counter the threat ... and Churchill begins: "Think about booking a nice cottage on the Isle of Wight later this summer. I strongly recommend the Seaside Inn. The crumpets are to die for." Not quite up to: "We shall fight on the beaches, we shall fight on the landing grounds, we shall fight in the fields and in the streets, we shall fight in the hills; we shall never surrender."[25]

Yes, the challenge the United States faced in 2001 was fundamentally different from the one England faced in 1940. But where a great leader, Winston Churchill, made it clear that sacrifices were required, George Bush's promise was that nothing would be asked of America's citizens (except those who actually served in the military, which was a very small minority of its citizens). Bush served up guns and butter, with future generations responsible for footing the tab somewhere down the road.

Here are the annual deficits for the years of the Bush Presidency:[26]

2002	$158 billion
2003	$378 billion
2004	$413 billion
2005	$318 billion
2006	$248 billion
2007	$161 billion
2008	$458 billion

The last full year that George Bush was president was 2008.

What exactly did $158 billion represent? It meant that every man, woman and child got to spend $550 that year that hadn't yet been earned. That would increase to more than $1,000 per year for 2003, 2004, and 2005, before it briefly dipped, and then exploded in 2008.

The illusion of prosperity was being built on a mountain of public debt — and there was an ocean of private debt on top of that! In *constant* dollars (which means inflation-adjusted), average debt per household increased from $50,971 to $72,862 between 2000 and 2009.[27]

Maybe Canadians felt that we were late to the party, but we did our darndest to catch up to our southern neighbours. Someone who works in radio generally argues that one word is worth a thousand pictures, but here I'll show the ratio of household debt to GDP for Canada during the period from 1990 to 2013 ... you could run the a Grand Prix downhill ski race on it.[28]

Household debt-to-income ratio

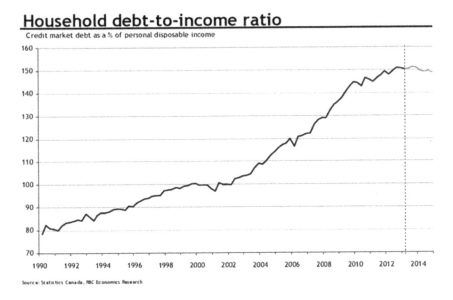

Credit market debt as a % of personal disposable income

Source: Statistics Canada, RBC Economics Research

Yet we were pikers compared to Americans. I don't generally agree with economist Paul Krugman, who can't find a government spending program he doesn't like, but even the blind squirrel occasionally finds half a nut. In 2010 he wrote: "The root of our current troubles lies in the debt American families ran up during the Bush-era housing bubble. Twenty years ago, the average American household's debt was 83 percent of its income; by a decade ago, that had crept up to 92 percent; but by late 2007, debts were 130 percent of income."[29] The part that Krugman left out (for ideological reasons) were the Bush deficits that were instrumental in creating that false sense of prosperity. When people feel that they're rich and going to get richer, they're more apt to increase their personal debt.

You combine that private debt with $10 trillion of public debt and something had to give — and it did.

I've been talking a lot about the United States and I'm going to continue to talk a lot about the United States, because what happened within its borders, starting in 2008, affected Canadians profoundly. The American experience should teach us volumes about effective and ineffective public policy, and that culture and values are decisive in determining the economy's direction.

The trouble that Paul Krugman alluded to was, of course, the pronounced economic downturn that began at the end of the Bush era. It has been called the Great Financial Crisis of 2008. I take issue with this moniker, for three reasons.

First, it doesn't qualify as "great." The two recessions of the 1970s, as measured by the Misery Index, were both worse and longer-lasting. Second, I would argue that it was less *financial* and more *economic*. To me, *financial* implies that the issue is about money, which is just paper, while an economic crisis implies deeper problems. Finally, crisis? Crisis suggests that you've got two hours to live unless you find that magical elixir. Crisis is where England was in June of 1940, with German forces massing along the northwest coast of France. The "crisis" of 2008 might qualify as a difficult period, but nothing more than that.

Let's call it the Not-so-Great Economic Difficulty of 2008 and understand how it came to be.

The popular interpretation is that the bubbling of the U.S. housing market and its subsequent bursting was the fault of "greedy bankers." Barack Obama said so repeatedly as he successfully ran for election in 2008.

There was no shortage of optimism after Barack Obama triumphed over John McCain. For one thing, Obama had a law degree, and from no less an institution than Harvard.[30] If anyone could fix the housing crisis, it was Barack Obama.

Here's something you may not know about Barack Obama. When he ran for president he was asked to release different bits of confidential information, one of which was his LSAT score for admittance to Harvard Law School.[31]

Some of you may not be familiar with the LSAT. The letters stand for Law School Admission Test. It's a standardized test that everyone writes under the same conditions — my sister went through the experience herself before attending law school at the University of Toronto.

What's the purpose of the LSAT? It provides the only opportunity in the admissions process to level the playing field. Typically when you apply for law school, you provide your undergraduate transcripts. But different programs and different teachers rate things differently — how can anyone actually compare them intelligently? You can submit a letter or essay introducing yourself — but who knows who actually wrote it? But that's not possible with an LSAT score. Finally, there's nowhere to run, nowhere to hide.

Barack Obama was asked to reveal his LSAT score ... and he refused.

Why do you think that was? I suppose that there are a couple of possible explanations. Because I'm generally one who sees the glass as half full, not half empty, and I like to give people the benefit of the doubt, it could be that he had an incredibly high score. I mean he might have knocked his LSAT out of the ballpark and he was just being modest. He didn't want to put it out there because people might have thought he was being boastful.

Or maybe it's because it was embarrassingly low and he didn't want people to know that he had no business being admitted into Harvard Law School in the first place and he could thank his lucky stars that his father was born before he was.

QUESTION 44

What do you think of the last sentence?

☐   It is a clever lampooning with oh-so much truth to it.

☐   It is a scurrilous attack on a great American.

QUESTION 45

How did you answer Question 42 and Question 44?

☐   The same.

☐   Differently.

Why does a LSAT score even matter? It speaks directly to how a society's most treasured prizes are allocated. A pure merit-based system —

which is what the LSAT represents — had been replaced by something else. In Obama's case, it was family lineage.

This was a time that required someone with the vision to see that for a variety of reasons, things were very different and the conventional responses to economic difficulties would no longer be effective.

QUESTION 46

What was the cause of the U.S. mortgage meltdown of 2008–2009?

☐   Greedy bankers.

☐   Irresponsible public policy.

☐   Something bigger than both of those things.

If the housing bubble of 2008 were a weed, you could say that the Community Reinvestment Act (CRA) of 1977 was the seed that it grew from. The CRA was consistent with a wide variety of affirmative action programs of the 1970s.[32]

The purpose of the CRA was to "encourage" lending institutions to meet the needs of borrowers in all segments of their communities. If you didn't play ball, then you would be denied insurance from the Federal Deposit Insurance Corporation — this effectively meant you'd be out of business.

The CRA was passed late in 1977. Take a look at the foreclosure rates that decade:[33]

Year	1970	1971	1972	1973	1974	1975	1976	1977	1978	1979
Foreclosure Rate	0.3%	0.3%	0.5%	N/A	0.5%	0.4%	0.4%	0.4%	0.4%	0.4%

Even with two severe recessions, they barely budged.

Then came the decade of the 1980s — a period of strong economic growth — and falling interest rates. You would think that foreclosure rates would remain stable or fall, wouldn't you? Except they didn't.

Year	1980	1981	1982	1983	1984	1985	1986	1987	1988	1989
Foreclosure Rate	0.5%	0.5%	0.8%	0.8%	0.9%	1.0%	1.2%	1.3%	1.2%	1.0%

It's not fair to blame the CRA entirely — or even mostly — for the upward drift of default rates during this period. I think that climb is more indicative of how Americans increasingly came to look at personal debt: something that would be paid off only if it didn't put them out too much — a kind of choice rather than obligation.

Then came the 1990s and the Clinton presidency. Bill Clinton received 80 percent of the black vote that election and owed that constituency.[34] Small-town bankers tend to vote Republican and Clinton was singularly adept at not only rewarding friends but punishing enemies. Commencing in 1994, the Department of Housing and Urban Development (HUD) launched a series of high-profile cases against financial institutions. The onus fell on the accused to prove that their lending practices did not discriminate on racial grounds. HUD frequently based its analysis on a naive statistical approach: If one thousand mortgage applications came from whites and one thousand from blacks, there should be a proportionate rejection rate. This approach ignored the fact that black applicants *should* have had a higher rejection rate based on income *alone*.[35]

In 1995, the median income of white families was $45,496. The median income of black families was $28,485. Twenty-seven percent of white families made $25,000 or less; 45 percent of black families made $25,000 or less.[36] It is logical that this discrepancy in income is what accounted for the higher rejection rates for black applicants.

Assume that there's a town with 100,000 families; 90,000 are white and 10,000 are black. Twenty-five percent of the white families are poor while 50 percent of the black families are poor. The chance that any poor family will be rejected if it applies for a mortgage is 50 percent. All families that are not poor will be accepted.

Non-poor white families rejected	90,000 x 0.75 x 0%	0
Poor white families rejected	90,000 x 0.25 x 50%	11,250
Non-poor black families rejected	10,000 x 0.50 x 0%	0
Poor black families rejected	10,000 x 0.50 x 50%	2,500

Even though black families make up only 10 percent of the town's population, they would account for 18.2 percent of the rejections based on the bank's model for assessing risk. There's nothing remotely racist here. And so it was decided not to let reason get in the way of a good, old-fashioned political vendetta. It was time for the authorities to put on some storm trooper boots and kick some Republican bankers' butts!

Financial institutions did the only logical thing to protect themselves. They lowered lending standards for everyone. Which is why — even as the economy boomed in the late 1990s — foreclosure rates were more than twice as high as they had been in the recessionary years of the 1970s:

Year	1990	1991	1992	1993	1994	1995	1996	1997	1998	1999
Foreclosure Rate	0.9%	1.0%	1.0%	0.9%	0.9%	1.0%	1.0%	1.1%	1.1%	1.1%

There were two more factors, one of which has received lots of commentary, and one of which has been largely ignored, that contributed to the collapse in the housing market.

Regulatory changes increased systemic risk. In 1998, the Glass-Steagall legislation — around since the Great Depression, separating lending banks from investment banks — was repealed. Then, in 2004, the Securities and Exchange Commission reduced the capital requirements for five Wall Street banks: Goldman Sachs, Morgan Stanley, Merrill Lynch (now part of Bank of America), Lehman Brothers (now defunct) and Bear Stearns (now part of JP Morgan Chase). Leverage was ramped up from approximately ten to one to forty to one. What that meant was that in 2003, for every $10 loaned, the banks had $1 to cover defaults and one short year later, that ratio increased to for every $40 loaned, $1 to cover defaults.[37]

This contributed to the collapse. But it overlooks what *really* caused the meltdown: People who borrowed money chose not to honour their debts.

It is as simple as that.

There was a very instructive story that came out of mainland China a short time ago. In 1990, a peasant, Mei Guanghan, went door to door, borrowing 70,000 yuan ($11,000 Canadian) from his neighbours to pay for his wife's medical bills after an accident put her in a coma.[38]

He noted how much he took from each person, vowing to eventually repay his debts. He was true to his word. Early in 2014 — twenty-four years later — he had paid everyone back every single yuan.

Why did he do it? I'll let him speak for himself: "Honour is honour and I don't believe in taking something for nothing."[39]

What did Mr. Guanghan *value?*

Taking care of his wife. And honour, which to him meant paying back what he owed.

QUESTION 47

Once ... even once during 2008 and 2009 ... do you remember hearing a single American politician say: "If you borrowed money from a financial institution, you are responsible for paying that money back"?

☐   No.

☐   Happened pretty much every day of the week and twice on the Sunday morning talk shows!

QUESTION 48

Once ... even once during 2008 and 2009 ... do you remember hearing a single American politician say: "If you borrowed money from a financial institution and you are currently in arrears, you are responsible for working out a repayment schedule and paying back everything you owe"?

☐   No.

☐   Happened pretty much every day of the week and twice on the Sunday morning talk shows!

QUESTION 49

Once ... even once during 2008 and 2009 ... do you remember hearing a single American politician say: "I am introducing a bill today that rewards those who are making timely payments of interest and principal on their outstanding loans and penalizes those have who defaulted"?

☐ No.

☐ Happened pretty much every day of the
week and twice on the Sunday morning talk
shows!

QUESTION 50

How do you think the mainstream press would have characterized a politician who made *any* of those statements?

☐ A leader.

☐ A fascist.

There have been any number of easy questions in *Stalled* but that was probably the easiest one of all.

QUESTION 51

What do you think the so-called Financial Crisis of 2008–2009 would have been like if every American who owed money looked at paying back his debts the way that Mr. Guanghan did?

☐ The "crisis" would have been worse.

☐ The "crisis" would have been exactly the
same.

☐ There wouldn't have been a "crisis" in the first
place.

There's a joke about a guy who falls from the balcony of a fifty-storey building, and as he's hurtling past the forty-ninth, then forty-eighth, then forty-sixth, then … you get the idea … he keeps saying to himself: "So far, so good!" That was a little bit like the Canadian economy in the mid-years of the 2000s. The fiscal stimulus in the United States helped us immensely because many of those dollars were spent on goods and services produced here.

The dominoes started falling in 2007. In February, Freddie Mac announced it would stop buying the riskiest subprime mortgages. In July, Bear Stearns liquidated two hedge funds that invested in similar products, and the next month Fitch started cutting the ratings of Countrywide Financial, although it was still judged investment grade.

In January 2008, Bank of America bought out Countrywide Financial in a move that was supposed to shore up the financial system. Not quite. After a several month lull, things developed quickly in September:

- **September 7:** Mortgage giants Fannie Mae and Freddie Mac are taken over by the government.

- **September 15:** Bank of America agrees to purchase Merrill Lynch for $50 billion.

- **September 15:** Lehman Brothers files for bankruptcy-court protection.

And then the bailouts began:

- **September 16:** American International Group, the world's largest insurer, accepts an $85 billion federal bailout that gives the government a 79.9 percent stake in the company.

- **September 21:** Goldman Sachs and Morgan Stanley, the last two independent investment banks, become holding companies, subject to greater regulation by the Federal Reserve.

- **September 25:** Federal regulators close Washington Mutual Bank and its branches; its assets are sold to JPMorgan Chase in the biggest U.S. bank failure in history.

- **September 29:** Congress rejects a $700 billion Wall Street financial rescue package, known as the Troubled Asset Relief Program or TARP, sending the Dow Jones Industrial Average down 778 points, its single-worst point drop ever.

In November, the CEOs of the Big Three North American automakers rode their corporate jets to Washington to ask for loans from the Troubled Asset Relief Program, or TARP, which had been designed to assist financial institutions.[40]

And just around this time, the reins of presidential power were being handed over from Republican George Bush Jr., to Democrat Barack Obama.

What the Republicans had presided over in the past eight years, even as the real economy stagnated and the illusion of growth was maintained by debt, was a significant increase in one "industry": lobbying of government. In 2000, 12,536 registered lobbyists (or more than twenty-three lobbyists for each Congressperson) spent $1.57 billion. In 2009, when the economy was apparently reeling — remember, the party line was that these were the worst conditions since the Great Depression — 13,788 lobbyists (a healthy increase of 10 percent) greased the pockets of elected officials to the tune of $3.5 billion.[41]

In underdeveloped countries, when public officials take money from private interests we call it bribery. In developed countries, when public officials take money from private interests, we celebrate it as democracy.

Of course the government bailed out the financial services industry. No major U.S. corporation provided more money to Obama in 2008 than Goldman Sachs, the "Financial Services Devil Incarnate" according to some. *Of course* the U.S. government bailed out the auto sector, which was really about bailing out the UAW on the backs of the secured creditors. Without the help of the unions, Obama would never have been elected in the first place, and without their support in 2012, he would have been a one-term president.

Back to our guy who has fallen from the fiftieth-floor balcony. He's just sped past the second floor and he continues to say: "So far, so…" *Splat.* That's what the global economy did in 2008 as the you-know-what hit the fan.

The United States faced difficult times in 2009 — I still don't think it deserves the term "crisis" — because of two reasons:

- George Bush had worked hand-in-glove with Federal Reserve Chairman Alan Greenspan to push interest rates down to 1 percent.

- George Bush ran deficits that saw the United States amass over $2 trillion of debt in seven years.

So what — according to Barack Obama — was the solution?

- Work hand-in-glove with Federal Reserve Chairman Ben Bernanke to lower interest rates to 0 percent.

- Run deficits that saw the United States amass over $4 trillion of debt in four years.

Let me repeat the Bush deficits:

2002	$158 billion
2003	$378 billion
2004	$413 billion
2005	$318 billion
2006	$248 billion
2007	$161 billion
2008	$458 billion

The year 2009 was a "shared" year:

2009	$1.4 trillion

Here are Obama's deficits:[42]

2010	$1.3 trillion
2011	$1.3 trillion
2012	$1.1 trillion
2013	$680 billion

QUESTION 52

Who said: "Those who don't learn from history are doomed to repeat it."?

☐ George Santayana.

☐ Forrest Gump.

QUESTION 53

Who said: "Stupid is as stupid does"?

☐ George Santayana.

☐ Forrest Gump.

And the irony is that while Bush's supporters would never identify with Obama's — and vice versa — there have never been two presidents who occupied the Oval Office who were more friendly to the interests of the so called "1 percenters" than these two. I'll explain this, but first I'd like to show that when talking about inequality things are not always as simple as they seem.

There are two numbers that are bandied about that highlight the wealth disparity in the United States. The top 1 percent controls 40 percent of the country's wealth, and the assets of the top 5 percent exceed the assets of the bottom 95 percent.[43] There is something more than a little bit disingenuous about these numbers because they don't take into consideration something significant, and that's the value of benefits like pension plans that working people enjoy.

There's an entrepreneur that started a business which employed ninety-nine people who made a middle-class wage throughout the years. The entrepreneur sells the business for $20 million and retires. Meanwhile, the ninety-nine people who worked for him have all paid off their homes but have no other financial assets. The average house is worth $200,000.

The 1 percent's assets are approximately equal to the 99 percent's:

1 x $20 million ≈ 99 x $200,000

Or is something missing?

It's likely that those ninety-nine people have pensions. For the next twenty years, they'll draw $30,000 annually. The undiscounted value is $600,000 and we can put the present value at half that, or $300,000.

This changes the equation somewhat:

99 x $200,000 + 99 x $300,000 ≠ 1 x $20 million.

It's important to consider everything when talking about inequality. Is there a great disparity of wealth on this continent? Of course. And I would prefer it if wealth were more broadly distributed. The question is: What is the appropriate mechanism?

It is 2014. There is broad agreement that the average working American is worse off today than she was in 2007. This is after a huge amount of fiscal and monetary stimulus. What we have seen, however, is asset inflation that disproportionately benefits the 1 percent.

Why didn't the deficit spending accomplish what it was supposed to do: stimulate the American job market and increase wages? It's hardly a mystery.

In a very short time, you will have a total grasp of why, in an open economy, deficit spending is singularly ineffective in creating domestic employment. Then you can speculate why this very simple concept hasn't been explained to you before.

There are two ways to measure gross domestic product (GDP), which is the value of all goods and services produced in an economy in a given period of time: the income approach and the expenditure approach.

We'll demonstrate with yours truly. Last year, George Brown College paid me $100,000. I made $50,000 from the University of Toronto and $10,000 from CBC. Using the income approach, I contributed $160,000 to Canada's GDP.

Alternatively, we could have tracked my spending. I paid $60,000 in taxes. My mortgage payments were $30,000. I spent $25,000 on food and clothing, $15,000 on vacations, and saved $30,000. By the expenditure approach, I contributed $160,000 to Canada's GDP.

A way to understand the expenditure approach across the entire economy is to add up:

Household consumption (C)

Investments (I)

Government spending (G), and

Net exports (X – M), i.e. (Exports – Imports)

GDP = C + I + G + (X – M)

A way to understand the income approach across the entire economy is to look at gross domestic product (GDP) plus transfer payments from government (F) minus business savings (SB) minus taxes (R). This will be equal to what households end up with, which can be divided between consumption (C) and household savings (SH). Formulaically:

$$GDP + F - SB - R = C + SH$$

We combine SB and SH to get total savings, S.

$$GDP + F - R = C + S$$

We can combine transfer payments (F) with taxes (R) to get T.

$$GDP - T = C + S$$

We rearrange terms:

$$GDP = C + S + T$$

We've established the equivalency of the equations, therefore:

$$C + I + G + (X - M) = C + S + T$$

The Cs cancel each other out.

$$I + G + (X - M) = S + T$$

If we want to isolate the impact of government deficits, we can re-arrange terms one last time, subtracting T from both sides, and carrying both investment (I) and net exports (X – M) to the right side of the equation:

$$(G - T) = (S - I) - (X - M)$$

What this tells us is that if there is an imbalance in government spending, the adjustment — BY DEFINITION — must be made in the savings/investment process and/or terms of trade with the rest of the world.

Imagine that the government is currently balancing its budget, that domestic savings are equal to investments, and that trade is balanced, with exports and imports the same. Let's try putting some numbers to it:

$$(40 - 40) = (20 - 20) - (10 - 10)$$

Then the government spends more than it collects to "stimulate" the domestic economy:

$$(50 - 40) = (?? - ??) - (?? - ??)$$

It stands to reason that savings would increase. At least some of the money would be put away for a rainy day:

$$(50 - 40) = (22 - ??) - (?? - ??)$$

There is no reason to think that investment would either increase or decrease.

$$(50 - 40) = (22 - 20) - (?? - ??)$$

The only possible adjustment is to the terms of trade. There is no logical reason why a country's exports would increase, just because its government is spending more money. Therefore the only reasonable adjustment *must* be to imports:

$$(50 - 40) = (22 - 20) - (10 - 18)$$

Imports would increase to re-establish the necessary equilibrium condition.

QUESTION 54
Was this example particularly difficult to follow?

☐   No.

☐   Yes.

QUESTION 55
Why have you never heard this explained by any politician before?

☐   They don't understand it themselves.

☐   They don't understand it themselves, but even if they did, they wouldn't want citizens to understand that this is what deficit spending leads to.

When a sovereign government runs a trade deficit in an open economy, the only certain impact is that it creates jobs ... for its trading partners.

And the only *certain* impact of printing money is to create inflation, in one form or another. The inflation of the 1970s was reflected in the consumer price index. The inflation of the past five years has been seen in the capital markets.

The S&P 500 closed at 676.53 on March 9, 2009. It has almost tripled since then.[44] The International Monetary Fund warns that another housing bubble might be forming in the United States.[45] Even though gold has pulled back from its all-time highs, it has still appreciated by more than 10 percent compounded annually, since Bush ran his first large deficit in 2001.[46]

You tell me who's benefitted from deficit spending and loose monetary policy.

QUESTION 56

Who do you think the prime beneficiaries of the deficit spending in the United States over the past decade have been?

☐   Working people in the United States.

☐   Working people in the People's Republic of China.

QUESTION 57

Who do you think the prime beneficiaries of the low interest rate policy of the past decade have been?

☐   The 1 percent.

☐   The 99 percent of working people.

One of the reactions against the 1 percent was various "Occupy" movements held across North America. Canada holds the dubious honour of getting this singularly useless ball rolling.

On June 9, 2011, Vancouver-based *Adbusters* magazine registered the domain name OccupyWallStreet.org. A month later, it called for a September 17 rally, hoping that twenty thousand would show. As it turned out, there were only one thousand, but they stubbornly held on. And very soon a gaggle of celebrity supporters showed up to offer support: Roseanne Barr, Michael Moore, Noam Chomsky, and Susan Sarandon among them.[47]

Copycat protests sprang up all over North America, including a tent city in St. James Park, very close to George Brown College. I walked through that encampment every morning on my way to school.

There was an assortment of groups in the park with somewhat different agendas, but the common complaint revolved around the unequal distribution of wealth.

There are two possible ways to achieve a more equal distribution. One is for the have-nots to create more of it. That requires doing something, something that someone else covets. The essence of that activity is selflessness because you benefit precisely to the extent that you provide the greatest benefit to others.

The other way to achieve a more equal distribution of wealth is to take what has already been created. The essence of this activity is selfishness. The occupiers in St. James Park were indifferent, it seemed, from whom the wealth was taken, because it was reported that food bank trucks delivered provisions to them.

I couldn't help but notice the stark contrast between the occupiers and most of my George Brown College students. I had the sense that many of those who were camping in St. James Park had but fed on the lilies and lain in the roses of life. Meanwhile, many of my GBC students work part-time or even full-time hours, sometimes supporting their families as they try to grind out an education. I know that for some international students, it takes the pooling of their grandparents', parents', and even aunts' and uncles' money to afford the tuition. All these students ask for is a chance to compete and make the pie bigger, which would benefit everyone, including the protestors.

I'll come back to that word again: *values.*

You can get ahead by working, if this is what you value.

You can illegally occupy a public park and whine about the unfairness of life, if this is what you value.

The second option was taken by many young Canadians. I saw it with my own two eyes. It should be recognized for what it was and treated with the contempt it deserves.

QUESTION 58

If the Occupy protestors had spent the same time and energy working at minimum wage jobs instead of sitting around and doing nothing but complaining, what do you think it would have accomplished?

☐   Lessened income inequality.

☐   Worsened income inequality.

Throughout this book, I've referred on numerous occasions to different economic metrics: inflation, unemployment, and GDP. Most people don't know how each is measured, and the manner in which they are distorted by those whose interests are served by presenting a picture that is better — or worse — than it really is.

Inflation is tracked by the consumer price index, or CPI. Every month, Statistics Canada purchases a fixed basket of six hundred goods and services. The sample is based on "representativeness" and "expected continuous availability" and is updated every two years.[48]

There are several sources of bias in the CPI: commodity substitution bias, new goods bias, quality change bias, and outlet substitution bias.

Commodity substitution bias refers to the fact that, in the real world, if one product gets more expensive relative to another, less of it is purchased. Let's say that 1 percent of the CPI is tied to the price of beef and 1 percent is tied to the price of chicken. If beef doubles in price, it's a pretty good bet that consumers will buy less beef and more chicken. This isn't captured by the way the CPI is measured in Canada. In this model, an equal amount of beef and chicken is bought every month irrespective of how the prices change vis-à-vis each other.

New goods bias is a product of the fact that the relative price of new products frequently falls sharply after their introduction. If these goods come to market *after* the CPI basket is updated, then the true cost of living may be overstated.

Quality change bias derives from the fact that quality improvements may increase the functionality of products and these are not fully captured by the price adjustments made by the statisticians.

Finally, outlet substitution occurs when people change their shopping habits, going to discount retailers, when prices increase. Ignoring this biases the CPI.

All of these biases tend to overstate inflation.

Why does government want to overstate inflation? Because so many government benefits are tied to it. If you're a senior who is receiving Old Age Security, would you rather be given a 2 percent increase in a given year or 3 percent? The answer is self-evident. You've been told by your country's statistical bureau that your cost of living has increased by 3 percent. Are you really going to look that gift horse in the mouth?

Any ruling party wants to be popular with its electorate because that's how it stays in office, which is why, as long as benefit programs are tied to the consumer price index, there is all the political incentive in the world to overstate, rather than understate, the actual increase in the cost of living.

Government has an even stronger interest in understating unemployment, and in the '00s, came up with a creative way of doing so.[49]

Calculating unemployment starts with the labour force. This is everyone aged fifteen to sixty-five who is either working or actively looking for work. If you're working part-time, you're considered fully employed, a clear distortion. If you're unemployed and have stopped looking for work, you're out of the labour force and therefore not unemployed. There's distortion number two.

The labour force also excludes full-time students — and that's the new, creative way that the Ontario government came up with to make the employment numbers look better than they are. The rate could be lowered if the number of students enrolled in post-secondary education was increased and the length of the programs was stretched out.

When I joined George Brown College in 2000, I was one of a handful of instructors in the two-year Financial Planning Program. It required students to achieve twenty-four credits, and was as focused as a laser beam. The emphasis in the first year was on helping students pass the Canadian Securities Course, the bedrock designation in the financial services industry. In the second year, we instructed in other licensing courses, including life insurance, derivatives, and the professional financial planning course. Everything we did was directed toward the vocational goal of filling a role in the financial services industry.

This lean offering was transformed into a flabby three-year designation, which now includes electives that have nothing to do with financial planning. Some of the courses that my students might take this semester include film studies (as if they need to go to school to watch movies!) and sexual diversity (can't you learn about that from the Internet?). Several years ago, George Brown College rolled out a four-year Applied Degree in Financial Planning: What we used to accomplish in two years now takes twice as long.

Who wins? People like me! Higher education has become a job-creation program for educated members of the New Elite, those who have graduate degrees of one sort or another (as if there is any connection between the ability to teach and the number of years spent in school). The more students there are in the system, the more bureaucratic positions needed in the education establishment. The growth in the size and length of educational programs was also a boon to politicians. Unemployment seems low; however, that number is artificial. Full-time students are not included in the unemployment figures, even if it would be their strong preference to work.

We know who loses. Society at large and, more particularly, students. Society loses because any time that resources are misallocated, wealth is destroyed, not created. And what graduating students are increasingly finding is that they are leaving school with a crushing burden of debt, entering a market where the jobs just aren't there.

In 2010, the amount of money students owed to the government exceeded $15 billion[50] ... and it's only been growing since then. Indeed, for several years now in the United States, student debt has exceeded debt on automobiles.[51]

But there's an important difference between a car and many college diplomas and university degrees. You know that a car will get you somewhere.

For many students, however, the diplomas and degrees they have spent years and small fortunes to acquire are taking them nowhere. They are being encouraged to enroll in programs and take courses that offer no hope of actually landing them jobs. *Forbes*, the U.S. business magazine, printed a list of the ten worst college majors (pertaining to employment rates and median income); the list includes English language and literature; history; commercial art and graphic design; physical fitness and parks and recreation; music; liberal arts; philosophy and religious studies; fine arts; film, video and photographic arts; and anthropology and archeology.[52] Most of these shouldn't even be understood as disciplines. They're hobbies, and expensive ones at that.

At the same time that more and more students were graduating from Canadian colleges and universities with diplomas and degrees that were essentially worthless in the job market, something else was happening — an expansion of the Temporary Foreign Worker Program (TFWP) — that spoke volumes about how many Canadians had come to view work.[53]

Canada's first formalized migrant worker program was the 1973 Non-Immigrant Employment Authorization Program. It established a new class of temporary resident tied specifically to non-permanent employment. The program remained small for a number of years: There were fewer than 40,000 workers in the early 1980s. The number climbed to the 70,000 range and by the 1990s, the Temporary Foreign Worker Program (TFWP) had evolved into a program primarily for *high-skill* occupations with two exceptions: agricultural workers and live-in caregivers (rich matrons need their Filipino nannies; otherwise they might miss their Pilates classes!).

In 2000, the TFWP program started to take off. There were about 100,000 TFWPs in 2000 and the number had pretty much tripled by 2010. In 2000, the majority of TFWs were classified as being in "high-skill" occupations. In 2005, the top five non-live-in caregiver occupations were musicians and singers, actors and comedians, producers, directors, and related occupations; specialist physicians; and other technical occupations in motion pictures and broadcasting. Just three years later, the top five categories were food-counter attendants and kitchen helpers; cooks; construction-trade help and labourers; light-duty cleaners; and musicians and singers.

In ten years, the TFWP had evolved from a program that filled temporary shortages in high-skill occupations to a program that depressed wages for the working poor and allowed Canadians to remain on Employment Insurance (EI) and welfare, rather than fill positions that they felt were beneath them.

The Temporary Foreign Worker Program is wrong in every way possible.

If there is one group that is consistently mistreated in Canada, it is the working poor. These are the people who get up every morning, put in their eight hours — or more — and in many cases have little more to show for it than those who stay at home and receive social assistance. The way a market economy is *supposed* to work is that if there are shortages of anything (for example, non-skilled labour), the invisible hand of the marketplace should bid the price up until equilibrium is reached. Guest worker programs that target low-paying occupations cut that invisible hand off at the wrist.

Let me pose a question about the other cohort, the unemployed and those on welfare.

QUESTION 59

Should someone on EI or welfare be allowed to refuse work they are capable of performing, yet continue to draw benefits?

☐　　No.

☐　　Yes.

This is something, by the way, I would love to have seen put to a plebiscite in 1954 and to compare the result from that to one from today, 2015. I am borderline certain that it wouldn't have even been close sixty years ago. The vast majority would have voted "no." Today? My guess is that it would be close with those answering in the negative taking it, but I wouldn't bet the farm on it. And while we're in the country…

Each year, about 30,000 migrant workers are brought here under the Seasonal Agricultural Worker Program to harvest crops.[54] This is unskilled labour. It was once done by Canadians. It should be done by Canadians. During the years from 2000 to 2009, the unemployment rate never dipped below 6 percent, which means that there was no shortage of people available.[55]

Any government would like to overstate gross domestic product, but that's a bit trickier, isn't it?

Not really. According to the income approach measurement for GDP, your contribution is based on how much money you make, not what you actually do. The easiest way to increase GDP is by expanding government.

Look at this following table. It was created by excerpting from two Labour Force Surveys by Statistics Canada, one at the end of 2002, the other from 2013:

Employees (thousands)	12/31/2002	12/31/2013
Private Sector	12,696.4	11,480.7
Public Sector	2,956.3	3,620.4[56, 57]

There were *fewer* people employed in the private sector at the beginning of 2014 than there were at the beginning of 2003. And in the past eleven years, the ratio of workers in the private sector to workers in the public sector has declined from 4.3 to 3.2. Is anyone surprised that the Canadian economy is having difficulty getting out of its own way? In too many cases not only are public sector workers doing nothing of value, they're getting in the way!

Rumour has it that the following sign sits in several different government offices in Ottawa:

> Every morning in Kanata, a domesticated house cat gets up. It knows it must not run around the house or do anything at all or it will not be fed. Every morning in Kanata, a domesticated dog wakes up. It knows it must not chase the cat or do anything at all, or it will not be fed. It doesn't matter whether you're a cat or dog — when the sun comes up, you'd better not do anything if you want to be sure that you're fed.

QUESTION 60

Based on my experience with government agencies/departments, what do you believe?

☐   That sign is already in several different government offices.

☐   That sign should be in several different government offices.

Allow me to introduce Yuri the Apparatchik.

You know that I work with the University of Toronto School of Continuing Studies. I have designed two different programs for them: Passing the CFA, and Passing the Canadian Securities Course. We have agreed upon a "shared revenue" model of compensation. I do well if the programs do well and I do poorly if they do poorly. This allows me the discretion to hire whom I work with, because the money comes out of my pocket, not the school's.

In the summer of 2011, I decided that I needed a full-time teaching assistant (TA). I knew the perfect candidate. But there was one problem. He wasn't a permanent resident of Canada. He was here on a student visa. But he told me about a program that the Canadian government offered, and he collected the forms I had to fill out in order to secure a temporary work visa.

It would be a ten-month contract, running from September 2011 through June 2012 inclusive.

The first requirement was to advertise the position to see if there were any qualified Canadian candidates. I followed the instructions to the letter, and didn't receive a single application. This suggested to me that approval should come quickly.

I filled out the necessary documentation, then went to the Human Resources website to learn how to submit it. I was to mail everything in one envelope to Human Resources' downtown Toronto office.

Just one problem. There was a postal strike at the time.

I telephoned the Human Resources office and explained that I had a package to submit and wanted to know where I should deliver it.

"It has to be mailed," I was told.

"But there's a mail strike," I replied.

"It has to be mailed," the woman on the other end of the line said. And then she giggled.

Why wouldn't she? The joke was on the two of us: a sucker who was trying to grow his business and an international student who had been dinged at the rate of $12,000 a year to study in Canada. Whether the application was submitted or not submitted, whether it was approved or not approved, she knew she was safely ensconced in a job where, once past the probationary period, it didn't matter how much she did or how little she did. One way or the other, she was as safe as the gold in Fort Knox.

The mail strike was settled a couple of weeks later. I sent off the envelope and followed up a week later to make sure it had been received.

"Yes, we've got it," I was told.

Great! I called my prospective TA to tell him the good news. They had it. It was surely only a matter of time. And then he asked me if he could see me, with some good news of his own.

Of course, I said.

The next day, he told me that because of the opportunity he was being given, he had proposed to his long-time girlfriend and asked if I would be best man at his wedding.

Like I said earlier, you couldn't get me out of this job with attack dogs and water cannons.

Two more weeks passed. It was now late August and I needed my TA to start very soon. I called the Human Resources office and asked when I could expect an answer and was told: "Two or three months."

Two or three months? To approve a ten-month (oops, better now make it seven- or eight-month) contract.

I asked if I could speak to the case officer, and that's how I got to know Yuri the Apparatchik.

My question was a simple one: "Why was this taking so long?"

Yuri told me that he had to "check" certain things.

What was there to check? I had advertised the position, following both the spirit and letter of the Human Resources instructions to a "T," and I hadn't received one single application. Game, set and match, no?

"That didn't matter," I was told. "Certain things had to be 'checked.'"

"Is there a way to expedite the process?"

"No," Yuri said impatiently. "I'm *very* busy."

"Busy making puppies," I said to myself (think about it a second) as I bit my tongue.

Several weeks passed — it's getting late into September — and I picked up a telephone message from Yuri, which I eagerly returned.

Yuri needed "clarification" on a few things.

Let us clarify away!

"What," he asked, "is the teaching assistant going to do?"

I thought he was joking. On the application I had bullet-pointed the responsibilities. Some of it was low-value-added: taking care of photo-copying, marking multiple-choice tests, and entering grades on an Excel spreadsheet. Some of it required greater expertise: preparing quizzes and tests and tutoring students. If you're running a small business — which surely describes mine — everyone does what needs to be done at the time.

We went through everything, point by point, and I was told that the decision would be forthcoming soon.

Classes were about to begin and I had to work frantically to get every-thing done. My potential TA was twisting in the wind. The wedding went ahead, but he didn't have the security of the job that he should have already been working at. I still hadn't heard anything from Yuri by the end of October — at which point classes had started — and then in mid-November I received a letter — delivered by first-class mail — indicating that my application had been denied because the wage I was offering was insufficient.

I was guaranteeing $17.50 per hour, which works out to an annualized salary of $35,000 with performance bonuses. The wage was twice what is routinely paid agricultural workers. If instead of working with me, he had sought employment on a farm, it would have been rubber-stamped weeks ago. But did that matter? Of course not.

Yuri the Apparatchik had made his decision.

QUESTION 61

Do you agree that the first person that Yuri should have spoken to was the job applicant to see if he felt that the wage was a fair one?

☐   Yes.

☐   No.

I don't know what kind of "checking" Yuri did. I do know that he never spoke with the potential hire. Shouldn't that have been the first — and really only — person he consulted? It was no one else's business; no one else would be directly impacted. But bureaucrats are bureaucrats. They live in their own world and there is nothing that an ordinary citizen can do about it. Welcome to government in action or government inaction … it's six of one, half a dozen of the other.

Yet it did provide a valuable lesson. I would do everything in my power to avoid dealing with idiots like Yuri from that day forward.

I will not spend my life filling out forms. I will not hire anyone full-time. I will contract work out. I will scale back my business before I have to jump through silly hoops created by the Overpaid and Underworked.

And I would be shocked if I'm the only Canadian who feels this way.

I consider myself somewhat of an expert in working for government because that's what I've done for the past fifteen years at George Brown College.

QUESTION 62

In a world of slaves and masters, which would you choose to be?

☐   A slave.

☐   A master.

Private sector workers are the slaves; public sector workers are the masters.

The evening I signed the contract that formalized my relationship with George Brown College, I said to a friend: "I've just taken early retirement."

My vacation time — over the Christmas holidays — exceeds what most Canadians in the private sector have in a year. I know that I can't be replaced by someone better, and it's borderline impossible to get fired.

In fact, I have thought at some length what it would take to get dismissed ... not packaged out, but stone-cold fired.

I suppose that if I missed class after class without properly notifying my supervisor, this might result in dismissal. But doing that wouldn't cross my mind in a million years!

I suppose that if I openly started dating students in my class, this might result in dismissal.

I suppose that if I used particularly abusive homophobic or racist language, this might result in dismissal. But doing that wouldn't cross my mind in a million years!

You have it very good when you work in the public sector.

But there's more. The pension I will one day receive is astonishingly generous, and because it is a defined benefit plan, there's no investment risk for me. In the meantime, as a government worker, I make significantly more than those in the private sector. This is true for all of us, even if we do less!

A 2013 study by the Fraser Institute estimated that public sector workers earn a 14 percent wage premium compared to their brethren in the for-profit sector.[58] The Institute for Competitiveness and Prosperity put out its own research that indicates that there is a 5 percent public sector wage premium in Ontario that costs taxpayers $1 billion a year.[59]

I think that both of those numbers wildly understate what that gap is, and I'll use my occupation as an example. If I were performing similar duties at a private college, my suspicion is that my workload would be 20 percent heavier and my wage would be 25 percent lower. And this applies to a variety of different occupations.

There were twelve thousand people employed by the Toronto Transit Commission (TTC) in 2012 and almost 1,400 earned over $100,000 — including twenty-one people who sold Metropasses![60] How many cashiers in the private sector make $50,000? The salary for a Toronto Police Service constable starts at $57,777 for a cadet-in-training and it goes up to $90,623 for a first-class constable.[61] How many security guards in the private sector

— whose jobs are arguably far more dangerous — would come close to $55,000 at the peak of their careers?

These numbers grossly understate the pay disparity, however, when sick days are factored in. According to a report from Statistics Canada (keep in mind that it is staffed by government employees so its objectivity can surely be questioned), provincial and federal government employees take fifteen days a year, compared to eight in the private sector.[62]

There is a government worker who makes $55,000 per year. His counterpart in the private sector makes $50,000 — allowing for a very conservative 10 percent premium for the public sector employee. Before statutory holidays, each would be expected to work 260 days. Take the stats off, it's down to 250. Each gets the same fifteen vacation days, meaning 235 days working. But our public sector worker takes another fifteen days off, meaning 220 days, versus the eight for the private sector employee.

The wage differential is now $250 versus $220 and now the wage gap is 14 percent.

The word is out and increasingly *rational* economic actors bend heaven and earth to "work" in the public sector, because boy-oh-boy, do we have it good!

This past year, there were approximately eight thousand students who graduated from Ontario's teachers' colleges.[63] Think about the tens of thousands of hours that were spent in training for this profession. At the same time, surveys of recent graduates suggest that the unemployment rate for new teachers in Toronto is 50 percent.[64] This is well known. Yet highly educated people are making an informed decision about pursuing this career. Why? Because there isn't a job that exists in Canada today that pays more, requires less, and provides so much personal satisfaction. This supply glut would be solved overnight if the same market forces that determine the number of convenience stores and dry cleaners applied to teaching.

This would be the intelligent response to the oversupply of teachers. Let market forces determine the appropriate wage. What is the province of Ontario doing? It is reducing the number of teachers admitted into the system, then doubling the number of years of training.[65]

At the same time that government employment has been ballooning, it has managed to increasingly fail in providing the basic services citizens once expected.

In May 2009, David Chen, a store owner in Toronto's Chinatown district, chased down a man who earlier in the day had stolen plants from him. He detained the criminal until police arrived, but it was Chen, not the shoplifter, who was charged by the police. The forcible confinement charges were subsequently dropped during his trial.[66] But what was largely overlooked was *why* he took the law into his own hands in the first place.

On a previous occasion, Chen called the police when a shoplifter was in his store and he had to wait five hours until anyone arrived. (The local police station, 52 Division, is several hundred metres from his store. Unfortunately for Mr. Chen, he's not beside a Tim Hortons.) Is it any wonder he acted to protect his property? The police didn't.

Then there was the G20 Summit.

In June 2010, leaders from the world's major economic powers assembled in Toronto. Police from all over Canada were called in to maintain order. It was like nothing I had seen before in this city.

Yet still a tiny number of protestors were allowed to run amok, holding their own personal *Kristallnacht*, as the police watched. Then later, when law-abiding citizens were exercising their right to assemble (wasn't that supposed to have been protected in the Charter?), at least some cops acted like thugs.

And no one in a position of authority — not the chief of police, whose competence surely had to be questioned; not the mayor, who throughout his two terms in office ran interference for the unions responsible for his election — no one was held accountable in any meaningful way.[67]

Meanwhile, taxes continue to go up and up and up …

Then there was the TTC ticket-taker who was caught sawing logs on the job.

On January 9, 2010, a TTC rider snapped pictures of George Robitaille, asleep at his post, in the McCowan LRT station. The photograph became a lightning rod for the frustration that people have with the service itself, and the protection that pampered public sector workers are provided compared to those who toil in the private sector.[68]

A disproportionate number of the working poor rely on the TTC to get to work. A disproportionate number of the working poor are employed in the private sector. There is a very strong likelihood in most workplaces that if one were caught sleeping on the job, it would result in immediate termination with cause. But from the beginning, everyone knew that nothing would happen to Mr. Robitaille. In fact, I recall that soon after he posed for the front cover of the *Toronto Sun*, a Cheshire-cat grin on his face.

Why wouldn't he be happy? Life is what you get away with and he knew he could sleep on the job and his job would be protected.[69] This is wrong, though, on so many levels. If you are being paid a premium wage, then a reasonable expectation is that there should be premium performance. If you are in an occupation that provides virtually complete protection from layoffs, the reasonable expectation is that you should be held to a higher, not a lower, standard of performance. Common sense has been turned on its head when it comes to labour markets.

It is the worst possible time for the public sector to become bigger and bloated, because Canada is facing the biggest demographic challenge in its young life. The population is aging rapidly. The 2011 census brought that point home very clearly. In that year there were five million seniors and they accounted for 14.8 percent of the population, up from 13.7 percent just five years earlier. The number of seniors is expected to double over the next twenty-five years, and by 2051, one in four Canadians is expected to be aged sixty-five or older.[70]

This has two important implications for the Canadian economy.

First, it means that the ratio of those working to those not working will decrease. This will put a great burden on the former.

There's another important implication. We're on the cusp of the biggest intergenerational transfer of wealth the world has ever seen. The estimates I've heard suggest that over the next twenty years, in Canada alone, $1 trillion will pass from generation to generation. This has impacted my generation's behaviour hugely.[71]

Quite simply, for many people in their forties, fifties, and sixties, the retirement plan is to wait for Ma and Pa (how can I say this as sensitively as possible) to take that Long Dirt Nap, so that the underachieving progeny can inherit the house and cottage they never worked for.

There's the old saw: Hard work never killed you — but why take the chance? There is far less motivation to set your alarm early, shorten your lunch breaks, and work longer into the evening, when instead you can go home and switch on your HDTV, knowing that there's a windfall coming your way somewhere down the line.

Perhaps that looming transfer of wealth isn't unrelated to some research that recently came out of the U.S.-based Brookings Institution. The authors, Ian Hathaway and Robert E. Litan, state:

> Business dynamism is the process by which firms continually are born, fail, expand, and contract, as some jobs are created, others are destroyed, and others still are turned over. Research has firmly established that this dynamic process is vital to productivity and sustained economic growth. Entrepreneurs play a critical role in this process, and in net job creation.[72]

QUESTION 63

Does entrepreneurial activity play a key role in economic growth and job creation?

☐   Yes.

☐   No.

Hathaway and Litan examine "firm entry rate." It measures the number of firms that have been in business one year or less as a ratio of all firms. In 1978, it was 15 percent. It had contracted to just over 8 percent by 2011.

What does this tell us? It means that the economy is increasingly becoming less dynamic. Why is that? Because if there are lots of businesses that have been operating for one year or less, it means that there are both a tremendous amount of start-ups … and failures, but the failure isn't deterring people from giving it another shot.

It evokes Carl Sandburg's wonderful poem, "Chicago":

> … Fierce as a dog with tongue lapping for action, cunning
> as a savage pitted against the wilderness,
> > Bareheaded,
> > Shovelling,

Wrecking,

Planning,

Building, breaking, rebuilding...[73]

That is the "creative destruction"[74] of capitalism that libertarian economist Joseph Schumpeter celebrated. You start a business that falls flat on its face. So you try again. Then again. You keep throwing stuff against the wall until something sticks. You're like one of those inflatable toys you had when you were a kid — the ones you would keep punching in the nose. They would fall over then come upright again, only to get knocked down, only to get up again and again and ...

Increasingly, though, the State arranged things so that there is no need to get up. Indeed, increasingly there is no need to even get knocked down in the first place. There are paths that offer less resistance.

Find a do-little job in the bureaucracy.

Get a job with the TTC and nap while you're being paid.

Inherit money.

Why work hard? What is the point of working hard if it's not necessary and it's not something that you value?

This decline in the work ethic has been accompanied by a huge rise in behaviours and attitudes, with serious negative consequences — both personal and economic. According to the Canadian Obesity Network, one in four adults and one in ten children are clinically obese. Its website states: "A 2010 report estimated that direct costs of overweight and obesity represented $6 billion — 4.1 percent of Canada's total health care budget. However, this estimate only accounts for health care costs related to obesity, and does not account for productivity loss, reductions in tax revenues, or psychosocial costs."[75]

American studies suggest that annual health care costs were $1,429 higher per person for obese people compared to people of normal weight. Obesity-related conditions include heart disease, stroke, and Type II diabetes.[76] Another particularly troubling consequence of obesity is that it leads to some truly frightening sights around public swimming pools in the summertime.

To the best of my knowledge, no one in this country is being tied to dining room tables and forced, against their will, to eat bacon-wrapped meatloaf and deep-fried ice cream. It's a choice that people make, fully knowing that if they are obese and need medical attention, all you have to do is call 911 and the ambulance will be there soon; and when it's all said and done, it won't cost them a cent.

QUESTION 64

Does obesity cost the Canadian economy a great deal, both directly and indirectly?

☐ Yes.

☐ No.

This is something that could be solved overnight. This is something that should be solved overnight.

It just requires the slightest amount of will.

In Canada, about 25 percent of children are born out of wedlock.[77] In the United States, it's 40 percent.[78]

Why are these numbers so high — and so much higher than they were fifty years ago?

The message has gotten out. You will be taken care of no matter what and if you have children, they will be taken care of. The Welfare-State mentality has become firmly ensconced.

It would be irresponsible to ignore the implications. According to the latest American census, there is a high correlation (0.6) between "State-level poverty" and out-of-wedlock births. There is ample evidence that there is a relationship between poverty and crime. Common sense, then, would inform anyone that there's a causal relationship between out-of-wedlock births and crime.

Not every child born out of wedlock will turn to a life of crime. It's equally true that only a small minority of impaired drivers get into accidents. That doesn't mean that driving impaired is a good thing.

QUESTION 65

Should public policy attempt to discourage drunk driving?

☐   Yes.

☐   No.

QUESTION 66

Should public policy attempt to discourage out-of-wedlock births?

☐   Yes.

☐   No.

Approximately 16 percent of Canadians still smoke — and this is after it has been proven beyond any reasonable doubt that there is a clear connection between tobacco products and myriad serious illnesses.[79]

About 10 percent of Canadians use marijuana, even though it is illegal.[80]

Canadians are among the highest users of antidepressants in the world according to the Organization for Economic Co-operation and Development (OECD),[81] and in 2013, the Canadian Pediatric Society — in its oh-so-finite wisdom — officially approved the use of one class of antidepressants (which includes Prozac) for children.[82]

An estimated 4 percent of the Canadian population is dependent on alcohol, and 20 percent of current and former drinkers state that their drinking negatively affects either their jobs or finances.[83]

Obesity. Children born out of wedlock. Tobacco consumption. Illegal drug use. Legal drug use. Alcoholism.

These are social problems, yes, but with important economic implications.

Along with these problems, advanced industrial nations all face the drags to their economies caused by the high cost of maintaining infrastructure. Let me give an example.

In the midst of writing *Stalled*, I accidentally bumped the USB key that I was working on and it bent. Days of work were temporarily lost.

First, I did what anyone would have done in my position: I cursed a blue streak. Then, after I calmed down, I consulted a colleague, who suggested that I look for a repair service.

It was almost 5 p.m. The only shop that was open where the owner sounded confident the USB key could be fixed was located in Mississauga. I Googled the shop's location and learned that it was a forty-five minute drive away. I jumped into a cab, and one hour and forty minutes later, there I was.

Why did it take so long? The arterial highway heading west out of Toronto was down to two lanes because of repairs. A 2013 study from the Canadian Chamber of Commerce estimated that congestion costs the Canadian economy $15 billion a year, and that this country's infrastructure deficit could be as large as $570 billion.[84]

Maintaining the existing infrastructure, which is the first priority, won't be accretive to growth in the way that originally building it was. Let's go back to the three towns from earlier in *Stalled*. The years go by and the road that connects them must be repaired. To do so means closing two of the four lanes, which means that even as money is being spent on the repairs, efficiencies are lost. Once these two lanes are fixed, the other two must be shut down. The end result is that after all that lost time and all that expense, the road will function exactly as it did before.

Is the expenditure necessary? Unquestionably. But it will slow down the economy. The spending that we are required to do on infrastructure will not have the same positive impact that it once did.

There was so much hope in the year 2000 after twenty years of strong economic growth. But the wheels started coming off … gradually … and what had *seemed* to work in the past — cutting interest rates and government spending — just didn't have the same stimulative effect to the economic activity that creates goods and services of real value.

Infrastructure spending just got us back to where we were — it didn't move the ball down the field.

Lots more people worked in government, but rather than facilitating productive activity, in many cases they just got in the way of it.

The demographic reality meant that fewer working-age people would have to support more of the aged.

We tried to mask the problem with debt. The U.S. solution was public borrowing; the Northern Way saw households owe more than ever before … yet that didn't lead to anything close to full employment.

And the "leaders" that the public relied on — politicians and central bankers — not only could not provide solutions, they seemed unable to even recognize what the real problems were.

In June of 2013, John Sawyer, president of the Oakville Chamber of Commerce, very graciously invited me to hear newly appointed Bank of Canada Governor Stephen Poloz speak. The topic was "Reconstruction: Rebuilding Business Confidence in Canada."[85]

The speech, Poloz's first as governor, was about the "structural" damage done to the Canadian economy in 2008 and 2009, and how long the economy would take to mend.

Poloz suggested that it was a good thing Canadians had gone so deeply into debt (facilitated by cheap money from the Bank of Canada) and that everything would be just hunky-dory once businesses started investing again. The suggestion was that Canada was on the right course and that everything would take care of itself. We would be back to full employment soon and the trend growth that men of our generation (I believe that Mr. Poloz is about my age) had come to expect.

Almost exactly a year later, Statistics Canada released its employment report for June 2014, in which it noted the following:

- Employment was little-changed in June and the unemployment rate rose by 0.1 percentage points to 7.1 percent as more people were searching for work.

- Compared with twelve months earlier, employment increased by 72,000 or 0.4 percent. This was the lowest year-over-year growth rate since February 2010, when year-over-year employment growth resumed following the 2008–2009 labour-market downturn.

- The number of hours worked was little changed in the twelve months to June.[86]

Perhaps the governor of the Bank of Canada believes that this indicates an economy that is reconstructing.

It seems to me that this is the definition of an economy that has stalled.

PART FOUR

Jump-Starting the Canadian Economy

We've just passed what Syd Field would call Plot Point Two.

Many years ago, I thought I would find the most satisfaction in life by writing screenplays. There were two remarkable books I came across, both written by Field: *Screenplay* and *The Screenwriter's Workbook*. They taught me a great deal about that craft, and provided some even more important life lessons.[1]

The key teaching is that structure is critical to any film's success. Structure is everything.

A movie is typically two hours long, and it should have three acts. Act One — about half an hour — is the Set-Up. In Act One, generally after about ten minutes, a device is used to grab the viewer's attention. Act Two takes us through the Confrontation. It should be about one hour long, with a clearly defined midpoint where the action turns in an important way. Act Three is the Resolution. There are also two Plot Points. One is just before the end of Act One, the other just before the end of Act Two. A Plot Point is defined as "any incident, episode, or event that hooks into the action and spins it around in another direction."[2]

Let's apply this framework to *Stalled*.

The device in Act One was the statement *Israel has … Israelis.*

Plot Point 1 was the statement, *By any reasonable definition, poverty was eradicated from this continent decades ago, but it wasn't in the self-interest of the New Elite to accept "yes" as an answer.*

Act Two, the Confrontation, started with the 1970s. The economy struggled, then took off again. The midpoint was the end of the 1990s, where it seemed that life was only going to get better. The second half of Act Two was the period 2000 to 2014 ... when an economy that had been going gangbusters slowly ground to a halt.

It would be possible to stop right now.

Except.

Except what kind of a film would *Jaws* have been had it ended with Roy Scheider, Richard Shaw, and Richard Dreyfuss deciding *not* to set out after the great white shark? *Mad Max 2: The Road Warrior*, would *not* be my favourite movie of all time had it ended with Mel Gibson limping out of the tent and declaring, "I am *not* driving that rig."

I owe it not only to you, but to Syd Field and all the legendary screen-writers — Goldman, Stone, Coppola — to provide a rousing Act Three and deliver a clear Resolution.

The Canadian economy has stalled and here are the *structural* changes required to jump-start it!

Fixing It – Point by Point

From this point forward, *Stalled* will be pure Canadiana.

I will lay out as explicitly as possible my program to fix the Canadian economy.

Here are the five bedrock principles that are the foundation for everything that follows:

1. People of working age should be responsible for taking care of themselves, and during their working years should be responsible for ensuring that their retirements are comfortable.

QUESTION 67

Do you agree with Principle 1?

☐ Yes.

☐ No.

2. Government should intrude minimally on the voluntary contracts that individuals and collections of individuals negotiate between each other.

QUESTION 68

Do you agree with Principle 2?

☐ Yes.

☐ No.

3. The tax code should be designed to encourage productive activity and discourage unproductive activity.

QUESTION 69
Do you agree with Principle 3?

☐   Yes.

☐   No.

4. Social systems should be designed to not only prevent "gaming," but to penalize it.

QUESTION 70
Do you agree with Principle 4?

☐   Yes.

☐   No.

5. There should be a clear and direct connection between the contribution to society that people make and the benefits that they derive from it.

QUESTION 71
Do you agree with Principle 5?

☐   Yes.

☐   No.

Fair warning: If you disagree with any of these, do yourself a favour and put the book down right now. Because you will be tortured by what follows.

The problems have already been identified:

- Government is bloated. There are too many people who are paid too much who do too little.

- Big budget social programs — the Canada Pension Plan, Old Age Security, and Employment Insurance — have not adapted adequately to reflect how times have changed.

- The two most important government spending programs — education and health care — require overhaul.

- Welfare provides all the wrong incentives.

- Canada's human capital is not being maximized by today's immigration system.

- Labour markets are frequently incontestable, for a variety of reasons, leading to gross inefficiencies. Government too often intrudes in these markets.

- The tax code does not provide the proper incentives to encourage wealth-generating activity.

- Values: There is far too little personal responsibility; there are far too many people who expropriate wealth rather than create it, and individual rights are routinely trampled.

We're getting very close to indicating what exactly is needed to jumpstart the Canadian economy ... or as Pink would say, "Getting the party started."

Here are the latest federal and Ontario budgets to give you an idea how revenues are currently being generated, and where the money is going. I've included both because provincial spending, particularly in the areas of health and education, accounts for such a large part of government expenditures in Canada. The budget of Ontario is used as an example of a provincial budget; however, any province's budget could be substituted.

Revised budgets will be presented at the end of this section, reflecting the changes that would occur were the recommended program adopted.

FEDERAL BUDGET SUMMARY FISCAL 2013–2014
(PROJECTION)[1]

Budgetary Revenues	264.0
Program Expenses	251.2
Debt Charges	29.3
Total Expenses	280.5
Deficit	-16.6
Federal Debt	616.0

PROGRAM EXPENSES

Elderly Benefits	41.8
EI Benefits	17.0
Children's Benefits	13.2
Transfers to Persons	**72.0**
Health Transfer	30.3
Social Transfer	12.2
Fiscal Arrangements	18.7
Gas Tax Fund	2.1
Other Transfers	0.7
Alternative Payments	-3.5
Transfers to Government	**60.5**
Operating Expenses	76.2
Transfer Payments	37.4
Capital Expenditures	5.1
Direct Program Expenses	**118.7**
TOTAL EXPENSES	**251.2**

REVENUE SOURCES

Personal Income Tax	130.1
Corporate Income Tax	35.0
Non-resident Income Tax	5.5
Income Taxes	**170.6**
GST	29.9
Customs Duties	4.2
Other Excise/Duties	10.6
Excise Taxes/Duties	**44.7**
EI Premiums	21.5
Other Revenues	27.1
TOTAL REVENUE	**264.0**

* All numbers are in billions of dollars.

PROVINCIAL BUDGET INTERIM FISCAL 2013–2014 (PROJECTION)[2]

Revenue	113.8
Program Expenses	127.0
Interest on Debt	10.6
Total Expenses	127.0
Deficit	-13.2
Net Debt	269.2

PROGRAM EXPENSES

Health	48.8
Education	23.8
Community Services	10.1
Colleges and Universities	7.6
Children and Youth	4.0
Transportation	2.8
Attorney General	1.8
Municipal Affairs/Housing	0.8
Interest on Debt	10.6
Other	16.7
TOTAL EXPENSES	**127.0**

REVENUE SOURCES

Personal Income Tax	25.6
Sales Tax	20.4
Corporations Tax	11.4
Education Property Tax	5.5
Employer Health Tax	5.3
Ontario Health Premium	3.2
Gas Tax	2.4
Land Transfer Tax	1.6
Tobacco Tax	1.1
Fuel Tax	0.7
Beer and Wine Tax	0.6
Other Taxes	0.8
Tax Revenue	**78.6**
Govt. Canada	22.4
Govt. Enterprises	4.8
Other	8.0
TOTAL REVENUE	**113.8**

* All numbers are in billions of dollars.

Before we go any further, a reminder about the Cobb-Douglas production function.

Every recommendation will positively impact one or more of these key drivers of economic growth:

- Quantity of labour (number of hours worked producing goods and services of *real* value);

- Amount of capital employed (think machinery);

- Total factor productivity (an encompassing phrase that captures both technological advances and the possibility that we can organize ourselves more perfectly to produce more, given the same hours worked and the same amount of capital employed).

And perhaps *most* importantly:

- Motivation

> **QUESTION 72**
> How important do you think motivation is in driving economic growth?
>
> ☐　　　Extremely important
>
> ☐　　　Important
>
> ☐ ·　　Unimportant

It's Go Time!

We've discussed the performance of the American economy from 2000 to 2014 at length. It was pushed into recession in 2001 — for no good reason — because of the Fed's interest rate increases. Then a combination of reckless monetary policy and irresponsible fiscal policy led to the reckoning of 2008–2009. In an economy that is increasingly service-based, where just-in-time inventory methods are the rule, not the exception, the business cycle is far less cyclical than it was in previous decades.

The days of an activist fiscal policy and monetary policy are long gone.

Keynes said, "In the long run, we're all·dead." Let me break it to the Keynesians: Keynes died years ago and it's far past time to bury his ideology.

There should be a constitutional requirement for every level of government — federal, provincial, and municipal — to balance budgets every single fiscal year. Politicians have demonstrated that they can't be trusted to discipline themselves.

There should also be additional constitutional requirements around elections. When they're held — and they should be at regular intervals, every three years, alternating between federal, provincial, and municipal — each party should be required to submit its platform and budgets until the next election, then should be legally required, on penalty of perjury, to honour them. The carpetbaggers who would campaign against wage- and price controls, then institute them almost immediately, or promise to maintain the trust structure only to do a 180 after being elected, would be put out of business.

If there were a true crisis — like war — that required short-term deficit spending, then a snap election should be called. The people should decide whom they want to lead them under those changed circumstances.

There is no need for the Bank of Canada. It should be replaced by a computer that grows the money supply at a constant rate, consistent with non-inflationary growth. Three percent would be about right.

Steady fiscal and monetary policy would provide the underpinning that is the precondition for steady economic expansion.

To help balance budgets, governments need to either cut spending, raise taxes, or do some of both. No one wants higher taxes, of course, so governments need to cut spending. The best place to start is with itself.

QUESTION 73

Would you agree that the most effective leadership, the most powerful leadership, is leadership by example?

☐   Yes.

☐   No.

If you believe that government in this country is too big, the place to start is in Ottawa with Parliament.

Let's contrast Canada with the United States.

There are 35 million Canadians.[3] There are 315 million Americans.[4]

Our House of Commons has 308 seats.[5] The ratio of population to parliamentarians is 114,150:1. The American equivalent, the House of Representatives, has 435 elected officials.[6] Its ratio is 726,437:1.

Does anyone think that there is a fundamental difference between representative democracy Canadian-style and American-style? There are some constitutional scholars who might point out that in Canada the legislative and executive branches are combined while they are separated in the United States, but this difference is trivial.

This should be the formula for our MPs. Each of the thirteen provinces and territories get one off the bat. Then, for every 250,000 or fewer in population (based on the most recent census), an extra seat would be allocated to that province.

This is what this formula would mean for Canada, as of 2013:[7]

Province/Territory	Population	Seats in Parliament
Newfoundland and Labrador	526,700	4
Prince Edward Island	145,200	2
Nova Scotia	940,800	5
New Brunswick	756,100	5
Quebec	8,155,300	34
Ontario	13,538,000	56
Manitoba	1,265,000	7
Saskatchewan	1,108,300	6
Alberta	4,025,100	18
British Columbia	4,582,000	20
Yukon	36,700	2
Northwest Territories	43,500	2
Nunavut	35,600	2
Canada	35,158,300	163

The ratio of population to elected officials would be 215,695:1 — still more than three times the U.S. rate — but much more reasonable than it currently is.

The savings would be significant. MPs make a base salary of $163,700.[8] But that's not close to what each costs. Expenses add another $300,000.[9] Reducing the size of the House of Commons would save $66 million annually.

And who decided that reasonable compensation for an MP is $163,700 annually? Silly me — they did!

The median wage for a Canadian who works full-time is $50,000 per year.[10] It's ludicrous to classify sitting in Parliament as a full-time job. The total number of days that Parliament was in session in 2011 was ninety-eight. For 2012, it was 131, and 111 in 2013.[11] Those are part-time hours. But let's be charitable and call it a full-time occupation.

What is a fair premium? The salary for an MP is now in excess of 300 percent of the median full-time wage in Canada. A 50 percent premium sounds right to me. That would put the annual salary at $75,000 and the sweet pensions parliamentarians currently receive would be eliminated. They would enjoy the same access to the revised Canada Pension Plan (explained later) as every other citizen.

What would the impact be of this admittedly drastic cut in wages?

One argument against cutting MPs' salaries has always been that if this were done the "best" people would no longer run for office. To refute that argument, let me present Exhibit A, Exhibit B, and Exhibit C: Stephen Harper, Justin Trudeau, and Thomas Mulcair. My hunch is that you could visit any Investors Group office in Canada and find three more gifted people.

The counter-argument is far more powerful. If the compensation were $75,000 annually, it would be much more likely that people who ran for office weren't doing it for the money. They would have already achieved success in a previous career. They would be above the political fray. Then, if we allowed that their office expenses would be twice their salary, now each of the 163 MPs is costing the taxpayer $225,000, saving another $60 million.

If there were fewer MPs, doesn't it stand to reason that the quality of decision-making would be higher? Presumably, each party would now put its best 163 people forward, not dilute the talent pool with the next best 145. The answer is self-evident.

It's taken fewer than six hundred words to save the people of this country $126 million while improving the quality of leadership.

QUESTION 74

What would be the effect of reducing the number of MPs and their compensation?

☐   It would save money and improve government.

☐   It would save money but worsen government.

We can debate whether reducing the number of MPs and their compensation would improve or worsen government, but there's no question it would save money, which really means that it would allow more people to create goods and services of value, making the pie bigger.

Let's continue exploring this. The United States has nine times Canada's population.

QUESTION 75

Which country has more senators?

☐   Canada.

☐   The United States of America.

The edge goes to us: 105[12] to 100.[13]

There's been much attention paid recently to various Senate scandals. In the eye of the storm are two ex-journalists: Mike Duffy and Pamela Wallin. The scandal around Duffy was that the prime minister's chief of staff reimbursed him for expenses that were improperly charged to us, the Canadian people. To many, it looked like a cover-up.[14] Wallin was accused by her peers of wrongfully claiming expenses, and although she paid back in excess of $100,000, she issued a statement: "I have not done anything wrong. I am not guilty of any misconduct. Accordingly I will not resign as a senator."[15]

QUESTION 76

Under what circumstances do people typically give back money?

☐   When they've done nothing wrong.

☐   When they've done something wrong.

The first thing that came to mind when I heard about these incidents: Why were two former journalists appointed to the Senate in the first place? The popular explanation seems to be that they would help the Conservative Party in its fundraising efforts. There is likely some truth to that. Both have name recognition. But if Senate appointments were really about celebrity and fund-raising, wouldn't it have made more sense to appoint a couple of former hockey players?

It strikes me that there is a much more plausible explanation *why* Mike Duffy and Pamela Wallin were appointed to the Senate.

The prime directive for any politician is to be elected, then once in office, re-elected. Public perception is formed by large media sources, such as CBC and CTV. By appointing two ex-CTVers to the Senate, the Conservatives were sending a powerful message to all journalists whose politics might be perceived as centrist or even, in common vernacular, right-wing: "You do right by us, we'll do right by you."

This should concern anyone even tangentially interested in the democratic process. We already have a serious problem with the media in this country. There is and always will be a strong institutional bias in the CBC, the public broadcaster, to support any government initiative that promises to extend government's reach. This is understandable. Under the current funding model, the CBC's existence depends on the largesse of politicians. There is an unspoken, but obvious, quid pro quo: We, the CBC, will run interference for all government spending programs, and in turn, both the beneficiaries of those programs and the ruling party will support the funding of us, the public broadcaster. One hand washes the other which washes the other.

That leaves the private media to act as government's watchdog. But government has found a way to co-opt the Fourth Estate and turn watchdog into lap-dog: advertise!

I consume very little media. If it weren't for sports, I would not own a television set. My radio broke three years ago. I do not subscribe to any newspapers or magazines.

Yet even with the miniscule amount of media I receive, I can't help but notice how frequently I see messages from the government. For months, I heard about Canada's "Economic Action Plan." The Ontario government also produced taxpayer-funded propaganda about how much it was doing for this province's working folk. As I was researching *Stalled*, for weeks on end I learned about initiatives aimed at helping former members of Canada's military find civilian employment. And while I whole-heartedly supported what was being done, I couldn't help but think, *Wouldn't it be more cost-effective to just email former servicemen? Surely their location is known.* But the purpose of the ads wasn't to assist veterans. It was to help the Conservative Party get re-elected.

Here is what the federal government has spent on advertising in recent years:

2009–2010	$136.3 million
2010–2011	$83.3 million
2011–2012	$78.5 million
2012–2013	$69.0 million[16]

While the downward trend is encouraging, the amount spent is still troubling. It's not reasonable to expect that mainstream media will criticize the idea of bigger government, and those outlets that do are not going to see much government ad money come their way.

QUESTION 77

What is the best way to enhance the democratic process in this country?

☐　　　Have the government spend more money on advertising.

☐　　　Have the government spend less money on advertising.

As for the Senate: The real scandal is that we have one. It exists for the ruling party — whichever it might be — to reward those who are loyal to its interests, not the people of Canada.

Tweedledee, the Conservative Party, has acted no different than Tweedledum, its predecessor, the Liberal Party; and if the New Democratic Party, Tweedledummest, ever had a majority, it would also ensconce party loyalists to this corrupt institution.

The Senate should be abolished immediately.

The costs savings would be significant. Each senator gets a base salary of $138,700.[17] Even without any expenses (something that every Canadian should be very wary of!), that's another $15 million that could be given back to those taxpayers who actually do useful work.

QUESTION 78

What should happen to the Canadian Senate?

☐　　　It should be abolished.

☐　　　It should be allowed to continue as is.

Let's not stop there.

The governor general is the queen's representative in Canada. For discharging these duties, the governor general receives $270,602 a year, an unconscionable waste of money.[18]

The institution of the monarchy should have ended decades, if not centuries, ago. It's offensive to anyone who thinks for even a nanosecond about the symbolism around it. The philosophical underpinning is the intellectually bankrupt doctrine of the Divine Right of Kings. It posited that kings and queens derive their authority from God, and therefore they couldn't be questioned by mere mortals. It provided the justification for a minority to expropriate value from hard-working peasants, with the sword of the State literally hanging over their heads if they didn't accede to the monarch's wishes.

No one believes in the Divine Right of Kings anymore. Then why maintain the monarchy? The argument I've head is that it's part of Canada's "tradition." (Yes, I remember singing "God Save the Queen" in public school.) I've heard this same argument invoked by some southern Americans as a justification to fly the Stars and Bars, which was the Confederate flag during the American Civil War, to this day. Rattle your brain. The Stars and Bars was a symbol of the right of one race to enslave another. It is grotesque to celebrate that.

The essence of the monarchy is privilege without merit, and bloodlines determining your future. It is equally grotesque to celebrate that. Free men and women should not on bended knee refer to anyone as Her Majesty or His Excellency.

Give the governor general and the lieutenant-governors from all the provinces mops and buckets and get them to do something useful.

Some of you may be thinking: "Didn't Canada have a Senate and a governor general during the 1950s and 1960s, two decades of strong economic growth? You can't blame flat economic performance on these two institutions."

This objection is easily answered: the growth occurred in spite of, not because of, the Senate and the queen's representatives in Canada.

The demographics today are fundamentally different and when things are different, they are not the same. Canada's population is aging; in the future, the ratio of seniors to younger people will increase. The reality is that this increased population of aged people can't be expected to help grow the economy.

For everyone else, it must be all hands on deck. We need all who can to contribute in a meaningful way, and we need to be sure that government is as lean and efficient as possible. So, in lockstep with streamlining government, there should be an immediate rollback of public sector wages.

I will repeat something for the last time: Two of my three jobs are in the public sector. There's nothing morally wrong with getting your paycheque from the government. Much of the work — not all, but much — is both necessary and honourable. But it doesn't follow that there should be the gulf in pay and benefits that exists today between public and private sector employees.

Here is a formula the government should use to bring compensation in line between these two classes of workers. There should be an immediate clawback of public sector wages as follows: The first $50,000 of income should be left alone. On the next $50,000, 5 percent would be cut. Therefore, if you currently earn $75,000, after the clawback you would make:

$$\$75,000 - [(\$75,000 - \$50,000) \times 0.05] = \$73,750$$

On everything above $100,000, 10 percent would be taken back. Therefore, a tenured professor (like yours truly) who earns $102,000 annually from George Brown College, would now take home:

$$\$102,000 - [(\$102,000 - \$100,000) \times 0.10] - \$2,500 = \$99,300$$

Tom Mitchell, the president and CEO of Ontario Power Generation, would see his salary drop from $1,710,000 to $1,546,500.[19]

No one is going to starve.

The savings would be enormous. If average compensation were reduced by $1,000 per employee (a conservative estimate), $3.6 billion of value would be redirected toward the private sector. It's a step in the right direction, but it can't stop there.

After the rollback, there should be wage freezes in the public sector, until labour shortages develop. Then, as market forces dictate, wages would increase — or decrease — to fill those necessary positions.

The ripple effects would create a tsunami. The most talented people would leave the public sector and gravitate toward the private sector to benefit from greater rewards. And it is the private sector that drives the wealth-generation process.

A final point must be made about public sector employment. It is unconscionable that an already privileged group abuses the system even more by taking significantly more fully paid sick days than Canadians in the private sector. From this day forward, all government employment contracts should be structured so that workers receive a stipulated number of paid days off in a given year. Let's make the number twenty. Those twenty days could either all be vacation days, or all sick days, or a combination of the two. This should also be adopted in the private sector.

Ivan Rand talked about the problem of "free riders" in labour markets. There is no more egregious example of free-riding in the Canadian workplace than those who consistently game the system by taking sick days, leaving others to pick up the slack and receive lower compensation (based on an hourly wage) at the same time.

QUESTION 79

What do you think would be the result of combining sick days and vacation days?

☐   Less equity in the workplace.

☐   More equity in the workplace.

QUESTION 80

Do you think that combining sick days and vacation days would lead to more hours worked in the year?

☐   Yes.

☐   Yes.

There is only one intelligent way to answer Question 80.

Of course, government expenditures encompass much more than the salaries and benefits of those that it employs directly. Government programs cost us all a huge amount. Some operate quite well, but there is a great deal of room for improvement with most. And some should just be gotten rid of entirely.

The three most important social programs are the Canada Pension Plan (CPP), Old Age Security (OAS), and Employment Insurance (EI). Both the CPP and OAS were introduced in the 1960s and the most important EI reform occurred in the 1970s, although eligibility benefits have been tightened since then.

Let me underscore once more why the CPP is borderline perfect: there is a direct connection between what you put in and what you get out. Currently, CPP contributions max out at $51,100.[20] In other words, what is deducted from your paycheque and the benefit you will receive from the CPP is the same if you make $51,100 or $151,100.

Two changes should be made to the CPP. Both are minor.

First, the basic benefit should start at the age of seventy rather than sixty-five. This addresses the fact that people are living much longer now than could ever have been anticipated in the 1960s.

The median wage in this country is $50,000. If a woman started working at the age of twenty-five and saved 10 percent of that, or $5,000 per year, and the Canada Pension Plan Investment Board generated a real return of 3 percent, then by the time she retired at seventy, there would be a nest egg of approximately $465,000 in real dollars. Then, if she lived another twenty years (a realistic estimate), she could draw $30,000 annually and provide a comfortable and dignified retirement for herself.

The second change would be to allow Canadians to make additional contributions into the CPP and enjoy a proportionately higher benefit during retirement.

The biggest flaw with today's Canada Pension Plan is that it doesn't address the needs of upper-income Canadians. Allowing additional voluntary contributions would correct this.

Imagine that there's another woman who also starts working at twenty-five, but she makes $100,000 per year. Currently, she can supplement her CPP savings with a registered retirement savings plan (RRSP). However, it is very unlikely that the same returns to scale on those investments will be enjoyed. Her $5,000 contributions to the CPP would grow to $465,000. But because of the higher fees in the RRSP account, her $5,000 contributions would grow to $360,000, assuming that the real return was 2 percent. If she could put $10,000 into the CPP, her retirement benefit would be $60,000. If she had to split the $10,000 between the CPP and an RRSP, her retirement benefit would be $52,000.

There has been discussion recently that the Province of Ontario may introduce its own pension plan to supplement the CPP. This is a terrible idea. It would be like digging up the streets to lay another set of water pipes. The infrastructure already exists with the CPP.

There are some businesses where economies of scale are more important than others and the investment industry is one of them.

The Old Age Security Act was passed in 1951. Originally, the qualifying age was seventy.[21] But if someone was born in 1900, the expectation was that they'd most likely never receive the benefit. OAS was designed as a program to deal with exceptional Canadians whose lifespan made them outliers.

In the 2012 budget, the Harper government announced three changes to OAS:

- The age of eligibility for Old Age Security (OAS) pension and the Guaranteed Income Supplement (GIS) will gradually increase from sixty-five to sixty-seven over six years, starting in April 2023. The ages of eligibility for the allowance and the allowance for the survivor will also gradually increase from sixty to sixty-two;

- As of July 2013, a voluntary deferral of the OAS pension allows you to delay receipt of your OAS pension by up to sixty months after the first date of eligibility in exchange for a higher monthly amount;

- An automatic enrollment process will eliminate the need for many seniors to apply for the OAS pension. This change is being phased in gradually starting in April 2013.[22]

These are baby steps in the right direction, but they don't go nearly far enough. A much more prudent phase-in would allow for business-as-usual for those currently receiving benefits. But if you're sixty-three years old, your benefit will start at the age of sixty-six. If you're sixty-one, your benefit will start at sixty-seven. If you're fifty-nine, your benefit will start at sixty-eight. If you're fifty-seven, your benefit will start at sixty-nine. If you're fifty-six, your benefit will start at seventy. This scaling would continue so that in the future OAS would commence at the age of seventy-five.

The benefit should be de-indexed, that is, it should not increase with inflation. There would be two important consequences.

First, there would be pressure on the political classes not to solve the country's economic woes by inflating our way out of them. The requirement to balance budgets and consistent monetary policy would be important bulwarks against this tactic. De-indexing OAS would complete the loop.

Second, with the new and improved CPP, there is a clear path provided by the State to a comfortable retirement. You know how long you have to work. You know how much you have to contribute to guarantee the retirement you want. Canadians could stand on their own feet and take care of their own futures.

Last: Employment Insurance (EI).

This program is wrong-headed in almost every way possible.

First, it is a middle-class entitlement program. It victimizes the working poor by its very construction.

The maximum insurable earnings is $48,600.[23] If you lose your job, you're entitled to 55 percent of your earnings, to a maximum of $514 per week.

There are two workers. One makes $50,000 ($960 a week) and the other $26,750 ($514 a week.) Both lose their jobs and are eligible for EI.

The worker who previously made $960 a week will receive the maximum benefit of $514. The worker who previously made $514 a week will receive $283. It is possible to live on $514 per week for an extended period of time; it is virtually impossible to live on $283. The worker who was already poorer is forced by economic necessity to re-enter the workforce immediately. Meanwhile, his EI contributions subsidize the wealthier worker, who can afford to take what frequently amounts to a paid vacation.

The last words are chosen carefully. I often speak to former students who have lost jobs and are looking for new work. It is not uncommon for them to wait as long as possible — which means until their EI benefit runs out — before re-entering the workforce. Their rationale: Why not, if I'm being paid reasonably well not to work? This isn't true of everyone, but it is true of some, and any program that *rewards* people for staying out of the workforce, reducing total hours worked, impedes economic growth.

There's another problem. If someone accepts a part-time job, EI benefits end. A couple of years ago, I offered an unemployed ex-student part-time work, and she refused. I didn't blame her. It would have been foolish to work for a couple of hundred dollars a week when she was receiving over five hundred.

The most sensible thing to do with EI is to phase it out over the next five years. Shrink both the maximum dollar benefit and number of weeks by 20 percent until in five years, EI no longer exists.

There might have been an argument for EI in a manufacturing-based economy, with its booms and busts. But today's economy is service-based. And as long as fiscal policy and monetary policy are consistent, there won't be the same cyclical swings in the future as there were in the past.

And if someone is worried about the security of his employment, the remedy is simple. Save independently or understand that if you lose your job, you'll be required to start another sooner rather than later. It's called individual responsibility and something that should be embraced, not shied away from.

Welfare sends the wrong message. It implies that there is such a thing as a free lunch.

Workfare sends the right message. It recognizes that sometimes the market can't react fast enough to provide opportunities for everyone.

Welfare rewards people for doing nothing and erodes the human spirit.

Workfare rewards people for contributing and helps develop skills that will lead to gainful employment.

There is no shortage of unskilled work that needs to be done. Instead of importing people temporarily to do Canada's dirty work, our citizens can and should perform these tasks.

Health care is the single biggest budget item for provinces across this country, and given the demographic reality — older people require more health care — there will be increasing strains on our system. My position on the single-payer system is clear. It is the most sensible funding model I know of. However, as currently practised, it's not perfect, and there are common-sense changes that should be made to make it better.

Neither of the parties in the system, the providers — the doctors — or the users — the public — has a compelling interest to minimize costs. Doctors are paid by the number of procedures that they perform. And no patient feels the hit directly if something unnecessary is done. I was once hit by a car when I was riding my bike. X-rays were taken to determine if a finger had been broken. My doctor instructed me to book an appointment to review the results. I asked why we just couldn't handle it by telephone and was told that it would be much better were it done in person.

My guess is that visits were covered by OHIP and telephone calls were not. Of course I made the visit, which meant that I had to miss work and an unnecessary procedure was billed to the system.

Another issue with the current system is that not enough attention is paid to preventative medicine. The old saying "An ounce of prevention is worth a pound of cure" is profoundly accurate. There should be economic penalties for those who voluntarily engage in unhealthy behaviour, and it's hard to think of two better examples than smoking and overeating.

We know that smoking costs the system dearly. In Ontario alone, direct costs range from $3 billion to $4 billion, with indirect costs twice that magnitude.[24] Obesity consumes more than 4 percent of Canada's health care budget.

What if smokers were required to pay an additional premium in the form of a special tax? What if the obese were required to pay an additional premium in the form of a special tax? What impact would that have on health care spending?

By the way, additional premiums exist now in this province. But they're based on income. The more money you make, the more you pay.

Ontarians are penalized precisely to the extent that they are productive. And only a fool would think that these premiums in any way moderate health care spending.

It would be equally foolish to think that special health care premiums for smokers and the obese would *not* reduce health care spending.

QUESTION 81

If you could wave a magic wand and have all smokers immediately quit, would you wave that wand?

☐   Yes.

☐   No.

QUESTION 82

If you could wave a magic wand and have all obese people immediately revert to — and stay — at normal weight, would you wave that wand?

☐   Yes.

☐   No.

Only tobacco farmers and Weight Watchers' franchise owners would have voted no to either of those questions.

Unfortunately, there are no magic wands. However, there are carrots and sticks.

For smokers and obese people who want to access the provincial health care system, an annual levy of $500 and $1,000 respectively would over time lead to a healthier population and less spending on health care.

Let me stop the "can't-afford-to-pay" canard in its tracks. Five hundred dollars is the annual cost of buying a pack of butts a week. And if you can afford to buy enough groceries to push your body mass index over 30, you can surely find the $1,000 to help you carry your weight (oops!) in funding the health care system.

The revenue raised in this province would be approximately $1 billion from smokers and $3 billion from the obese, with the intent being that as the years went by, less and less money would be raised, as fewer people lit up and those ugly pounds melted away.

Supplemental premiums would help control costs. But they don't go far enough. There should be an annual "deductible" for health care services used in any one year, up to a maximum of 5 percent of the previous year's income.

So, when your doctor suggests you need that visit after your finger is X-rayed when you're sure there's no need for it, you would push back. So, when your doctor casually prescribes "happy" pills, you'd think about how much unhappiness you're going to feel when your bill arrives. So, when your psychotherapist suggests you come back next week for the seven thousandth time so you can "talk out" how your life would have been so much better if Mommy and Daddy had only bought that puppy for you when you were five years old, you'd think about whether it's worth it.

And at the same time, if someone was suffering from a truly catastrophic illness, all the resources that could be mustered would be there, and that individual would not face financial ruin.

Just as health care accounts for a large part of provincial spending, so does education. Everyone agrees that the youth will determine this country's future. You'd think, then, that making sure that all of our children have a first-class education would be a top priority for everyone. You'd think.

In the 2013 International Ice Hockey Federation (IIHF) Championships, Canada lost to Russia in the bronze medal match, and it seemed to shake the country to its very core.

Was it — as Don Cherry claimed — political? Rather than selecting the best players, did Hockey Canada opt for a broad geographical distribution?[25] Was coach Brent Sutter right when he said that minor hockey looks at the "wrong" thing — it's more concerned with winning than skill development?[26] Or did columnist Steven Hume of the *Vancouver Sun* hit the nail on the head when he wrote: "It's time for a major re-think of how the game is evolving elsewhere while we paddle in the back eddy of the obsolete attitudes epitomized by Don Cherry"?[27]

Let me weigh in on this: Who cares?!

QUESTION 83

What is more important to Canada's future?

☐ The performance of our minor league hockey teams.

☐ The performance of our public education system.

In a world where knowledge is shared, neither capital nor technology will provide a long-term sustained competitive advantage for any country. The game-changers will be human capital and motivation, and if you believe, as I do, that the public education system is critical to developing human capital, then there should be a concerted effort to make it excellent.

I take public education very seriously. The same can't be said for the provincial politicians and trough-feeding education establishment, who have overseen its demise over the past few decades.

Last year, the OECD released a study of sixty-four countries, ranking their students based on performance in science, reading, and mathematics. Canada ranked thirteenth in mathematics; our results had dropped by 14 percent in the last decade.[28]

This is while — at least in Ontario — more resources have been poured into the public education system than ever before. In the past decade, while student enrolment declined by 5 percent, the number of teachers and non-teaching staff increased by twenty-four thousand. In 2002–2003, per-pupil funding was $7,201; it went up to $11,207 in 2011–2012.[29] When you pay more for something, you should get better results, not worse. What we're seeing indicates both indifference and incompetence. And the only tangible consequence that I can see is that one of the architects of this debacle, the minister of education from 2006 to 2010, was recently elected premier.[30]

The standardized tests administered to this province's students demonstrate how brutally bad the system is:

Primary Division: Grades 1–3

Reading	68 percent pass rate
Writing	77 percent pass rate
Math	67 percent pass rate

Junior Division: Grades 4–6

Reading	77 percent pass rate
Writing	76 percent pass rate
Math	57 percent pass rate

Grade Nine

Academic Mathematics	84 percent pass rate
Applied Mathematics	44 percent pass rate[31]

QUESTION 84

What is more important to this country's future?

☐   Ensuring that our children are well-educated.

☐   Ensuring that people who don't work get their welfare cheques.

Here's a thought experiment. What if, for just one month, only 75 percent of welfare cheques were successfully delivered? The other 25 percent went missing and that was that. Could you imagine the uproar? Would there be a media frenzy, demanding answers and asking for heads on platters? This question is rhetorical, because the answer is self-evident.

Then why isn't there the same uproar when barely half the children in Grades 4–6 pass a basic math test? It comes back to what we value, or at least what the elite, who have hijacked the education system, *value*.

QUESTION 85

Which would you much rather see?

☐   100 percent of children pass these standardized tests.

☐   100 percent of welfare recipients get their cheques on time.

The education establishment *values* protecting the people who work in the system. The education establishment does *not* value delivering an excellent educational experience for the children in the system.

This is a hard one for me to let go.

QUESTION 86

Where do you think that the children represented by that 43 percent failure rate come from?

☐   Poor neighbourhoods.

☐   Wealthy neighbourhoods.

Public education, which was supposed to be the great equalizer, has transformed itself into the opposite.

Public education in this province, public education in this country, stinks. That's the bad news.

The good news is that it's easy to fix.

Have you visited a primary school lately? I've been to a couple in the past year. What struck me was how similar they looked to the classes I attended during the 1960s. Things need to change.

First: Every desk should have a tablet or computer. This is the work tool of the twenty-first century — our children should be familiarizing themselves with modern technology as soon as possible. Tablets or computers should be the primary delivery method, and in the long run, much money and paper will be saved as textbooks are replaced with Web content.

Second: The curriculum should focus on *basic* skills: reading, writing, arithmetic, physical fitness — and a component that, for lack of a better phrase, I'll call "life skills" (more about that to follow). There should be province-wide examinations annually, and each student should be required to pass every section in order to move on to the next level.

Third: Teachers and administrators should be judged on the basis of the success of their students in these tests. Bonuses should be paid to teachers and schools that outperform, and if your students fail it means you're finding a new job. Am I the only one find who finds it mind-boggling that a brutally incompetent math teacher basically has a job for life, yet if there was a high-school coach whose football team was lousy year after year, you know he'd be replaced without a second thought?

There's that issue of values again.

Four: Efficiencies should be imposed on the public school system that are similar to those forced on the private sector. In the Province of Ontario, there are currently just over two million students and 127,210 full-time equivalent teachers.[32] That's a ratio of *sixteen* students per teacher. That's absurd. A much more reasonable ratio would be 20:1, meaning that twenty-five thousand of the least effective teachers and administrators would get their walking papers, leaving the province's students to benefit from instruction from the top 80 percent, with cost savings of $2 billion.

I would now like to talk briefly about two of the cornerstones of a revamped education system: physical fitness and life skills.

Obesity is a structural problem that will hold Canada back from realizing its full potential. The economic costs are very high, let alone the human toll. I don't believe that severely overweight people are happy and lead lives that are as full as those of the rest of us. The best way to deal with obesity is through a combination of education, diet, and exercise — and having children understand from a young age that they will not advance in their academic careers unless they can run a given number of kilometres in an hour, unless they can lift some fraction of their weight, unless … it's a model that armies have used successfully for centuries.

Life skills would vary, grade by grade. What someone should know at the ages of seven and seventeen are fundamentally different. However, a few of the skills that everyone graduating from high school should have as they enter the workforce are:

- the ability to understand concepts like the time value of money, and how to save for retirement;

- basic instruction in first aid such as the St. John Ambulance training course;

- the ability to perform simple home/apartment repairs: fixing a leaky faucet and electrical wiring are a couple of examples;

- driver's education should be conducted through the public school system as a *reward* for achieving "stretch" targets in the core courses; and

- resumé and cover letter preparation, and coaching in interview skills.

The objective of the public school system should be to give students the foundation skills they need to participate successfully in public life. It is crucial that we not lose sight of the fact that public education should exist to serve the needs of students and society, not the preferences of the education establishment.

There is a mistaken belief that more formal education is always better. The following excerpt from a 2012 report from the Canadian Centre for Policy Alternatives makes that case:

> Using data from Canada's 2006 Census, it is estimated that the average university-educated man pays about $140,000 in additional income taxes (compared to the average male high-school graduate) and receives $15,400 less in transfer payments (such as welfare and EI) over his working life due to his higher earnings, for a total of $155,400 in additional net taxes. University-educated women pay over $80,300 in higher income taxes and receive $18,100 less in transfer payments (compared to the average female high-school graduate), for a total of $98,400 in additional net taxes.[33]

The implication is that there is a direct correlation between getting a university education and achieving economic success. I'm not sure that this holds today to the same extent as it did in the past. It seems more likely that education and economic success are caused by other factors.

First, there's an inherent bias because of who goes to university in the first place. Overwhelmingly, the people who go to colleges and universities are the children of at least the middle and upper-classes. Based on their contacts alone, these kids have an above-average chance of success in the work world, which translates into higher income.

Moreover, the New Elite have frequently used education as a means to create false barriers to entry to various professions, leading to inflated wages. Much government work that requires a university education could just as easily be done by high school graduates.

This is not to say that education — at least in the past — hasn't frequently been a good investment. It is to say that we have to think critically about whether it will be an equally good investment in the future.

College and university education is heavily subsidized by the Canadian government. At George Brown College, Canadian-born students pay about 25 percent of the actual cost of their education while international students pay the full tab. (This year's tuition for the Financial Planning Certificate program is $3,471 for Canadian students and $12,880 for international students.[34]) Yet, in spite of this subsidy, we see students leaving school more in debt than ever before, and the system churns out thousands of graduates every year from a myriad of programs who have close to no hope in finding work in their field of study.

I've already reflected on my experience at George Brown College with the changing financial planning programs. A two-year diploma was transformed into a three-year program, and then a four-year degree program was introduced. Yes, if you can convince someone to take twice as many courses, there are twice as many teaching jobs. But it's a case of the education establishment putting itself first.

At least financial planning designations are defensible, since every year the banks, and the insurance and investment companies of Toronto hire hundreds of new staff. George Brown College has an excellent hospitality program and there are thousands of opportunities in the country's restaurants and hotels for these graduates.

I wonder whether the same can be said for its theatre arts program. George Brown College offers a three-year diploma in theatre arts, which is "vigorously concentrated, career-oriented training in the fundamental skills, practicalities, traditions and professionalism needed to work as a professional actor."[35]

But what kind of opportunities await? The barriers to entry in the acting profession are almost non-existent. We know that the majority of professional actors in this city could not possibly support themselves from this source of income alone. It would make more sense and be more honest if theatre arts were an elective course in the hospitality program.

The State should not be subsidizing theatre arts programs. It's unfair to taxpayers and many of the young people who naively believe that they have a reasonable chance of success in the profession.

Within the CBC, on numerous occasions I've seen veteran journalists shake their heads in dismay at the number of colleges and universities that offer journalism diplomas and degrees, because they know that the jobs simply aren't there.

The Ministry of Education should look at every community college program and ask one question: "Is there a market-driven need for its graduates?" The question now is: "If we open it up, will we be able to fill it?" Those are two very different propositions.

If the answer is "Yes, there is a market-driven need," the next question should be "How can we make it as cost-efficient as possible for the students?" The ideal would be a part-time school/part-time work model, combining education with practical work experience. To illustrate the point, here's how it could work with financial planning, the field with which I'm most familiar.

There are hundreds of call-centre jobs in the Greater Toronto Area. There are hundreds of customer service representative jobs. The financial planning program should be organized to allow students to perform paid work three days in private industry, and then offer them instruction on the other two. It would be the perfect marriage of theory and practice and it would mean that students could leave school with jobs lined up and without the same crushing debt burden.

For those programs where there isn't a market-driven need, but would be filled with students were they opened, there's an obvious solution. Make every student who wants in, Canadian-born or international, pay full freight. The invisible hands of the marketplace would quickly strangle the life out of most of them.

The questions should be similar at universities. There is nothing wrong with full-time liberal arts programs (other than that they are generally a waste of time), and as long as students and/or their families are willing to pay their full cost, by all means let them continue.

On the other hand, there are some university programs where there is a discernible public good. Medicine. Engineering. Computer science. The current funding model should be continued for those — government picks up the majority of the tuition cost — with one important difference: if you're in the top 10 percent of your class, 100 percent of your education is taken care of, and if you're in the top 1 percent, you get paid for going to school.

QUESTION 87

What would be the result of a system that rewarded the top students?

☐   It would encourage excellence.

☐   It would be excellence-neutral.

If everything I've suggested for higher education were adopted, my guess is that full-time enrolment would drop by 50 percent and would be replaced by what should be the dominant post-secondary education model, and that's part-time studies.

Allow me to reflect on my experience.

There are two degrees/designations that are recognized as being most important if one wishes to make one's way to the highest echelons of the financial services industry. One is the Master of Business Administration (MBA) and the other is the Chartered Financial Analyst® (CFA) designation.

I have both, so I think I come to the table reasonably well-informed.

The MBA requires students to leave the workforce for approximately a year and a half. Typically, one goes to school for eight months, breaks for four in the summer, then returns for another eight months.

It is very different with the CFA designation. There are three examinations. You must pass each in turn before proceeding to the next one. There are only two opportunities each year to sit Level I: the first Saturday of December or June; while the only opportunity to write Level II and Level III is the first Saturday of June. After a candidate passes the Level III examination, he has completed his educational requirement. Finally, there is a work-experience requirement in order to become a CFA charterholder.[36]

The CFA program is designed to allow people to work full-time as they are studying. The candidate develops the practical side of her career, honing her theoretical skills at the same time.

Another important difference is cost. Full-time tuition at my alma mater, the Rotman School, exceeds $41,000 annually,[37] while the CFA Institute charges candidates approximately US$1,500.

And, last but not least, the CFA examinations are competitive.

The bar for clearing the CFA examinations is set notoriously high. The pass rate for Level I is typically around 40 percent, for Level II 43 percent, and 50 percent for Level III.[38] If you've attended business school in the past few decades, you know that it requires something akin to an act of will not to complete it successfully. After paying $80,000 (for two years), you'd better give me that master's degree!

The CFA model should be the template for "higher" education in this country. Work productively during the day, then fill evenings and weekends with study. There is simply no doubt that this would increase aggregate hours worked immensely, pulling the Canadian economy up along with it.

A quick aside: The education establishment is no fan of the CFA program — for understandable reasons. When I started teaching at George Brown College, I commenced my CFA studies. A year into them, a new departmental chair joined the school and addressed the staff, telling us that she was supportive of any educational initiatives that we would undertake. She would see that we were reimbursed for anything that would improve our professional skills.

I teach in financial planning and the CFA designation is the gold standard in this field.

I was thrilled to hear her words: $1,000 (it was cheaper then) is $1,000. I introduced myself and told her that I was a Level II candidate in the CFA program and would love to take advantage of her very kind offer. I was told in no uncertain terms that the CFA Institute was not "recognized" and I could pay for it myself.

The education establishment does not recognize the CFA Institute, but it does recognize a threat when it sees one.

I believe that excellence in educational achievement should be celebrated, and that all should be judged by the same standards. That's one of the reasons that I love sports. It's one of the few areas in life where objective excellence is embraced unabashedly. And there is no sports tournament I enjoy more than the NCAA Men's Basketball Division One single-elimination tournament, a.k.a. March Madness. Each year, I'm amazed at how many talented teams there are — and there's a very good reason for that. Powerhouses like Kentucky, North Carolina, and Kansas recruit selectively, bringing only the best into their programs.

What would Canada look like in twenty years if we adopted this as our immigration model?

In *Stalled*, I have returned time and time again to the critical importance of highly motivated human capital. Canada is fortunate in that we have an astonishing competitive advantage in this contest. We are a desired destination for people from all four corners of the globe, yet we squander the opportunity with a sloppily conceived immigration system.

The current process starts with admissibility. There are a number of reasons to disqualify someone from the beginning, ranging from security concerns to health. If someone makes it past those screens, then she should be slotted into one of the following classifications: federal skilled worker; federal skilled trade; self-employed person; live-in caregiver; and refugee among them. Family class programs allow a Canadian citizen or permanent resident to sponsor children, aged eighteen and under.[39]

In 2012, 257,887 immigrants were admitted into Canada, with the breakdown as follows:

- family class — 23 percent

- economic immigrants — 62 percent

- refugees — 14 percent

- "others" — 1 percent

These percentages have been constant over the last decade.

Studies indicate that immigrants are falling farther and farther behind native-born Canadians. In the 1980s, new immigrants earned $0.85 for every dollar earned by the Canadian-born. By 2000, immigrant men earned $0.67 and women $0.65. By 2005, the gap had widened to $0.63 for men and $0.56 for women. And unemployment rates are higher for immigrants than native-born Canadians.[40]

The system could be improved so easily. Rather than passively processing applications, Canada should be actively recruiting those whom we want to join Team Red and White.

The first step would be to determine the number of immigrants that fits Canada's needs. The most recent ten-year average is 250,000 and it's a nice round number to work with.

We've decided on the number. Next, we need to decide how to allocate among the different classifications: family, economic immigrants, and refugees. This is a matter that should be debated in Parliament, but to keep the math simple, let's say 62,500 family class (25 percent); 162,500 economic immigrants (65 percent), and 25,000 refugees (10 percent).

The fairest and most transparent method to allocate the 62,500 family class immigrants would be through a modified auction. Canada currently charges immigrants anywhere from $500 to $1,000 under the existing system, so charging for the right to come to this country has a precedent. Preference would be given to family members of working age, and the younger the better. Someone who is twenty-five has more years of productive work in them than someone who is fifty-five.

This class of immigrants would have special restrictions. It would take a minimum of ten years before family class immigrants would be covered by Canada's health care system (they could purchase their own medical insurance in the meantime); otherwise, there would be the understandable temptation for families to bring in kin with existing medical conditions to take advantage of our medical system. It would take minimal resources to process these 62,500 applications — a team of one hundred immigration officers would be more than enough. And if the *average* amount paid for family class immigrants were $25,000, this would raise more than $1.5 billion in revenue for government coffers.

Refugee status would be determined on humanitarian grounds. Difficult decisions would have to be made, no different than what happens today. Part and parcel of being granted refugee status, however, would be settling requirements (Canada would have the right to choose where refugees would live) and employment requirements (Canada would have the right to determine the occupation this class of immigrant would pursue upon landing in Canada). For true refugees, this would be a small price to pay. Those who aren't willing, but are instead attempting to game the system, would be weeded out very quickly.

For the 162,500 economic immigrants, it would no longer be "business as usual" either. Six hundred and fifty immigration recruiters should be hired to deal with the potential immigrants for this class. Each recruiter should be responsible for bringing in 250 economic immigrants a year, which means one a day. And compensation for these recruiters would be directly tied to the contribution that those immigrants make in their first five years in Canada, essentially a probationary period.

It would be immigration in stages. For five years, immigrants would have the same right to work as all other Canadians. However, criminal behaviour — for example, possession of firearms, or conviction for certain classes of crimes (we're not talking about parking tickets) would result in immediate revocation of citizenship and return to country of origin. Assuming that an economic immigrant kept her nose clean for five years, full citizenship would be granted.

This is how the logistics might work. I'm an immigration recruiter. I determine that Vivian and Gurmanik, two excellent students who just graduated from the Financial Planning Certificate program at George Brown College, would be valuable additions to the Canadian workforce. It would be my responsibility to determine interest on their part, and then perform my own due diligence. They both check out. Presumably I would have cultivated contacts with important employers like the big banks and major insurance companies. Or I've established relationships with placement firms. We would work together to get firm job offers, and once those were in place, probationary status as a Canadian citizen would be granted.

Both Vivian and Gurmanik would be given social insurance numbers, as would the other 248 economic immigrants that are my responsibility. At the end of the year, the total income of the 250 economic immigrants would be tallied. If some of them opened and owned their own small business, other data would be collected: total revenue generated and full-time equivalent jobs created. Then, as the immigration recruiter, my compensation would be determined by *their* success.

This system replicates how hiring decisions are made in the real world. I own a small business. I only work with people I know, or who come highly recommended, the "friend of a friend" network. Similarly, immigration recruiters would reach out to university professors and college instructors to find out which of their international students have "the right stuff." There's an old saying about law school: The "A" students end up working for the "C" students. Transcripts and a GPA tell some things. They don't tell everything.

QUESTION 88

What would the result of "recruiting" immigrants most likely be?

☐ It would worsen the results of recent immigrants.

☐ It would improve the results of recent immigrants.

It would make perfect sense for the lion's share of Canada's economic immigration to flow through the country's college and university programs. We've talked about the demographic challenge that Canada faces: the country is aging. If economic immigration were driven by recent graduates (instead of workers with years of experience), it stands to reason that the average age of the country would be lower. A student visa would allow an international student the same right to work as a native-born Canadian. Through the years, many of my students at George Brown College have worked part-time in the financial services industry, gaining valuable practical experience while they were refining more theoretical skills. This opportunity would be extended to international students as well. However, to ensure that they weren't gaming the system, (that is, coming to Canada only to work), one of the requirements for obtaining a visa would be successful completion of their program of study.

Recruiting has been used for years to build winning athletic programs. If the future of this country is more important than any collegiate basketball game — and I'd like to believe that it is — then perhaps we should start acting like it is.

So, we have students graduating from high schools and colleges and universities looking for work, and we have immigrants coming to Canada who want to find a job. What's the best strategy to help make sure that there is work for them? Simply stated: the government should stop interfering in the job market.

In 1983, Michigan was the car capital of North America. That year, Nissan opened its first automotive plant in North America in the State of Tennessee. Fast-forward to 2013. Alabama is ranked the number one automotive state in the United States, breaking a four-year run by Tennessee. Kentucky rounds out the top three. Michigan doesn't even medal.[41]

Tennessee, Alabama, and Kentucky have all been "right-to-work" states for an extended period of time. Michigan became a "right-to-work" state in 2012 and there are signs that there may be a renaissance in the auto industry.[42]

Right-to-work legislation would result in an immediate surge of capital investment into this country. And there's an important principal behind right-to-work. It's called individual freedom. I should have the right to join a union and I should have the right not to join the union. An employer should have the right to negotiate with a union as well as the right not to negotiate with it.

More freedom, more investment, and more opportunity would be the direct result of right-to-work.

What would Canada look like if there were no such thing as "wrongful dismissal"?

If you are an employee dissatisfied with your situation, you can walk off the job and that's that. Your employer is legally required to pay you for all the hours you spent there. Perhaps you weren't dissatisfied but you have a better offer. An employee is always free to pursue better opportunities.

What if employers had the same option? What if the law of the land was that — with two weeks' notice — an employer could notify an employee that his services were no longer required and he could be replaced with someone who could do the job better?

QUESTION 89

What would the result be of making labour markets contestable?

☐   It would increase productivity.

☐   It would not impact productivity.

☐   It would reduce productivity.

This employment model is not unprecedented in North America. If you are a fan of the National Football League — as I am — on a weekly basis you see workers (football players) who can be cut from the team at any time, with their contracts terminated immediately. It drives persistent excellence.

Of course, working at a bank or on an assembly line is different from being a professional football player, isn't it? For one thing, the football player's career is shorter, suggesting that more employment protection is required. For another thing, football players make more money, suggesting that more employment protection is required, because if they lose their jobs, the downside is that much steeper. There isn't that much difference between football players and bank employees or manufacturing workers, after all.

There would be several direct consequences if Canada made it possible to replace a worker with someone else — just because that other person is better — separate and apart from increased productivity. Enlightened employers would work very hard to establish the reputation that they use this option very selectively. Anyone who runs a business knows that it is very expensive to train new people. There would be a strong tendency to keep the workers you know, rather than take a chance on a new one. Employers who replaced people capriciously would suffer because word would get out and they would not attract the best. This is the era of social media. Bad publicity goes viral in milliseconds.

However, employees — for good reason — would also be more nervous than they are today. The smart ones would try not to expose themselves to this vulnerability. Everyone knows that no one can replace you if you're the boss! There would be an outbreak of entrepreneurialism, one of the most important pistons that drives the economic engine. Common sense tells us that when people work for themselves, they work harder.

I'll use myself as an example. I am an employee at George Brown College and instruct in various industry-licensing courses. I am a self-employed contractor with the University of Toronto School of Continuing Studies and instruct in various industry-licensing courses.

QUESTION 90

Where does Michael Hlinka's teaching priority lie?

☐   With George Brown College.

☐   With the University of Toronto School of Continuing Studies.

Making all labour markets contestable would have three immediate results:
1. increasing hours worked;
2. increasing the motivation of the workforce across a whole spectrum of jobs; and
3. causing an explosion in entrepreneurialism.

Once again: government should intervene minimally in labour markets.

For those who need more convincing, here is some data from Alberta and Ontario.[43]

Province	Minimum Wage
Alberta	$9.95
Ontario	$11.00

Alberta's minimum wage is the lowest in Canada. Ontario's is among the highest.

Here is some additional data:[44]

Province	Minimum Wage	Average Weekly Earnings
Alberta	$9.95	$1,108.01
Ontario	$11.00	$920.12

Ontario's minimum wage is 10 percent higher; Alberta's average weekly earnings is 20 percent higher.

QUESTION 91

Where would you prefer to live?

☐   In a place where the minimum wage is high but average earnings are low.

☐   In a place where the minimum wage is low but average earnings are high.

If we could generate real economic growth by raising the minimum wage, then I'd be all for making it $100 an hour! Based on a forty-hour work week and fifty weeks in the year, everyone would now be making $200,000! But why stop there? Raise it to $1,000 an hour ... now we're all millionaires.

But perhaps — just perhaps — there'd be fewer jobs ... which means that less work would be done ... which would mean that we'd all be poorer.

There are other problems with minimum wage laws. They are insensitive to the nuances of the marketplace. I visit Las Vegas frequently. On one of my last trips, I was in a busy bar on the Strip, and was struck by how much business it generated at all times of day and night. When I was younger, I worked in restaurants as a server and bartender so I was curious to know how much these bartenders made in tips on a typical day. I asked one. After consulting with a colleague, he estimated that the average was between $300 and $350 a shift, or about $40 an hour.

His employer still has to pay him a wage on top of that.

It doesn't make sense. There's only so much money to divide among everyone who works in that establishment. Bartenders get a bigger cut of that money — at the expense of kitchen help. It's not right; it doesn't make sense.

There's also the issue of unpaid interns. One of the ways for inexperienced workers to get a foot in the door is to volunteer — I'm regularly approached by ex-students who want to transition their careers into something education-related and who offer to work for free. There are tens of thousands of situations like this in Canada every day. It would be impossible to provide this opportunity if it were necessary to pay for their services. Minimum wage laws can't possibly address this issue. The minimum wage is a crude and irrelevant tool and should be done away with immediately.

There are other labour issues that need to be dealt with:

QUESTION 92

Compensation should be tied to productivity. Do you agree that the more productive workers are, the more compensation they should receive?

☐ Yes.

☐ No.

Government-mandated time-and-a-half pay for overtime turns that common sense proposition on its head.

At the end of the working day, people are tired. It stands to reason that according to the diminishing-return concept we discussed earlier, each hour of extra work is marginally less productive than the previous one. It makes absolutely no sense to require employers to pay more for it — clearly it has the impact of reducing aggregate hours worked.

Now, it may be that for a worker to be enticed to put in overtime, she might require time-and-a-half. Or double time. That should be worked out between employee and employer. Government should not be involved.

Compensation and benefits should be determined by market forces. We would see that as the pro-growth initiatives I've been suggesting take hold, both would increase. But very importantly, the existing loopholes that allow some employers to game the system should be eliminated, too.

I'm talking about the Temporary Foreign Worker Program. End it immediately. The only exception would be a "permit system" that would allow a business to bring a non-Canadian resident into this county. The permit would cost $500 per day, or twice the average daily wage. This would allow, for example, a film company to "import" a star actor for a shoot, or an international business to hire specialized consultants for short periods of time. It would not allow the agricultural sector to bring in unskilled labour from Mexico to undercut Canadians who would do the work — as long as their wages were being determined in markets that were both fair and competitive.

Those not born in Canada who are present in the country should be categorized in one of five ways:

- Visitors: Canada welcomes people from all around the world to visit us; however, it would be illegal for a visitor to work in this country;

- Visa students: They would have the same right to work as any Canadian student; however, they would be required to successfully complete the academic program in which they are enrolled;

- Guest workers: They would be allowed to work by permit only, and only with payment of a daily fee of $500;

- Canadian residents: Those on the path to citizenship; and

- Canadian citizens.

Okay, we've dealt with cutting government spending through cutting the government workforce and the money it spends on social programs. We've dealt with the problems with the health, education, and immigration systems. That was just a warm-up. Now we're going to tackle something big: taxes.

QUESTION 93
Do you think that incentive systems determine behaviour?

☐   Yes.

☐   No.

The tax code should encourage productive economic activity.

Earlier, interim budgets for both the federal government and the Ontario provincial government were provided. The Feds derive more than half their revenue from income taxes; Ontario close to one-quarter. This dulls the incentive to work. Taxing earned income is the worst tax of all.

Here are the principles for the new, improved tax code. After stating them, we'll get down to the details — because as everyone knows, that's where the devil is:

- Personal income tax on *earned* income should assume far less importance. No one who makes $60,000 or less in earned income annually should pay income tax.

- The tax rate on passive income (or investment income) should exceed the tax rate on earned income. Inheritance taxes should be reinstated and treated as passive income.

- Consumption taxes should assume far more importance, with focused user fees as appropriate.

- Taxes on corporate profits should be eliminated.

Now let's explore these points one at a time.

There is earned income and investment income. The latter includes realized capital gains, dividends, and interest. Right now, both dividends and realized capital gains are taxed at a lower rate than earned income.

The argument is that this is necessary to escape "double taxation." When a company makes money, it must pay taxes before it returns anything to owners or shareholders in the form of either dividends or capital gains. In this new system, corporate profits would no longer be taxed, so double taxation would no longer be an issue.

Here's how the income tax system should work: You receive your first $60,000 of earned income, tax-free. All earned income in excess of that and all investment income would be taxed at a rate of 25 percent — that's the federal rate; the provinces would take their cut on top of that. There would be no deductions. There would be no tax credits. It would be simple, transparent, and clean.

Here's what *everyone's* income tax return would look like from this point forward:

Personal Tax Return Form — Revenue Canada

	Earned Income	Unearned Income
Total Income (TI)		
Less Base Deduction	−$60,000	$0
Taxable Income (TxI)		
Taxes Owed (TxI x 0.25)		
Total Taxes Owed		

Print name: _____

Signature: _____

Dated: _____

QUESTION 94

Do you like this tax form more than the one you have to fill out now?

☐ I like it *less.*

☐ I like it *more.*

Only chartered accountants and Canada Revenue Agency employees ticked the "less" box.

There's a guy who works in the oil sands. He made $90,000 in salary and $10,000 in investment income last year. This is what he would pay in taxes:

	Earned Income	Unearned Income
Total Income (TI)	$90,000	$10,000
Less Base Deduction	−$60,000	$0
Taxable Income (TxI)	$30,000	$10,000
Taxes Owed (TxI x 0.25)	$7,500	$2,500
Total Taxes Owed	$30,000	

There's a guy whose trust fund returned $100,000s in investment income last year:

	Earned Income	Unearned Income
Total Income (TI)	$0	$100,000
Less Base Deduction	−$60,000	$0
Taxable Income (TxI)	$0	$100,000
Taxes Owed (TxI x 0.25)	$0	$25,000
Total Taxes Owed	$25,000	

QUESTION 95

How do you think income should be taxed?

☐ I believe that earned income should pay a lower rate.

☐ I believe that unearned income should pay a lower rate.

This is not class warfare. This recognizes that earned income drives real economic growth in a way that unearned income does not.

The GST/HST should increase so that revenue collected across the country would increase by 50 percent. This would result in $45 billion collected annually rather than the current $30 billion.

GST/HST rates vary greatly across Canada. They are as low as 5 percent in the western provinces (because of zero provincial sales taxes) and range from 13 percent to 15 percent in the provinces (Ontario, Prince Edward Island, New Brunswick, Nova Scotia, and Newfoundland and Labrador) that harmonized their provincial sales taxes with the GST. Therefore, the relative amount of the increase would differ from province to province.[45]

Intelligent exceptions to GST/HST charges would continue.

Gasoline taxes should be higher. Currently, the federal excise tax is ten cents a litre on gasoline and four cents a litre on diesel.[46] And about forty billion litres of gasoline and seventeen billion litres of diesel are consumed annually in Canada.[47]

Taxes should be increased to $1 a litre on both gasoline and diesel.

Speaking of gasoline and diesel, one topic I have not addressed directly is the environment and climate change. There are a couple of reasons. First, the focus of *Stalled* is the economy and there is no tension between prudent environmental practices and a vibrant economy. It's a false dichotomy.

Second, I don't understand the science well enough. In my lifetime, I've heard how CO2 emissions can reflect heat away from the Earth and trap it. Both sound equally plausible.

Therefore, I admit that I am skeptical about what is now termed "climate change." Ten short years ago, it was "global warming." I was part of a panel discussion in 2005 and expressed doubt about the doomsday scenario that was being presented, and was assured by a leading scientist that unless CO2 emissions were curbed immediately, within five years (2010), the city of Toronto would never see snow in winter and our summers would become so unbearably hot that people would be dropping dead like flies from heatstroke.

Oops. There's been a strategic retreat. It is no longer global warming. It's climate change. Our emissions are either going to make the climate warmer, or colder, or not impact it.

And each scenario is equally disastrous!

I remain skeptical.

However, there is one thing I am sure about: we become wealthier precisely to the extent that we use resources more effectively. A simple question: If you could snap your fingers and increase your car's fuel efficiency by 20 percent, would you? Of course.

I've got some bad news and some good news for you. The bad is that you can't snap your fingers and increase fuel efficiency by 20 percent. The good news is that this is a low-ball estimate of what is possible — right now — with existing technologies.[48]

However, there is a problem, and it's the payback period. Cars would *immediately* become more expensive and it would take years to make those investments pay off. But if gasoline were more expensive, the calculation changes overnight. Consumers would *demand* more fuel-efficient vehicles and everyone would be happy: red meat–eating capitalists (like yours truly) and vegan environmentalists.

We know that if gasoline and diesel were significantly more expensive, less would be consumed. My estimate is that if prices were shocked up that severely (close to 50 percent), consumption would drop by 25 percent, which means that instead of revenues being what they are currently (forty billion litres times ten cents per litre and seventeen billion litres times four cents per litre for a total of $4.7 billion) it would be thirty billion litres times $1 per litre and fourteen billion litres times $1 per litre for a total of $44 billion. Rounding off, the increased revenue would be $40 billion.

Approximately 120 million people in Canada flew in a plane in 2012.[49] If each were charged $10 — which is less than the cost of a first-run movie — $1.2 billion would be raised.

The value of trading on the Toronto Stock Exchange and the TSX Venture Exchange routinely exceeds $5 billion a day.[50] If there were a transaction tax of even 0.1 percent every time shares traded, that would raise $20 million a day, or $1.25 billion annually. A tax that insignificant would have no impact on what real investors do, but it would reduce or even eliminate much of the program- and high-frequency trading that creates no real value.

It's estimated that Canadians spend about $3 billion annually on cannabis. If it were legalized and one-third of that value was captured by taxes, there's another $1 billion in revenue.[51]

Ireland's economy boomed after it dropped tax rates on corporate profits to 10 percent. Its economy doubled over the next decade. Imagine the impact if instead of 10 percent, we went to 0 percent. It is certain that capital — which is far more mobile than labour — would flood into this country, creating a plethora of jobs and instant shortages in a variety of different occupations.

And that's a good thing! We know what the market response is to shortages: prices (which means wages) are bid up. Canada would lure the industries of the future into our borders with a tax policy that has proven to be highly effective. And the quid pro quo for eliminating taxes on corporate profits would be an immediate end to government subsidizing any industry. Not oil. Not auto. Not film.

The Fraser Institute's work indicates that since 1981, all levels of government have forked over $684 billion to different businesses, with half of that federal, 40 percent from the provinces, and municipalities picking up the rest. In 2009, it was $25 billion.[52]

Here is what the federal government would collect in taxes, were this roughly revenue-neutral tax regime adopted. By my estimates, it actually generates slightly more revenue, but these are approximations.

	Current Tax Collected	Change	New Tax Collected
Personal Income Tax, Earned Income	$130 billion	-$46 billion[A]	$84 billion
Personal Income Tax, Investment Income		+$15 billion[B]	$15 billion
Personal Income Tax, Inheritance Income		+$10 billion[C]	$10 billion
Corporate Income Tax	$35 billion	$35 billion	$0 billion
Non-resident Income Tax	$6 billion		$6 billion
Goods and Services Tax	$30 billion	+$15 billion[D]	$45 billion
Customs Import Duties	$4 billion		$4 billion
Other Excise Taxes/Duties	$11 billion	+$40 billion[E]	$51 billion
Revenues from EI	$22 billion		$22 billion
Other Revenues	$27 billion	+$5 billion[F]	32 billion
Total Budgetary Revenue	$264 billion		$269 billion

Note: The numbers don't add up exactly because of rounding errors.

A. The mid-points of 2009 tax brackets and taxpayers were taken to derive this estimate.[53]

B. This estimate is based on 2012 investment income of $60 billion.[54]

C. One trillion divided by 20 is $50 billion.[55] Twenty-five percent of that (rounded down) is $10 billion (There would be avoidance).

D. GST increased to 7.5 percent.

E. This $40 billion comes from the fuel tax.

F. Other revenue is $1.5 billion from immigration, $1.2 billion deplaning, $1.25 billion TSX/trading fees, and $1 billion cannabis, with the total rounded up to $5 billion.

Let me stress one very important point: In order to have a tax system where EVERYONE who makes $60,000 or less in earned income pays ZERO income tax, and where ALL investment income is taxed at a rate of 25 percent and only earned income in EXCESS of $60,000 is taxed at a marginal rate of 25 percent, two things are necessary:

- ABSOLUTELY NO TAX CREDITS;

- ABSOLUTELY NO TAX DEDUCTIONS.

Even for charitable giving?

How about *especially* for charitable giving?

There are millions of Canadians who every year donate their money to charities for all the right reasons. There are millions of Canadians who every year donate their time to charities for all the right reasons. And because these folks would never think of abusing charitable giving, they have difficulty thinking that anyone else would.

It is precisely for that reason that I have so much concern with what happens in the world of charities.

Early in the 1990s, a weekly magazine appeared on the streets of Toronto: *Outreach*. It was sold on street corners by some of Toronto's homeless and unemployed. Its business model was simple: it cost the vendors forty cents to buy a paper from the publisher, and they turned around and sold the papers for one dollar, or whatever the buyer wanted to give them. It represented everything I believe in — a hand up, not a hand-out, with rewards directly tied to the effort put forward.

When I started buying *Outreach*, it had a sports columnist. But soon his work stopped appearing, and I thought that there might be an opportunity for me. I had written sports in the past and enjoyed the process. I submitted a column on spec, it was printed, and I was invited to send in a picture and contribute regularly, and my work appeared each week for the next twenty-one years, until *Outreach* folded in the spring of 2014.

Several years after I started contributing to *Outreach*, my financial fortunes took a turn for the better, largely because of the success I was enjoying in the stock market. Someone I considered a friend at that time was making his living directing infomercials. Paul asked to meet to discuss a business proposition. "I want to register a charity that will raise money for Toronto's homeless. I want to make infomercials that play on TV late at night with a 1-800 number attached to them. You'll seed the work with $50,000 to make the videos and buy time. Then what we'll do, as co-directors, is each take an annual salary of $75,000. Anything left over will go to the homeless. I've looked into it and it's perfectly legit."

It may have been legal, but it didn't feel right, so I said thanks but no thanks.

One of the recurring themes in *Stalled* is that when resources are misallocated or used inefficiently, all of us lose.

In 2006, there were fifty-six thousand registered charities in Canada. Today there are eighty-eight thousand.[55] I don't know of any other sector in the economy that has exhibited that type of growth, and in this proliferation, there must be a great deal of duplication and waste.

In addition, the compensation packages for many who work in the sector are astonishing. The CBC reported that in 2011, more than six thousand charity workers earned in excess of $120,000, and a few hundred made more than $350,000 anually.[56]

Early in 2014, the Canada Revenue Agency announced that it had revoked the charitable status of forty-seven different charitable organizations and denied more than $5.9 billion (this is not a typo) in donation claims. I have to say, $5.9 billion doesn't sound like a series of innocent errors. There is something insidious going on — I've heard the theory floated that organized crime might be muscling in on the charitable sector as a means of laundering money.[57]

Mismanagement is also an issue. The *Toronto Star* recently reported on the Leukemia & Lymphoma Society of Canada. It raised $30 million over the past two years for research, but only 11 percent of that went to researchers. What about the rest? The society rents two separate spaces in Toronto and two separate spaces in Montreal. A "design and brand" consultant charged $18,000 per month for its services. This is not where the people who in good faith donated that $30 million thought their money would go.[58]

Another recurring theme in *Stalled* is how the elite find ways to game the system. The infomercial venture is an excellent example. But there's an even better one. Then-MP — and now Liberal Party leader — Justin Trudeau took $20,000 to speak at a charitable fundraising event in June 2012.[59]

QUESTION 96

Do you think that actions speak louder than words and individuals demonstrate what is truly important to them by the actions they take, not what they say?

☐   Yes.

☐   No.

Trudeau was hired through an agency to talk about youth education. Money was being raised to buy furniture for a home for the elderly. As it turned out, the event was a dud and the charity lost $20,000. One of the board members wrote Trudeau, explaining the situation, and asked for the fee back.

Trudeau refused.

It became public and pressure started to mount. My hunch is that the Liberals did some snap polling and one of the sharper backroom boys called him. "Look, Justin, I don't give a &#! about that charity or any other, you don't give a &#! about that charity or any other. But believe it or not, there are some idiots — and we need their votes — who think that when they give money to charity, it should go to the needy.... Of course it's funny ... but it's what those morons think."

In taking the money, Justin Trudeau did nothing illegal. In keeping the money, he would have done nothing illegal. But if this is not the metaphor of metaphors for gaming the system, I don't know what is.

I am blessed to have a number of wonderful people whom I consider close friends and here's something I'm sure of. Fred would never take one cent from any charity. Neither would Ly. Or John or Kate or Pete.

Paul would.

Justin Trudeau did.

QUESTION 97

What would you a call a "public servant" getting a $160,000 salary, who then takes $20,000 from a charity, plus expenses, for a speaking engagement?

☐   A stand-up guy who represents my values.

☐   A weasel-and-a-half.

If charitable donations were no longer tax deductible and if special status were taken away from charities and they were treated like all other for-profit businesses, I don't think it would affect the giving most of us do. I don't think it would have much impact on how the legitimate charities are run.

I do think it would chase the money-changers out of the charity temple.

People should be allowed to give their money to whomever they want. And government should be neutral about it, with one exception: contributions to political campaigns.

Currently, political contributions enjoy favourable tax treatment. In fact, the tax credit is far more generous than the one given for charitable donations. You cut a $399 cheque to someone running for Parliament, you're credited with paying $300 in tax.[60]

QUESTION 98

If there are tax credits in Canada, who should they be more generous for?

☐   Those giving to charity.

☐   Those giving to political campaigns.

This is madness. The tax system should not reward those who attempt to buy influence. It should penalize them. Citizens should be free to give as much as they want, understanding that for every dollar contributed, two more dollars in taxes will be owed.

QUESTION 99

Do you think citizens should be encouraged through the tax code to contribute to political campaigns?

☐   Yes, I like the current system where citizens are encouraged through the tax code to con tribute to political campaigns.

☐   No, I would prefer a system where citizens are discouraged through the tax code from con tributing to political campaigns.

We also need to discourage the abuse of the court system by those filing spurious claims. Mention was made earlier of the explosion in class-action lawsuits filed by those seeking an easy way to get money.

These actions, and similar actions by individuals involved in civil litigation suits, are costly in terms of court time and resources. And under the current system, the plaintiff exists in a "heads I win, tails I don't lose" world. The system is stacked against the defendant and this isn't right. The system should be altered so that if a plaintiff sues unsuccessfully, he should owe the defendant 10 percent of the claim, and the judicial system 10 percent. This would reduce the number of lawsuits, and help get the public away from the "legal system as lottery" that diverts so many resources into this zero-sum game. It would also likely reduce the size of the court system, since there wouldn't be so many actions to deal with — a change that would save taxpayers money.

The Canadian economy will not achieve its full potential as long as government remains as big as it is.

There should be a simple rule that drives the number of departments and agencies. Is this an essential service, and can it be provided more efficiently by government than the private sector? Everyone wants the armed forces to be run by government. Everyone wants the fire and police departments run by government. Yet, even though food is "essential," everyone understands that the private sector delivers it more efficiently.

There are a number of federal departments and agencies that should be eliminated immediately.

- There is no need for the Canada Council for the Arts. There will never be a shortage of the arts in this country.

- There is no need for the Canadian Radio-television and Telecommunications Commission. The market is the only regulatory body we need for these industries.

- Canada Post is a relic from the past and should be phased out over the next five years.

- Given the changes in tax laws, the Canada Revenue Agency should shrink dramatically, by at least half its current head-count of 41,176.[61]

- Close all the "human rights" commissions immediately. They are not the solution; they are the problem.

- The Office of the Commissioner of Official Languages and its $24 million budget takes stupidity and meddling to an entirely new level.[62]

This is just a start. Other departments and agencies would start falling like dominoes, freeing people (like our friend Yuri) to direct their energies to create goods and services of real value.

The funding model for the Canadian Broadcasting Corporation should change, with government support replaced by voluntary contributions from Canadians, similar to what happens with National Public Radio in the United States.[63]

My experience with CBC radio and television has been life-changing. I have both tremendous respect and affection for many colleagues. I know that if not for the opportunity the CBC provided me, there would be no *Stalled*. But just as I have recommended that the Canada Pension Plan should be amended, just as I have recommended that Old Age Security needs a major overhaul, just as I have recommended that Employment Insurance be phased out, I believe that how the CBC gets funded needs to be changed, because under the current model the country's best interests are not being served.

If the CBC is as important to the lives of Canadians as its defenders believe, then it would have no difficulty raising $1 billion from private donations. On the other hand, if it is, as its critics suggest, irrelevant, then it would suffer the fate it deserves.

QUESTION 100
How would you prefer that the CBC be funded?

☐   With the current model.

☐   With an NPR-like model.

Here is what the interim federal budget for 2013–2014 would look like were all of the recommendations adopted:

EXPENSES (in $Billions)

Program Expenses	
Elderly Benefits[A]	40.0
EI Benefits[B]	0.0
Children's Benefits	13.2
Transfers to Persons	**53.2**
Health Transfer[C]	28.8
Social Transfer	12.2
Fiscal Arrangements	18.7
Gas Tax Fund	2.1
Other Transfers	0.7
Alternative Payments	-3.5
Transfers to Government	**59.0**
Operating Expenses[D]	59.4
Transfer Payments[E]	24.9
Capital Expenditures	5.1
Direct Program Expenses	**89.4**
TOTAL EXPENSES	**201.6**

REVENUE (in $Billions)

Revenue Sources	
Personal Income Tax[F]	105.0
Corporate Income Tax[G]	0.0
Non-Resident Income Tax	6.0
Income Taxes	**111.0**
GST[H]	45.0
Customs Duties	4.0
Other Excise/Duties[I]	51.0
Excise Taxes/Duties	**100.0**
EI Premiums[B]	0.0
Other Revenues[J]	32.1
TOTAL REVENUE	**243.1**

A. Elderly benefits would decline marginally as the retirement age is raised.

B. EI has been eliminated.

C. Health care expenditures would be reduced by 5 percent, given the deductible.

D. Operating expenses would decline by 20 percent as departments and agencies were eliminated and wages were restrained.

E. The $12.5 billion in subsidies to business was deducted from transfer payments.

F. Personal taxes were reduced by $25 billion, with a significant shift in the burden to unearned and inheritance income from earned income.

G. Corporate income tax comes down from $35 billion to zero.

H. GST increases by 50 percent from $29.9 billion to $45 billion.

I. Other excise/duties increase from $10.6 billion to $51 billion because of $40 billion from higher energy taxes.

J. Other revenues would increase by $5 billion from the taxes explained earlier.

The surplus of $9.6 billion could be used to retire the federal debt. Even if one were to assume that Canada experienced no economic growth and debt charges were fixed at $29.3 billion annually, it would still mean that the debt would be retired in fewer than sixty-five years.

Once the debt was eliminated, there would be more tax cuts, returning the value-added to the people directly responsible for weath creation.

Here is what the interim Ontario provincial budget for 2013–2014 would have looked like were the recommendations I made implemented:

EXPENSES (in $Billions)

Health[A]	46.4
Education[B]	17.9
Community Services[C]	0.0
Colleges and Universities[D]	6.0
Children and Youth	4.0
Transportation	2.8
Attorney General	1.8
Municipal Affairs/Housing[E]	0.0
Interest on Debt	10.6
Other[F]	6.7
TOTAL EXPENSES	**96.2**

REVENUE (in $Billions)

Personal Income Tax[G]	22.1
Sales Tax[H]	30.6
Corporations Tax[I]	0.0
Education Property Tax	5.5
Employer Health Tax	5.3
Ontario Health Premium[J]	4.0
Gas Tax	2.4
Land Transfer Tax	1.6
Tobacco Tax	1.1
Fuel Tax	0.7
Beer and Wine Tax	0.6
Other Taxes[K]	0.8
Tax Revenue	**74.7**
Govt. Canada	22.4
Govt. Enterprises	4.8
Other	8.0
TOTAL REVENUE	**109.9**

A. Health care expenditures would decline by 5 percent.
B. Education spending would decline 25 percent with increased efficiencies and market wages paid to teachers and administrators.
C. Community services would fall to zero as workfare replaces welfare.
D. College and university spending would decline by 20 percent as programs are eliminated and/or streamlined.
E. Municipal Affairs/Housing spending would be eliminated.
F. The $10 billion in business subsidies have been allocated to Other.
G. Provincial income tax reduced by same ratio as federal personal income tax.
H. Sales taxes have increased by 50 percent.
I. Taxes on corporate profits have been eliminated.
J. Increases by $0.8 billion because of new levies to smokers and the obese.
K. Other taxes would include the tax on stock market trading, the tax on marijuana, and the tax on flying.

The surplus of $13.7 billion could be used to retire debt. Even if one were to assume that Ontario experienced no economic growth and debt charges were fixed at $10.6 billion annually, it would still mean that the debt would be retired in fewer than twenty years.

Once the debt was eliminated, there should be more tax cuts, returning the value added to the people responsible for wealth creation.

Let's talk a little bit about what the transition would look like.

The tax code should be changed first. Corporate tax rates should be slashed to zero. Concurrently, right-to-work legislation should pass. That combination would result in an immediate flood of capital into the country, leading to the creation of hundreds of thousands of new jobs.

These opportunities would disproportionately benefit young Canadians, simply because this is the group that currently suffers from the highest rate of unemployment. Many students, seeing what they could earn immediately, would join the work force. Some would continue their education part-time. Some would not.

As well, there would be at least some people in the public sector who would see the writing on the wall and realize that the days of both higher wages and greater job security were over. The most ambitious would transition to the wealth-generating private sector.

There would be a flowering of entrepreneurialism with the new tax code that rewarded productive activity.

Would everyone like it? Of course not.

Canadians who had coasted for years in jobs, protected by seniority, would have a rude awakening as suddenly what mattered was what you actually did when you were there, not how long you'd been there. The elite, who have mastered the art of wealth redistribution, would have their day of reckoning as well.

But in those rude awakenings, in those days of reckoning, would be the kick in the pants they need to do what Canadians of past generations did to build the country we have … and that is put in an honest day's work.

EXTRO

Canada has been very good to the Borski family.

I was born in Toronto in 1958 and have lived here all my life.

My mother was born in 1935 in Toronto and lived here all her life.

My mother's mother was born in Lagow, Poland, and at a young age realized that there was no future for her there. She had an older sister, living in Toronto who sponsored her. When my grandmother arrived in Canada, she didn't speak a word of English, she didn't have a cent to her name, and the only person she knew was her sister.

And she was fourteen years old.

Stella Borski didn't come to Canada because of its generous unemployment benefits. Mike Hlinka didn't come to Canada because he anticipated that one day he'd draw Old Age Security and have the Guaranteed Income Supplement to fall back on. Stella Borski didn't come to Canada because when she felt sick and didn't go to work she would still be paid as if she were there. Mike Hlinka didn't come to Canada because there were human rights commissions to hear him whine if something wasn't quite going his way.

Stella Borski and Mike Hlinka came to Canada because it provided *opportunity*, the chance for a better life for them, and more importantly, a brighter future for the children they already had and one day would have.

I grew up listening to this mantra from my grandparents: "Each generation must surpass the previous one ... each generation must surpass the previous one..."

Both of my grandfathers were fiercely proud men — entrepreneurs — who ran their own small businesses and dedicated their energies to provide opportunities for their children that they, themselves, never had. They were brave and strong and independent. The values that my grandparents embraced were family, sacrifice, hard work, and self-sufficiency.

But there were expectations. They *expected* that their children would work equally hard. They *expected* that their children would accomplish things that they could not. They *expected* that their children would make similar sacrifices, so their grandchildren would surpass their children.

Stalled is dedicated to the values of my grandparents and the values of Mr. Smith, who risked his life for ten years — values that seem to have been misplaced.

But I don't think they're lost. I see the fire in the eyes of too many of my best students to believe that.

We can find those values again. If we choose to.

And when we find those values and reconnect with who we are and where we came from, we will accomplish great things, and live knowing that in two generations our grandchildren will stride across this country as giants, standing at least seven feet tall.

ACKNOWLEDGEMENTS

I don't know where to start.

I've been blessed with a wonderful, supportive family and if not for that …

So much in *Stalled* was formed with innumerable conversations with good friends.

Bill Harnum introduced me to the wonderful people at Dundurn Press. If not for his efforts, I might never have had this opportunity.

Nattaya Chaimahawong and Tom Sunsrangjoeren provided invaluable assistance, helping me with the tables and graphs.

I'm grateful for the yeoman work of Dominic Farrell in editing and shaping the final version.

And last — but certainly not least — I owe a debt of gratitude to all of the wonderful students it's been my pleasure to work with over the years, both at the University of Toronto School of Continuing Studies and George Brown College (even the ones who think I'm the "stupidest teacher they ever met").

NOTES

INTRODUCTION

1. www.ratemyprofessors.com/ShowRatings.jsp?tid=245283.

2. www.azlyrics.com/lyrics/saltnpepa/pushit.html.

PART ONE

What Is *Supposed* to Make an Economy Grow

1. http://switchboard.nrdc.org/blogs/kbenfield/us_home_size_preferences_final.html.

2. www.bloomberg.com/news/2013-08-29/saudi-oil-output-to-stay-near-10-million-barrels-a-day.html.

3. https://www.cia.gov/library/publications/the-world-factbook.

PART TWO

The 1950s

1. www.canadaatwar.ca/content-17/world-war-ii/canadian-war-industry/.

2. www.statcan.gc.ca/pub/98-187-x/4151287-eng.htm.

3. http://transit.toronto.on.ca/subway/5102.shtml.

4. www.statcan.gc.ca/pub/11-516-x/pdf/5220023-eng.pdf.

5. https://www.globalfinancialdata.com/news/articles/government_debt.pdf.

6. www.budget.gc.ca/2014/home-accueil-eng.html.

7. www.statcan.gc.ca/daily-quotidien/140626/dq140626c-eng.htm.

8. www.brookings.edu/~/media/events/2010/3/18%20china%20outlook/0318_china_outlook_bosworth.pdf.

9. http://data.worldbank.org/indicator/NY.GNS.ICTR.ZS.

10. Canada, House of Commons Debates (May 1, 1947), William Lyon Mackenzie King, PM.

11. www.cic.gc.ca/english/resources/publications/legacy/chap-5a.asp#chap5-6.

12. www.cybercollege.com/frtv/frtv025.htm.

13. Tom Wolfe, *The Right Stuff* (New York: Farrar, Straus and Giroux, 1979), 32.

14. www.crossingwallstreet.com/archives/2009/06/.

15. Patrick Foster, *American Motors Corporation: The Rise and Fall of America's Last Independent Automaker* (Minneapolis, MN: Motor Books, 2013).

16. https://www.policyalternatives.ca/ceo.

17. http://publications.gc.ca/collections_2012/banque-bank-canada/FB4-11-2010-eng.pdf.

Wealth Generation — and What Makes Wages Go Up

1. http://corporate.ford.com/news-center/press-releases-detail/677-5-dollar-a-day.

2. www.amazon.ca/Aftershock-Next-Economy-Americas-Future/dp/0307476332.

3. Michael Hlinka.

4. http://en.wikipediaorg/wiki/Ford_Model_T.

5. http://corporate.ford.com/news-center/press-releases-detail/677-5-dollar-a-day.

6. http://gspp.berkeley.edu/directories/faculty/robert-reich.

The 1960s

1. www.bartleby.com/124/pres56.html.

2. www.brainyquote.com/quotes/quotes/j/johnfkenn101159.html.

3. http://geography.about.com/od/globalproblemsandissues/a/greenrevolution.htm.

4. www.nobelprize.org/nobel_prizes/peace/laureates/1970/borlaug-bio.html.

5. http://www5.statcan.gc.ca/access_acces/archive.action?l=eng&loc=M1_11-eng.csv.

6. www.nber.org/papers/w1953.

7. Ibid.

8. http://economics.about.com/od/foreigntrade/a/bretton_woods.htm.

9. www.cbc.ca/news2/interactives/map-history-dollar/.

10. www.archives.gov/exhibits/charters/declaration_transcript.html.

11. www.smithsonianmag.com/history/the-dark-side-of-thomas-jefferson-35976004/?page=2.

12. www.h-net.org/~hst306/documents/great.html.

13. www.snopes.com/military/fonda.asp.

14. www.thecanadianencyclopedia.ca/en/article/health-policy/.

15. http://mapleleafweb.com/features/canada-pension-plan-overview-history-and-debates.

16. www.theguardian.com/news/datablog/2012/jun/30/healthcare-spending-world-country.

17. http://viewer.zmags.com/publication/37dab3ed#/37dab3ed/1.

18. http://alphaschool.ca/about/philosophy/hall-dennis-in-depth/.

19. http://cars.lovetoknow.com/Car_Ownership_Statistics.

20. www.econ.nyu.edu/dept/courses/gately/DGS_Vehicle%20Ownership_2007.pdf.

21. www.multpl.com/us-gdp-growth-rate/table/by-year.

22. www.statcan.gc.ca/pub/75f0002m/75f0002m2012002-eng.htm.

A Primer on Fiscal and Monetary Policy

1. www.brainyquote.com/quotes/quotes/j/johnmaynar380219.html.

The 1970s

1. www.automationinformation.com/DJIA/dow_jones_average_yearly_change.htm.

2. James Michener, *The Drifters* (New York: Fawcett, 1986).

3. Ralph Nader, *Unsafe at Any Speed: The Designed-In Dangers of the American Automobile* (New York: Pocket Books, 1966).

4. http://users.wfu.edu/palmitar/Law&Valuation/Papers/1999/Leggett-pinto.html.

5. www.history.com/topics/energy-crisis.

6. www.cato.org/publications/commentary/misery-index-reality-check.

7. www.miseryindex.us/indexbyyear.aspx.

8. www.thecommentator.com/article/1895/milton_friedman_and_the_rise_and_fall_of_the_phillips_curve.

9. www.statcan.gc.ca/pub/11-516-x/pdf/5500095-eng.pdf.

10. http://useconomy.about.com/od/usdebtanddeficit/a/National-Debt-by-Year.htm.

11. https://www.taxpayer.com/media/CoverStory24-27WEB.pdf.

12. https://www.ctf.ca/ctfweb/Documents/PDF/1995ctj/1995CTJ5_16_Goodman.pdf.

13. www.olg.ca/about/who_we_are/history.jsp?contentID=about_history_75-89.

14. www.olg.ca/about/public_disclosure/annual_report.jsp.

15. www.statcan.gc.ca/studies-etudes/75-001/archive/e-pdf/3828-eng.pdf.

16. www.stats.gov.nl.ca/statistics/Labour/PDF/UnempRate.pdf

17. www.cato.org/blog/unhappy-40th-anniversary-nixons-wage-price-controls.

18. www.canadahistory.com/sections/eras/trudeau/wage_&_price_controls.htm.

19. http://en.wikipedia.org/wiki/Public_Service_of_Canada.

20. http://en.wikipedia.org/wiki/Canadian_content.

21. http://cjc-online.ca/index.php/journal/article/view/605/511.

22. www.cbc.ca/news2/interactives/canada-deficit/.

An Economic Understanding of Unions

1. http://en.wikipedia.org/wiki/List_of_automobile_manufacturers_of_the_United_States.

2. www.britannica.com/EBchecked/topic/122178/closed-shop.

The 1980s

1. www.automationinformation.com/DJIA/dow_jones_average_yearly_change.htm.

2. http://www.taxfoundation.org/sites/taxfoundation.org/files/docs/ebf9a23d0bd0edc03bac0a2ce7321311.pdf.

3. http://taxfoundation.org/article/retrospective-1981-reagan-tax-cut.

4. www.cbc.ca/canadaus/pms_presidents1.html.

5. http://laws-lois.justice.gc.ca/eng/const/page-15.html.

6. http://thinkexist.com/quotation/my_people_and_i_have_come_to_an_agreement_which/206379.html.

7. http://laws-lois.justice.gc.ca/eng/const/page-15.html.

8. Ibid.

9. Canada House of Commons Debates (May 1, 1947), William Lyon Mackenzie King. PM.

10. www.csls.ca/journals/simp/simp05.pdf

11. www.wired.com/2011/08/0812ibm-5150-personal-computer-pc/.

12. www.globaltradealert.org/sites/default/files/GTA-AP1%20Vangrasstek_0.pdf.

13. www.automotive-fleet.com/article/story/1983/09/production-begins-at-u-s-nissan-plant1.aspx.

14. www.cbc.ca/news2/interactives/canada-deficit/.

15. http://en.wikipedia.org/wiki/Canada%E2%80%93United_States_Free_Trade_Agreement.

16. Laurier LaPierre, ed., If You Love This Country (Toronto: McClelland & Stewart, 1987).

17. www.samueljohnson.com/patrioti.html.

18. http://history1900s.about.com/od/coldwa1/a/berlinwall_2.htm.

The 1990s

1. http://bancroft.berkeley.edu/ROHO/projects/debt/1990srecession.html.

2. https://www.youtube.com/watch?v=BnFJ8cHAlco.

3. www.internethalloffame.org/inductees/jcr-licklider.

4. www.pewinternet.org/2014/02/27/part-1-how-the-internet-has-woven-itself-into-american-life/.

5. www.statista.com/statistics/191910/percentage-of-us-americans-with-internet-access-since-2000/.

6. www.cfr.org/defense-budget/trends-us-military-spending/p28855.

7. www.labourwatch.com/docs/decisions/LWDecision_Rand_Formula_English_2012_11_30.pdf.

8. http://scc-csc.lexum.com/scc-csc/scc-csc/en/item/774/index.do.

9. www.lectlaw.com/files/cur78.htm.

10. http://ir.lawnet.fordham.edu/flr/vol61/iss2/1/.

11. www.pbs.org/wgbh/pages/frontline/implants/cron.html.

12. Ibid.

13. http://en.wikipedia.org/wiki/NASDAQ.

14. https://ca.finance.yahoo.com/q/hp?s=NDAQ.

15. http://mapleleafweb.com/features/goods-and-services-tax-overview-history.

16. http://en.wikipedia.org/wiki/Celtic_Tiger.

17. www.thecanadianencyclopedia.ca/en/article/quebec-referendum-1995/.

18. www.cbc.ca/news2/interactives/canada-deficit/.

19. www.canadianforex.ca/forex-tools/historical-rate-tools/yearly-average-rates.

20. www.bankofcanada.ca/wp-content/uploads/2010/07/1914-26.pdf.

21. www2.econ.iastate.edu/classes/econ355/choi/1934jan30.html.

22. www.statista.com/statistics/188165/annual-gdp-growth-of-the-united-states-since-1990/; www.conferenceboard.ca/hcp/details/economy/gdp-growth.aspx.

PART THREE

The 2000s and Beyond

1. www.britannica.com/EBchecked/topic/382740/Y2K-bug.

2. www.miseryindex.us/indexbyyear.aspx.

3. www.stats.gov.nl.ca/statistics/Labour/PDF/UnempRate.pdf.

4. www.inflation.eu/inflation-rates/canada/historic-inflation/cpi-inflation-canada-1999.aspx.

5. www.newyorkfed.org/markets/statistics/dlyrates/fedrate.html.

6. http://georgewbush-whitehouse.archives.gov/president/biography.html.

7. www.businessweek.com/stories/2001-02-14/george-w-dot-s-b-school-days.

8. www.huffingtonpost.com/peter-dreier/how-george-w-bush-benefit_b_5814680.html.

9. http://pendientedemigracion.ucm.es/info/cet/documentos%20trabajo/DT16CET_impact_terr_boston.pdf.

10. www.newyorkfed.org/markets/statistics/dlyrates/fedrate.html.

11. www.cbpp.org/cms/?fa=view&id=2705.

12. http://economics.ca/2008/papers/0518.pdf.

13. www.financialpost.com/scripts/story.html?id=680330e6-ae7b-4aa9-8f06-cba3ddb8064f&k=72484.

14. www.cbc.ca/news/business/flaherty-imposes-new-tax-on-income-trusts-1.573751.

15. http://inflationdata.com/Inflation/Inflation_Rate/Historical_Oil_Prices_Table.asp.

16. www.nma.org/pdf/gold/his_gold_prices.pdf.

17. www.oecd.org/newsroom/34992235.pdf.

18. http://csis.org/blog/china-economic-reform-timeline.

19. www.wto.org/english/thewto_e/whatis_e/wto_dg_stat_e.htm.

20. Thomas Friedman, *The World is Flat: A Brief History of the Twenty-First Century* (New York: Farrar, Straus and Giroux, 2005).

21. www.worldsteel.org/dms/internetDocumentList/statistics-archive/production-archive/steel-archive/steel-annually/steel_yearly_1980-2012/document/Steel%20annual%201980-2012.pdf.

22. www.oica.net/category/production-statistics/.

23. www.oica.net/category/production-statistics/2013-statistics/.

24. www.washingtonpost.com/wp-dyn/content/article/2008/10/03/AR2008100301977.html.

25. www.winstonchurchill.org/learn/speeches/speeches-of-winston-churchill/128-we-shall-fight-on-the-beaches.

26. www.usgovernmentspending.com/federal_deficit_chart.html.

27. www.census.gov/people/wealth/files/Debt%20Highlights%202011.pdf.

28. http://research.stlouisfed.org/fred2/series/HDTGPDCAQ163N.

29. http://phdoctopus.com/2010/12/13/in-which-i-disagree-with-paul-krugman/.

30. www.biography.com/#!/people/barack-obama-12782369.

31. www.kidsiqtestcenter.com/obamas-iq.html.

32. www.federalreserve.gov/communitydev/cra_about.htm.

33. www.allcountries.org/uscensus/814_mortgage_delinquency_and_foreclosure_rates.html.

34. www.ropercenter.uconn.edu/elections/how_groups_voted/voted_92.html.

35. www.businessweek.com/the_thread/hotproperty/archives/2008/02/clintons_drive.html.

36. www.infoplease.com/ipa/A0104552.html.

37. www.unarts.org/H-II/ref/949-3747-1-PB-1.pdf.

38. https://ca.news.yahoo.com/blogs/good-news/determined-man-takes-24-years-repay-neighbours-charity-155454048.html.

39. Ibid.

40. www.usatoday.com/story/money/business/2013/09/08/chronology-2008-financial-crisis-lehman/2779515/.

41. www.opensecrets.org/lobby/.

42. www.usgovernmentspending.com/federal_deficit_chart.html.

43. http://thinkprogress.org/economy/2011/10/03/334156/top-five-wealthiest-one-percent/.

44. www.reuters.com/article/2013/05/06/us-usa-stocks-sp-timeline-idUS-BRE9450WL20130506.

45. www.thenewamerican.com/economy/markets/item/18481-chinese-economist-at-imf-warns-of-global-housing-bubble.

46. http://goldprice.org/gold-price-history.html.

47. https://www.adbusters.org/campaigns/occupywallstreet.

48. www23.statcan.gc.ca/imdb/p2SV.pl?Function=getSurvey&SDDS=2301.

49. www.statcan.gc.ca/pub/71-543-g/2012001/part-partie2-eng.htm.

50. http://cfs-fcee.ca/the-issues/student-debt/.

51. www.ibtimes.com/us-student-debt-reaches-11-trillion-surpasses-credit-card-debt-auto-loans-1583980.

52. www.forbes.com/sites/jennagoudreau/2012/10/11/the-10-worst-college-majors/.

53. www.statcan.gc.ca/daily-quotidien/030110/dq030110a-eng.htm.

54. www.statcan.gc.ca/daily-quotidien/100108/t100108a2-eng.htm.

55. www.stats.gov.nl.ca/statistics/Labour/PDF/UnempRate.pdf.

56. www.statcan.gc.ca/daily-quotidien/030110/dq030110a-eng.htm.

57. www.statcan.gc.ca/daily-quotidien/140110/t140110a002-eng.htm.

58. www.fraserinstitute.org/.../fraser.../publications/comparing-public-and-private.

59. www.competeprosper.ca/uploads/ICAP143_WP19_Insides_v3.pdf.

60. http://globalnews.ca/news/437719/over-1300-ttc-employees-on-sunshine-list/.

61. www.torontopolice.on.ca/careers/uni_benefits.php.

62. www.statcan.gc.ca/pub/75-006-x/2013001/article/11862-eng.htm#a5.

63. www.ouac.on.ca/statistics/teacher-education-applications/tapp_january/.

64. www.torontosun.com/2014/02/21/teacher-jobs-in-ontario-are-scarce.

65. www.cbc.ca/news/canada/toronto/ontario-to-overhaul-teachers-college-halve-admissions-1.1320533.

66. http://news.nationalpost.com/2010/10/07/david-chen-strip-searched-at-52-division/.

67. https://www.oiprd.on.ca/CMS/.../News-Release-G20-Report-release.pdf.

68. www.canada.com/story.html?id=5ac6a1b8-1c24-45a4-b1fd-d8527497b503.

69. www.citynews.ca/2010/11/28/ttc-mourns-as-sleeping-employee-dies-of-stroke/.

70. www12.statcan.ca/census-recensement/2011/as-sa/98-311-x/98-311-x2011001-eng.cfm#a1.

71. www.bmo.com/bmo/files/news%20release/4/1/Jul1509_inheritanceEN.html.

72. www.brookings.edu/.../declining%20business%20dynamism%20litan.

73. http://carl-sandburg.com/chicago.htm.

74. www.chamber.ca/media/blog/130917.../1309_50_Million_a_Day.pdf.

75. www.obesitynetwork.ca/obesity-in-canada.

76. www.cdc.gov/obesity/data/adult.html.

77. www.oecd.org/.../SF2_4_Births_outside_marriage_and_teenage_births_J.

78. www.brookings.edu/research/papers/
1996/08/childrenfamilies-akerlof.

79. www.hc-sc.gc.ca/hc-ps/tobac-tabac/
research-recherche/stat/
ctums-esutc_2012-eng.php.

80. www.ccsa.ca/Eng/topics/Marijuana/
Pages/default.aspx.

81. www.huffingtonpost.ca/2013/11/22/
antidepressant-use-world-
canada_n_4320429.html.

82. http://blogs.windsorstar.com/news/
canadian-paediatric-society-endorses-
antidepressants-for-children.

83. www.thecanadianencyclopedia.ca/en/
article/alcoholism/.

84. www.chamber.ca/media/blog/131218-
The-Foundations-of-a-Competitive-
Canada/131218_The_Foundations_of_a_
Competitive_Canada.pdf.

85. www.bankofcanada.ca/multimedia/
oakville-chamber-of-commerce-speech-19-
june-2013-video/.

86. www.statcan.gc.ca/daily-
quotidien/140711/dq140711a-eng.htm.

PART FOUR

Jump-Starting the Canadian Economy

1. Syd Field, *Screenplay: The Foundations of
Screenwriting*, revised edition (New York:
Delta, 2005); Syd Field, *The Screenwriter's
Workbook*, revised edition (New York: Delta,
2006).

2. Ibid.

Fixing It – Point by Point

1. www.budget.gc.ca/home-accueil-eng.
html.

2. www.fin.gov.on.ca/en/budget/
ontariobudgets/2014/.

3. www.statcan.gc.ca/tables-tableaux/
sum-som/l01/cst01/demo02a-eng.htm.

4. www.usnews.com/.../us-population-2013-
more-than-315-million-peoplePopulation
of USA.

5. www.parl.gc.ca/About/Parliament/
GuideToHoC/index-e.htm.

6. https://www.govtrack.us/congress/
members.

7. www.statcan.gc.ca/tables-tableaux/
sum-som/l01/cst01/demo02a-eng.htm.

8. http://canadaonline.about.com/od/
houseofcommons/a/salaries-
canadian-members-parliament.htm.

9. www.cbc.ca/news2/interactives/mp-cost/.

10. www.statcan.gc.ca/tables-tableaux/
sum-som/l01/cst01/labr69a-eng.htm.

11. www.parl.gc.ca/Parlinfo/Compilations/
HouseofCommons/SittingDays.aspx?
Chamber=03d93c58-f843-49b3-9653-
84275c23f3fb&Menu=HOC-Procedure.

12. www.parl.gc.ca/About/Parliament/
GuideToHoC/index-e.htm.

13. https://www.govtrack.us/congress/
members.

14. www.cbc.ca/m/touch/news/
story/1.1828437.

15. Ibid.

16. www.tpsgc-pwgsc.gc.ca/pub-adv/
rapports-reports/2012-2013/
tdm-toc-eng.html.

17. http://canadaonline.about.com/od/
senate/a/salaries-canadian-senators.htm.

18. www.parl.gc.ca/parlinfo/compilations/
GovernorGeneral/
GovernorGeneral_Salaries.aspx.

19. http://news.nationalpost.com/2014/03/28/
ontario-sunshine-list-topped-by-ontario-
power-generation-ceo-tom-mitchell-who-
made-1-71m-last-year/.

20. www.servicecanada.gc.ca/eng/services/
pensions/cpp/index.shtml?utm_source=
vanity+URL&utm_medium=print+
publication,+ISPB-185,+ISPB-41&utm_
term=/CPP&utm_content=
Mar+2013,+eng&utm_campaign=OAS+
Pension+2013,+Benefits+for+Low+
Income+Seniors.

21. http://activehistory.ca/2012/11/
a-short-historical-primer-on-canadas-
old-age-security-debate/.

22. www.servicecanada.gc.ca/eng/services/
pensions/oas/changes/index.shtml.

23. www.servicecanada.gc.ca/eng/sc/ei/
index.shtml.

24. www.rnaoknowledgedepot.ca/promoting_
health/sc_facts_about_smoking.asp.

25. https://ca.sports.yahoo.com/blogs/jrhockey-buzzing-the-net/world-junior-championship-don-cherry-slams-politically-correct-172107455.html.

26. http://o.canada.com/sports/theories-abound-for-canadas-junior-meltdown.

27. www.vancouversun.com/sports/Stephen+Hume+trouble+with+Canadian+hockey+starts+with+minor+leagues/7776668/story.html.

28. www.theglobeandmail.com/news/national/education/canadas-fall-in-math-education-ranking-sets-off-red-flags/article15730663/.

29. www.fin.gov.on.ca/en/reformcommission/.

30. http://news.ontario.ca/profiles/en/kathleen-wynne.

31. www.eqao.com/categories/home.aspx?Lang=E.

32. www.edu.gov.on.ca/eng/educationFacts.html.

33. https://www.policyalternatives.ca/.../eduflation-and-high-cost-learning.

34. www.georgebrown.ca/B150-2014-2015/.

35. www.georgebrown.ca/performingarts/.

36. https://www.cfainstitute.org/pages/index.aspx.

37. www.rotman.utoronto.ca/Degrees/MastersPrograms/MBAPrograms/FullTimeMBA/GettingIn/FeesandExpenses.aspx.

38. https://www.cfainstitute.org/pages/index.aspx.

39. www.cic.gc.ca/english/immigrate/index.asp.

40. www.cic.gc.ca/english/resources/research/2012-migrant/sec05.asp.

41. http://businessfacilities.com/tennessee-bfs-2013-state-year/.

42. http://manufacturingglobal.com/peopleskills/141/Alabama-Ranked-Top-US-State-for-Automotive-Manufacturing.

43. www.retailcouncil.org/quickfacts/minimum-wage.

44. www.statcan.gc.ca/tables-tableaux/sum-som/l01/cst01/labr79-eng.htm.

45. www.cra-arc.gc.ca/tx/bsnss/tpcs/gst-tps/rts-eng.html.

46. www.nrcan.gc.ca/energy/fuel-prices/4939.

47. www.statcan.gc.ca/tables-tableaux/sum-som/l01/cst01/trade37c-eng.htm.

48. www.scientificamerican.com/article/existing-technologies-could-cut-vehicle-fuel-use-in-half/.

49. www.statcan.gc.ca/pub/51-203-x/51-203-x2012000-eng.pdf.

50. http://web.tmxmoney.com/marketsca.php.

51. www.canadianbusiness.com/companies-and-industries/marijuana-inc/.

52. www.fraserinstitute.org/uploadedFiles/fraser-ca/Content/research-news/research/publications/government-subsidies-in-canada-a-684-billion-price-tag.pdf.

53. http://blogs.canoe.ca/lilleyspad/politics/the-rich-already-pay-their-fair-share-of-income-tax-in-canada/.

54. www.statcan.gc.ca/daily-quotidien/140321/dq140321d-eng.pdf.

55. www.charityintelligence.ca/.

56. www.cbc.ca/news/canada/thousands-of-charity-workers-earn-big-salaries-report-1.1022805.

57. http://news.gc.ca/web/article-en.do?mthd=index&crtr.page=1&nid=808689.

58. www.thestar.com/news/gta/2014/06/09/leukemia_society_spends_little_on_charitable_works_investigation_shows.html.

59. www.theglobeandmail.com/news/politics/trudeau-wont-refund-20000-speaking-fee-from-charity-fundraiser/article12573370/.

60. www.fin.gov.on.ca/en/credit/pctc/.

61. www.cra-arc.gc.ca/crrs/wrkng/menu-eng.html.

62. http://openparliament.ca/committees/official-languages/41-1/80/graham-fraser-1/only/.

63. www.washingtonpost.com/blogs/wonkblog/wp/2012/10/10/why-exactly-should-the-government-fund-pbs-and-npr/.

INDEX

Other Great Books on Economics, Business, and Finance from Dundurn

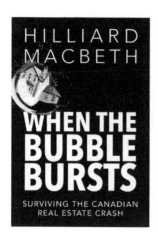

When the Bubble Bursts
Surviving the Canadian Real Estate Crash
Hilliard Macbeth

Starting in 2008, investors, upset by the stock market collapse, started to see real estate as a "safe haven" investment. While talking with numerous clients, investment manager Hilliard Macbeth realized that Canadians have far too much of their investment capital and savings tied up in expensive real estate when better opportunities are about to appear in other asset classes. He argues that Canada is in the midst of a real estate bubble, and there will soon be a crash in house prices.

What can Canadians do to be prepared financially for retirement and to take advantage of the "once in a lifetime" buying opportunity that will follow the bubble bursting? All these answers can be found in *When the Bubble Bursts*.

Sticky Branding
*12.5 Principles to Stand Out, Attract Customers
& Grow an Incredible Brand*
Jeremy Miller

Sticky Brands exist in almost every industry.

Companies like Apple, Nike, and Starbucks have made themselves as recognizable as they are successful.

But large companies are not the only ones who can stand out. Any business willing to challenge industry norms and find innovative ways to serve its customers can grow into a Sticky Brand.

Based on a decade of research into what makes companies successful, *Sticky Branding* is your branding playbook. It provides ideas, stories, and exercises that will make your company stand out, attract customers, and grow into an incredible brand. *Sticky Branding*'s 12.5 guiding principles are drawn from hundreds of interviews with CEOs and business owners who have excelled within their industries.

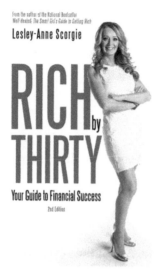

From the author of the National Bestseller
Well Heeled: The Smart Girl's Guide to Getting Rich

Lesley-Anne Scorgie

RICH by THIRTY

Your Guide to Financial Success

2nd Edition

Rich by Thirty
Your Guide to Financial Success
Lesley-Anne Scorgie

Think you can't be rich by thirty? Think again!

The earlier you make savvy decisions with your finances, the more successful you can be because time is on your side. And you don't need thousands of dollars or a hefty inheritance to get started. In fact, most young millionaires began by saving a few dollars each week — the cost of a bottle of water or a drop-in fitness class.

As a financially savvy young person, you will have the ability to choose the direction of your future rather than having to accept what life throws your way — and that's valuable because having choices will help you create a happy life. If you're ready to reach your financial potential, without sacrificing the best of what life has to offer, *Rich by Thirty* will show you how. In it you'll learn to:

- Maximize the value of your education;
- Live a frugal and fun life;
- Become debt free fast;
- Budget for the things you need and want;
- Save and invest like an expert;
- And choose a great career.

Forget about being broke! This guide will help you grow your money and empower you to create an awesome, and affordable, future for yourself.

Available at your favourite bookseller

DUNDURN

VISIT US AT
Dundurn.com | @dundurnpress | Facebook.com/dundurnpress
Pinterest.com/dundurnpress